WILLIAM BUTLER YEATS

WORLD DRAMATISTS

WILLIAM BUTLER YEATS

ANTHONY BRADLEY

WITH HALFTONE ILLUSTRATIONS

FREDERICK UNGAR PUBLISHING CO.

NEW YORK

80-27986

Copyright © 1979 by Frederick Ungar Publishing Co., Inc.

Printed in the United States of America
Library of Congress Cataloging in Publication Data
Bradley, Anthony, 1942–
  William Butler Yeats.

  (World dramatists)
  Bibliography: p.
  Includes index.
    1. Yeats, William Butler, 1865–1939—Dramatic works.
  2. Yeats, William Butler, 1865–1939—Stage history.
  PR5908.D7B7   822'.8   77–6953
  ISBN 0-8044-2068-8

For Patty and Mary

Acknowledgments

I wish to thank the many generous people who provided me with photographs of productions of Yeats's plays, in particular James Flannery, Reg Skene, and Irene Connors; their commitment to Yeatsian drama has helped me understand its significance. I am grateful to my colleague Michael Stanton for reading the manuscript of this book. I am most indebted to my wife, Patty, for her help with all aspects of this undertaking.

CONTENTS

CHRONOLOGY

1865	W. B. Yeats is born in Dublin on June 13.
1868	Yeats family moves to London.
1880	Family returns to Dublin.
1881–83	Yeats attends Erasmus Smith High School, Dublin.
1884	Writes the dramatic poems *Time and the Witch Vivien, The Seeker, The Island of Statues, Mosada.*
1884–85	Attends Dublin Metropolitan School of Art.
1885	Meets John O'Leary, founds Dublin Hermetic Society.
1887	Family moves to London; Yeats joins the Theosophical Society.
1888	*Fairy and Folk Tales of the Irish Peasantry* is published.
1889	Yeats's first volume of verse, *The Wanderings of Oisin*, is published. Meets Maud Gonne.

The dates of publication and of first productions are both important for the student of Yeats's plays. Accordingly, in the chapter headings I have cited, whenever possible, the dates of publication that Yeats gives in *Collected Plays;* in the Bibliography I have cited the dates of *first* publication. In the Chronology and in the discussions of individual plays, I have given the dates of first productions.

1890   Becomes member of the Order of the Golden Dawn.

1891   Parnell dies.

1892   Yeats founds the Irish Literary Society in Dublin.

1894   *The Land of Heart's Desire* is produced at the Avenue Theatre, London.

1896   Yeats joins the Irish Republican Brotherhood; meets Lady Gregory and Synge.

1897   Yeats discusses the possibility of founding an Irish theater with Lady Gregory, Edward Martyn, and George Moore.

1899   The Irish Literary Theatre is founded by Yeats, Lady Gregory, Edward Martyn, and George Moore. *The Wind Among the Reeds* is published. *The Countess Cathleen* is produced at the Antient Concert Rooms in Dublin.

1901   *Diarmuid and Grania,* by Yeats and George Moore, is produced at the Gaiety Theatre, Dublin.

1902   *Cathleen Ni Houlihan,* with Maud Gonne in the title role, is produced at St. Teresa's Hall, Dublin. *The Pot of Broth* is produced at the Antient Concert Rooms.

1903   *The Hour-Glass* and *The King's Threshold* are produced at the Molesworth Hall, Dublin. Maud Gonne marries.

1903–04 Yeats goes on lecture tour of the United States and Canada.

1904   *In the Seven Woods* is published. *Where There Is Nothing* is produced at the Royal Court Theatre in London. *The Shadowy Waters* is produced at the Molesworth Hall. *On Baile's Strand* is produced at the Abbey Theatre, Dublin.

1906   *Deirdre* is produced at the Abbey.

1907   *Playboy* riots. *The Unicorn From the Stars* is produced at the Abbey.

1910	*The Green Helmet* is produced at the Abbey.
1911	Yeats briefly accompanies Abbey Players on tour in the United States.
1913	Stays with Ezra Pound in England.
1914	*Responsibilities* is published. Second lecture tour of the United States and Canada.
1916	The Easter Rising in Dublin. Maud Gonne's husband, John MacBride, is executed by the English for his role in the insurrection. *At the Hawk's Well* is produced in London, in Lady Cunard's drawing-room.
1917	Yeats acquires Thoor Ballylee. *The Wild Swans at Coole* is published. Yeats marries Miss Georgie Hyde-Lees in London.
1919	Anne Yeats is born. Yeats goes on third lecture tour of the United States and Canada. *The Player Queen* is produced at the King's Hall, Covent Garden, London.
1919–21	Ireland fights war of independence.
1921	Michael Yeats is born. *Michael Robartes and the Dancer* is published.
1922	Yeats is appointed Senator in the government of the Irish Free State.
1922–23	Civil war in Ireland.
1923	Is awarded Nobel Prize for Literature.
1924	The Abbey is subsidized by the Irish government.
1925	*A Vision* is published.
1926	*The Only Jealousy of Emer, The Cat and the Moon,* Sophocles' *King Oedipus* are produced at the Abbey.
1927	Sophocles' *Oedipus at Colonus* is produced at the Abbey. The Peacock Theatre is opened. Yeats's health is bad—from this time he spends most winters in southern Europe.
1928	*The Tower* is published.
1929	*Fighting the Waves* is produced at the Abbey.

1930   *The Words upon the Window-Pane* is produced at the Abbey.

1931   *The Dreaming of the Bones* is produced at the Abbey.

1932   Lady Gregory dies. Yeats goes on his fourth and last lecture tour of the United States.

1933   *The Winding Stair and Other Poems* is published.

1934   *The Resurrection* and *The King of the Great Clock Tower* are produced at the Abbey.

1935   Yeats collaborates on a translation of the *Upanishads*.

1936   *The Oxford Book of Modern Verse,* edited by Yeats, is published.

1937   Second edition of *A Vision* is published.

1938   Yeats makes his last public appearance at the premiere of *Purgatory,* in the Abbey.

1939   Yeats completes *The Death of Cuchulain* just before dying, on January 28, at Cap Martin, on the French Riviera. *Last Poems and Two Plays* is published.

1948   Yeats is buried in Ireland.

1949   *The Death of Cuchulain* is produced at the Abbey.

1950   *A Full Moon in March* is produced at the Everyman Theatre, London. *The Herne's Egg* is produced at the Abbey.

I. YEATS'S LIFE AND WORK *

The oldest of five children, William Butler Yeats
was born in Sandymount, a suburb of Dublin, on
June 13, 1865. On his father's side, he was descended
from ancestors who had been Dublin merchants in
the eighteenth century. He could, however, lay some
claim to aristocratic origins, since one of those
merchants, Benjamin Yeats, married Mary Butler, a
descendant of the distinguished Anglo-Irish family
founded by the Earl of Ormond. Mary Butler brought
into the Yeats family the lands in County Kildare that
she had inherited through her relation to the Or-
monds. In more recent times the Yeats family had
tended to favor the church, rather than commerce,
as a vocation. Yeats's grandfather and great-grandfather were both clergymen in the Church of Ireland,
ministers of rural parishes in County Down and
County Sligo, and his father had been intended for
the church.

On his mother's side, Yeats was related to the Pollexfens and Middletons of Sligo, the prosperous little
county town on the northwest coast of Ireland. The
Pollexfens and Middletons were merchants, sailors,

* Readers unfamiliar with Irish history and culture may
wish to consult Chapter X, "Yeats and the Irish and Historical Cultural Background," before reading this chapter.

and shipowners. The poet's maternal grandfather, William Pollexfen, "must have been a man of personality, for the memory of him haunted his grandson to the end of his life, and Yeats has told us: 'Even today when I read *King Lear* his image is always before me, and I often wonder if the delight in passionate men in my plays and in my poetry is more than his memory.' " [1]

John Butler Yeats, Yeats's father, was prevented from becoming a clergyman by his agnosticism. It was only after he had qualified as a lawyer, however, that he realized his true vocation was to be a painter. As a consequence of his desire to study art in London, the family settled there when Willie, as he was called by his family, was only three. The child was soon very conscious of being unhappy at school and disliking London. During the next twelve years of the family's residence in London, however, there were frequent, prolonged visits with his mother's relatives in Sligo, where Willie always felt he really belonged. He loved the small, rocky seaport fringed by mountains and lakes, and was entranced by the conversation about ghosts and fairies that he would hear in his grandfather's house when his mother chatted with the servants. Because the beautiful landscape of Sligo came to figure so prominently in the poetry of his son, John Butler Yeats was moved to claim that by marrying a Pollexfen he had "given a tongue to the sea cliffs." [2] The elemental quality of the same landscape is also captured in the brilliant paintings of Jack Butler Yeats, the brother of the poet.

When their modest income from the heavily mortgaged land in Kildare was stopped in 1880 as a consequence of a rent strike, one of the tactics used by tenants against landlords in the Land War, the Yeatses returned to Ireland. It was this income that had allowed John Butler Yeats to marry in the first place, and it was what largely enabled him to support his family, for he was somewhat improvident about material concerns. To the distress of his prosperous, business-minded in-laws, he seemed either exasperatingly uninterested in making a living from his art or incapable of doing so. At any rate, it was doubtless to conserve money and to be nearer the Sligo relatives, whom Mrs. Yeats would often visit with the children, that the family moved back to Ireland.

On their return to Ireland, the Yeats family, now numbering four children, lived first in the Dublin suburb of Howth, then a fishing village. Willie and his mother were particularly happy in these surroundings, for the harbor and sea cliffs reminded them of Sligo. Mrs. Yeats had, by all accounts, no understanding of nor interest in her husband's work. It was clear that she much preferred to talk with the servant at Howth, the wife of a fisherman, than she had cared to be involved with her husband's artistic and intellectual friends in London. Willie spent a good deal of time wandering the hills and cliffs in a dreamy, exalted state. A thicket on the hill of Howth afforded him a delightful place to fantasize, and he actually invoked this thicket as a model for his early aesthetic theory of poetry as sanctuary from the real world: "That thicket gave me my first thought of what a long poem should be; I thought of it as a region into which one should wander from the cares of life. The characters were to be no more real than the shadows that people the Howth thicket. Their mission was to lessen the solitude without destroying its peace." [3]

The formal education of William Butler Yeats was irregular and deficient. One can understand why a close friend, the scholarly Lionel Johnson, later told the poet that he needed ten years in a library. The child's education was neglected partly, no doubt, because of the unsettling effect of frequent changes of residence, but mainly because of his lack of interest in the regular academic curriculum, a lack of interest that was reinforced by his father's outspoken opposition to the aims and methods of conventional education. The boy's earliest teachers (who included several Pollexfen relatives) thought his intelligence less than normal because he was so slow at learning to read. Willie never excelled at his studies, but his father, though often impatient with him, provided him with an infinitely more profitable education through his intellectual companionship. He would read Blake, and Shelley, and Shakespeare to the boy, and constantly discuss these and other writers with him, at the same time encouraging his son's literary efforts. Interestingly enough, Yeats remembered his father praising dramatic poetry as the highest form of literature. Though Yeats was to rebel against his father's influence, their intellectual companionship was to last for a very long time, until the father's death in 1922, in fact; the close relationship between the father and son is documented in their voluminous correspondence.

Yeats's formal education in Ireland consisted of two years' attendance at the Erasmus Smith High School in Dublin, followed by a further two years at the Dublin Metropolitan School of Art, where his father held a teaching post. Yeats enrolled in art school instead of in Trinity College, the university where his father, grandfather and great-grandfather before him had all had more or less distinguished careers. This decision doubtless had something to do with John Butler Yeats's convictions about the importance of art even for a general education, possibly had a little to do with the difficulty of meeting the expenses of a university education, and certainly had a great deal to do with the tacit acknowledgment that Willie was not well enough prepared to pass the university entrance examination.

If Yeats's painting did not reveal any great promise, it became very evident during his stay at the School of Art just where his interests and abilities lay. In 1884, when he was only nineteen, he wrote four verse plays —"dramatic poems" might be a more descriptive title for these closet dramas—*Time and the Witch Vivien, The Seeker, The Island of Statues,* and *Mosada.* All four reflect the same idealizing tendency as the rest of his early verse, that is, the constant need to escape from the real world and the constriction of time into some aesthetic, transcendent realm of existence. In the process of polishing the verse of *Mosada* only four years later, Yeats insightfully realized that his dramatic and lyric verse was "almost all a flight into fairyland from the real world and a summons to that flight." [4] At about this time, too, Yeats started to realize his identity as an Irish poet, and we find him committing himself to the idea of using Irish material for his poetry and plays. In "To Ireland in the Coming Times" Yeats asserts his Irishness: he wants to be mentioned in the same breath as the Irish nationalist poets of the nineteenth century, to be "counted one/With Davis, Mangan, Ferguson." His first volume of verse, *The Wanderings of Oisin* (1889), employs Irish mythology in the long narrative title poem, though the style is heavily symbolist and pre-Raphaelite.

Yeats's attraction to literary nationalism was widely shared in Ireland in the years after Parnell's downfall. Young men and women turned away from politics in disillusion toward societies that encouraged a cultural nationalism (or, alternately, far more radical and violent politics than Parnell had been associated with). Yeats founded the Irish Literary Society in Dublin in 1892 with the aim of promoting a distinctively Irish literature in the English language, a literature that would be identified with and help to create a noble and heroic nation. The society's president was the old Fenian, John O'Leary, who had been imprisoned and exiled for so many years because of his political beliefs. Yeats was drawn to O'Leary because of his nobility of character, his morality in politics, and his love of Irish literature. O'Leary never complained of his imprisonment, and fervid nationalist though he was, insisted that there were things a man could not do even to save a nation. It was no doubt under his influence and that of Maud Gonne that Yeats joined the secret revolutionary organization of the Irish Republican Brotherhood in 1896.

Maud Gonne's conscience was not so strict as O'Leary's on the point of what was and was not permitted in the struggle to free Ireland from English domination. One of the common ironies of Irish political life is that this nationalist political agitator, widely regarded as the Irish Joan of Arc, was of English parentage, and that her father had actually been a colonel in the British army. She was flamboyant as well as beautiful (she had been an actress for a short time), and was often accompanied by a small menagerie of dogs, pet monkeys, or caged birds. Yeats first encountered her in 1889, in London (the Yeats family had moved back to the city two years previously). He was captivated for life:

> I was twenty-three years old when the troubling of my life began. I had heard from time to time in letters from Miss O'Leary, John O'Leary's old sister, of a beautiful girl who had left the society of the Viceregal Court for Dublin nationalism. In after years I persuaded myself that I felt premonitory excitement at the first reading of her name. Presently she drove up to our house in

Bedford Park with an introduction from John
O'Leary to my father. I had never thought to see
in a living woman so great beauty. It belonged to
famous pictures, to poetry, to some legendary
past. A complexion like the blossom of apples,
and yet face and body had the beauty of lineaments which Blake calls the highest beauty because it changes least from youth to age, and a
stature so great that she seemed of a divine race.
Her movements were worthy of her form, and I
understood at last why the poet of antiquity,
where we would but speak of face and form, sings,
loving some lady, that she paces like a goddess. I
remember nothing of her speech that day except
that she vexed my father by praise of war, for she
too was of the Romantic movement and found
those uncontrovertible Victorian reasons, that
seemed to announce so prosperous a future, a
little grey. As I look backward, it seems to me that
she brought into my life in those days—for as yet
I saw only what lay upon the surface—the middle
of the tint, a sound as of a Burmese gong, an over-
powering tumult that had yet many pleasant
secondary notes.[5]

Maud Gonne wanted Yeats to write a frankly propa-
gandistic literature, but Yeats tried to cling to his
determination that, though his work must be distinctively national and Irish, it should not be nationalistic. He did write *Cathleen Ni Houlihan,* however, and
Maud Gonne starred in the lead role when it was produced in 1902. This was good theater, but it was also
excellent propaganda for the nationalist cause, as the
playwright must have realized. Yeats was with Maud,
too, in Dublin in 1897, during the violent riots that
she was largely responsible for instigating in protest
at the celebration of Queen Victoria's Jubilee. And
the following year, he worked with her on a commit-

tee responsible for commemorating the centenary of the Irish rebellion of 1798. Yeats was uneasy and wretched—he later said that these were the worst months of his life—because he could not commit his life and art to revolutionary politics, and it seemed that that would be the only way truly to impress Maud Gonne. Even more important than this ideological impasse was the unhappy reality that Maud Gonne preferred to have Yeats as a friend, rather than as a lover or husband. Despite the fact that there were other women in Yeats's life with whom he formed romantic attachments, it was to Maud Gonne that he repeatedly and vainly proposed marriage, and it was about her beauty and his "barren passion" for her that he wrote until the end of his life.

In addition to his growing involvement in Irish literature and politics, Yeats was also very much interested in eastern religions, the occult, and magic: we find him founding the Dublin Hermetic Society in 1885, joining the Blavatsky Lodge of the Theosophical Society in 1887, and the Order of the Golden Dawn in 1890. Because of the widespread interest in psychic phenomena during this period, both in Europe and America, Yeats's membership in such societies would probably have appeared much less eccentric then than it does today. Nonetheless, Yeats's belief in the supernatural was confirmed by the existence of these organizations. If he was not completely without skepticism, his need to believe was very great indeed. His belief in the occult can be accounted for partly as a reaction to his father's agnosticism, partly as a rejection of Victorian scientific materialism (a philosophy that had robbed the world, in Yeats's view, of spiritual significance), but most of all as evidence of his belief in an invisible world beyond the merely physical. The rituals of these societies were, for Yeats, comparable to the poet's use of literary symbols in their capacity to evoke an inexpressible world. There were also to be many similarities between his own symbolic system, *A Vision* and "traditional occult systems with which he was familiar." [6] His admiration for the symbolic and visionary English poet and painter, William Blake, moved Yeats to prepare an edition of Blake's works, in collaboration with his father's friend Edwin Ellis, which was published in 1893.

On a visit to the west of Ireland in 1896, Yeats met Lady Augusta Gregory, the widow of Sir William Gregory, governor of Ceylon. The nature of their lifelong friendship was something that Yeats keenly appreciated. As he eloquently acknowledged when she was ill: "I cannot realize the world without her. She has been to me mother, friend, sister and brother. She brought to my wavering thoughts steadfast nobility—all day the thought of losing her is a conflagration in the rafters." [7] Lady Gregory's translations from the Irish, especially *Cuchulain of Muirthemne* (1902), and *Gods and Fighting Men* (1904), are important sources for the mythological content of Yeats's poems and plays. Her role in the founding and managing of the Abbey Theatre, and her collaboration with Yeats on many of his early plays were no doubt fulfilling activities for her, but there can be little doubt that they were primarily designed to provide a theater for Yeats and to help him realize himself as a dramatist. She looked after Yeats's health and finances at a time when both were in a poor state, and she put her house, Coole Park, perennially at his disposal (Yeats was to spend many productive summers there). These actions are to be attributed not only to Lady Gregory's obvious love and admiration for Yeats, but also to her strong and magnanimous conviction that he was a great writer and circumstances ought to be arranged so as not to interfere with his writing.

Lady Gregory's importance to Yeats can be seen in many of his poems, plays, and letters. Her integrity and courage represented for Yeats all that was best in the Anglo-Irish tradition, and her house was to become an important symbol in Yeats's work of that tradition. The death of her son, who had designed stage sets for Yeats's plays, and had seemed to him a Renaissance combination of "soldier, scholar, horseman," was the occasion for Yeats's great elegy, "In Memory of Major Robert Gregory."

In the same year that he met Lady Gregory, Yeats met John Millington Synge in Paris. There is some uncertainty as to whether it was on this first meeting or a later occasion that Yeats, his mind full of a recent visit to the Aran Islands off the west coast of Ireland, encouraged Synge to give up writing criticism, to go to the islands and live as one of the people. Yeats admired the plays Synge came to write, finding in *Riders to the Sea* (1904) the compression and intensity he was to aim for in his own tragedies, and in *The Well of the Saints* (1905) and *The Playboy of the Western World* (1907), the opposition between natural passion and the institutional world which he incorporated into his own poems and plays. Yeats also admired what he conceived of as Synge's heroic ability to satirically unmask those traits in the Irish national character most Irishmen would prefer to leave concealed.

Yeats's poetry until the turn of the century had been marked by a number of influences and was as a consequence a rather conventionalized body of verse. (For the anthology of modern verse which he edited in 1936, Yeats refused to consider any of the poetry that he had written before the age of forty!) "In 1899 he published *The Wind Among the Reeds,* his most elaborate verse, his final poetry written for poetry's sake, for beauty's sake, and the swan song of

his *fin de siècle* composition."[8] Henceforth, Yeats
was to reject "the elaborate mythology which he had
created for himself out of the Romantic poets, the
Celtic legends, folk-lore and a smattering of symbolism."[9] Like the poetry, the early plays have sources
in Irish folklore, and always assert the superiority of
the spiritual to the material world; like the lyric
poetry, too, the verse of the plays is formed under the
influence of aestheticism and symbolism. But such
early plays as *The Countess Cathleen* (1892), *The
Land of Heart's Desire* (1894), and *Cathleen Ni Houlihan* (1902) do contain genuine dramatic conflict and
at least one essential characteristic of Yeats's later
dramatic style—those intense moments of spiritual revelation which distinguish the Noh plays. And Yeats
conceived of his dramatic work as exercising a much-
needed, salutary influence on his poetry: he associated
his plays with "the search for more of manful energy,
more of cheerful acceptance of whatever arises out of
the logic of events, and for clean outline, instead of
those outlines of lyric poetry that are blurred with desire and vague regret."[10]

With the very practical aim of making some money,
but also, no doubt, with the deliberate intention of
developing the public side of his personality, Yeats
embarked in 1903 on a four-month lecture tour of the
United States and Canada (there were to be another
three over the course of his life). He talked about the
Irish literary and dramatic movement then going on,
one of his aims being frankly to propagandize for it
in the colleges and universities where he lectured.
The American visit seems to have been enjoyable and
stimulating for him: he particularly enjoyed the air of
religious toleration, the lack of snobbery, and the emphasis he found on education as a preparation for
living. The Irish-American lawyer, John Quinn, who
was the chief promoter in the United States of the

Irish renaissance, said of Yeats's performance on this tour, "he got the chance, and made a great success. No Irishman since the time of Parnell's great trip here has made so grand an impression." [11]

After the turn of the century, in volumes like *In the Seven Woods* (1904), which contained *On Baile's Strand,* and *The Green Helmet And Other Poems* (1910), we find in Yeats's poems and plays a more personal, colloquial and energetic verse, and an attitude that engages more directly with the real world. (*In The Seven Woods* was, incidentally, the first book published by The Cuala Press, which was founded and managed by Yeats's two sisters, Elizabeth and Susan.) In such plays as *The King's Threshold* (1904), *On Baile's Strand* (1904), and *Deirdre* (1907), Yeats asserts aesthetic and human values in the face of the institutional, politicized world. And while he complains about the inroads made on his time and energy for writing poetry by "theatre business, management of men" (as he describes his activities in "The Fascination of What's Difficult"), this involvement and activity clearly helped bring about a remarkable improvement in his poetry. It is interesting to note that, even at this period in his life when he was so involved with the administration of the Abbey Theatre (from 1906–1910), Yeats spent at least half his time in London, and maintained rooms there, at Woburn Buildings, for twenty-four years. Despite his early distaste for it, Yeats must often have found London a more congenial and spacious city than the Dublin whose "casual malice" he loathed.[12]

The improvement in Yeats's work is unmistakable in his growing ability to write masterful poems about the world of public events in Ireland, an improvement demonstrated with singular clarity in the volume aptly named *Responsibilities* (1914). Sir Hugh Lane, Lady Gregory's nephew, had promised to endow the city of Dublin with his splendid collection of modern French paintings if a suitable gallery could be found to house them, but the influential and wealthy middle-class citizenry who could have subsidized such a gallery refused to do so. Yeats's indignation at their philistinism fills a number of satires in *Responsibilities,* the most memorable of which is "September, 1913." In this poem Yeats excoriates the huckstering mentality of modern Ireland, concluding that "Romantic Ireland's dead and gone/It's with O'Leary in the grave." Yeats's role as a personally involved chronicler of Irish public life is inaugurated in the poems in *Responsibilities,* and continued in such later poems as "Easter, 1916," "Nineteen Hundred and Nineteen," and "Meditations in Time of Civil War." These poems are not rhetorical or satirical, like so many of the poems in *Responsibilities.* Their greatness has much to do with Yeats's authoritative use of symbol, so that the poems entirely transcend the occasion of their inspiration. But one important aspect of their existence is that they are also poems, like those in *Responsibilities,* which are about Ireland's national life.

Certainly by the time *Responsibilities* was published, Yeats had become very disillusioned with the commercial theater. It was clear that the Abbey, insofar as it would be successful, would be successful in different ways than he had hoped. The surface of life in Ireland had found expression in the realistic comedies which were popular at the Abbey, but Yeats's poetic dramas, with their deeper sense of Irish identity as manifested in ancient myth and legend, were, by and large, caviar to the general public. It was with tremendous excitement, then, that Yeats encountered a form of drama that was an artistic paradigm and authority for the kind of plays he now realized he wished to write. His excitement was all the greater because this drama did not require a popular, commercial theater. Ezra Pound introduced Yeats to the Japanese Noh plays in 1913, and their influence can be seen on most of Yeats's plays after 1916.

The model of the Japanese play—its combination of verse, dance, and music, the use of masks by the players, the supernatural subject matter, its adaptability to private staging—encouraged Yeats to reject compromise with the restrictions of the conventional, realistic theater. In the model of the Noh, as Richard Ellmann concludes, "Yeats has at last found an adequate medium for his dramatic talents." [13] Consequently, there is an impressive authority and assurance in Yeats's dramatic treatment of the themes of love and death, the supernatural, the heroic, and his own philosophy in the group of symbolic verse plays spanning a period of more than twenty years—*At the Hawk's Well* (1917), *The Only Jealousy of Emer* (1919), *The Dreaming of the Bones* (1919), *Calvary* (1920), *The Cat and the Moon* (1926), *A Full Moon in March* (1935), and *The Death of Cuchulain* (1939).

Ezra Pound was best man at Yeats's marriage in 1917 to a young Englishwoman, Georgie Hyde-Lees, whom he had met some five years earlier. Yeats reported happily to Lady Gregory, who had been anxious to see him marry and settle down for some time —he was now fifty-two—that his wife "was kind, wise, and unselfish" and had made his life "serene and full of order." [14] The marriage seems, too, to have released great creative power in Yeats. The first volume of poems after his marriage, *The Wild Swans at Coole* (1919), is accomplished and varied beyond anything he had yet written. This was also the first volume of poems set in Thoor Ballylee, the Norman tower close by Lady Gregory's home, which Yeats bought in the same year as his marriage. The volume includes the elegy for Robert Gregory and other poems such as "The Wild Swans at Coole," in which the ordinary world is exalted to the status of symbol; it contains, too, erotic poems ("On Woman"), passionate, remorseful love poems ("A Deep-Sworn Vow"). It also contains poems that are strikingly new and different in the Yeatsian canon, poems like "The Phases of the Moon"; such poems reflect the speculations Yeats had started to systematize at this time as the result of his wife's discovery of her ability to produce automatic writing. Yeats was so excited by this phenomenon that he inquired of the spirits whether he should abandon poetry to study their revelations; luckily, they replied through Mrs. Yeats that their function was only to give him metaphors for his poetry. Yeats's organization of his thought in *A Vision* (1925, 1937) can best be understood as a symbolic patterning of human experience, and as the repository of his ideas about history and the human personality.

It is helpful to recall that Yeats's thought in *A Vision* is a countertruth to Victorian ideas of time and the human personality. At least, Yeats himself tells us, in a note to *The Resurrection* (1931), that this is the case: "For years I have been preoccupied with a certain myth that was itself a reply to a myth. . . . When I was a boy everybody talked about progress, and rebellion against my elders took the form of aversion to that myth." [15] Instead of the Victorian concept of time as linear progression, then, we have in Yeats's system the idea that historical and personal time is cyclical. Instead of the Victorian emphasis on sincerity, on being one's self, Yeats postulates a dynamic theory of the personality that expands the self by seeking to accommodate within it the very opposite characteristics to those which are a given of the personality. These ideas are expressed in a rather abstract system of symbols—a great wheel, gyres (interlocking cones), the mask, sun and moon, and so on. The relation of *A Vision* to Yeats's poetry and drama is important but problematical—it is typical of Yeats's attitude that he is not above mocking his own thought, as in *The Player Queen* (1922). If we accept the primary importance of the poems and plays, we may conclude that Yeats's philosophy is of compelling interest only when it is given a sensuous and vital embodiment in the poems and plays. And even then, what Richard Ellmann says of "The Second Coming," applies, I feel, to all of Yeats's poetry and drama: "an awareness of the system was more useful for writing than it is for reading the poem." [16]

Thoor Ballylee was, among other things, a wedding present for Yeats's young wife. So it comes that the following lines, written in 1918 while the crumbling tower was being repaired, are inscribed on its wall:

> I, the poet William Yeats,
> With old mill boards and sea-green slates,
> And smithy work from the Gort forge,
> Restored this tower for my wife George;
> And may these characters remain
> When all is ruin once again.

This consecration of the tower indicates that it was more than an impractical, draughty summer home for the Yeatses for the next ten years. Thoor Ballylee was, in fact, the symbolic locus for the poetry Yeats was to write during that period: the tower symbolizes Yeats's celebration of the creative impulse in the face of mortality, decay, and death.

Despite the serenity of his marriage and the birth of a daughter, Anne, in 1919, and a son, Michael, in 1921, Yeats was deeply troubled by a sense of impending historical cataclysm and the likely end of culture and civilization, a sense that had a good objective cause in the appalling war and vast social upheaval in Europe, and in the Troubles at home. This feeling was compounded by Yeats's personal sense of crisis at the approach of old age. A mood of bitter disillusionment dominates the poems of *The Tower* (1928); in such long poems as "Nineteen Hundred and Nineteen" and "Meditations in Time of Civil War," we find at times near-acquiescence in nihilistic destruction, at times a painful consciousness of the utter frailty of art, order, and ceremony as constructs with which to oppose the prevailing anarchy. Something of Yeats's mood during these years can be perceived in these lines from "Nineteen Hundred and Nineteen" (1921):

> Now days are dragon-ridden, the nightmare
> Rides upon sleep: a drunken soldiery
> Can leave the mother, murdered at her door,
> To crawl in her own blood, and go scot-free;
> The night can sweat with terror as before
> We pieced our thoughts into philosophy,
> And planned to bring the world under a rule,
> Who are but weasels fighting in a hole.

The war of independence fought against England in the years 1919–1921 was succeeded by civil war, the Treaty that ended the war with the English being the new source of contention. The Republicans rejected the Treaty's concept of an independent Ireland as one which was to be partitioned and to have the constitutional standing of a Free State (essentially, dominion status). They would have preferred to fight on to establish a united republic of Ireland. The Free Staters accepted the limitations of the Treaty, arguing that it gave Ireland the freedom to be free. In 1922, Yeats was appointed Senator by the new Free State government to advise on issues relating to education, literature, and the arts, and took up residence in a fine, eighteenth-century house in central Dublin on the eve of civil war. Like the other senators, Yeats was in some physical danger, and was given an armed guard. Characteristically, he could not but admire the spirit of the Republicans who fought against the government of which he was a member. He wrote to the English poet, Robert Bridges: "Life here is interesting, but restless and unsafe—I have two bullet holes through my windows—as it must always be when the sheep endeavour to control the goats who are by nature so much the more enterprising race." [17] The year after he entered the Senate, Yeats's status as a great modern writer was acknowledged by the award of the Nobel Prize for Literature. In his moving acceptance speech, Yeats shared his accomplishment with the dead John Synge and the failing Lady Gregory.

In the poem "Among School Children," occasioned by an official visit to a Montessori school in Waterford, Yeats displays some surprise and self-irony at his new identity as Senator:

> the children's eyes
> In momentary wonder stare upon
> A sixty-year-old smiling public man.

But he accepted his six-year appointment in the Senate very seriously. Yeats took a keen interest in everything that affected education and culture in Ireland, and he was an outspoken critic of the new government's anti-libertarian policies on censorship and divorce.

Yet Yeats identified, too, with authoritarian figures in the government, most obviously in his admiration for and friendship with Kevin O'Higgins, Minister of

Justice and External Affairs in the government until his murder in 1927. O'Higgins was the "strong man" responsible for the execution of many more Irishmen (who opposed the Free State government) than the British had executed during the war for independence. Moreover, Yeats's growing identification towards the end of his life with an idealized version of the eighteenth-century Anglo-Irish tradition often must have seemed like the worst kind of posturing to citizens of the new state. Yeats was against the proscribing of divorce, but the reason he gave was the wrong one: his argument was not that civil and religious liberty would be restricted for all by the passage of the bill that outlawed divorce in Ireland, but rather that it would discriminate against the Protestant minority, who were culturally superior to the majority because of their memorable eighteenth-century ancestors:

> We against whom you have done this thing are no petty people. We are one of the great stocks of Europe. We are the people of Grattan; we are the people of Swift, the people of Parnell. We have created the most of the modern literature of this country. We have created the best of its political intelligence.[18]

Yeats's increasingly conservative political sympathies led him (in the early 1930s) to write three marching songs for the Blue Shirts, the Irish fascists led by General Eoin O'Duffy, though he later changed his mind and re-wrote the songs so that they could not be claimed by the fascists. Yeats's radical conservatism was aristocratic in temper: he attempted to ignore the existence of democracy and the middle class. Paraphrasing Balzac, he once exclaimed, "There are only three classes I respect: the aristocracy who are above fear; the poor who are beneath it, and the artists whom God has made reckless." [19]

Illness during the last decade of his life required that Yeats spend most of his winters in southern Europe to escape Ireland's cold, damp weather. Illness and old age, however, seem only to have lent a new and compelling dimension to Yeats's celebration of life and his philosophical speculation. His volume called *Words For Music Perhaps* (1931) contains many poems that are expressly sexual and philosophic at the same time. These poems propound the truth that through the body and physical experience—and not by denial of it—one arrives at wisdom. In the words of Crazy Jane, the persona of the best of these poems,

> "A woman can be proud and stiff
> When on love intent;
> But Love has pitched his mansion in
> The place of excrement;
> For nothing can be sole or whole
> That has not been rent."

In 1934, Yeats rashly underwent the dubious Steinach (monkey-gland) operation which was supposed to result in rejuvenation. Yeats did have a particularly creative and productive period afterward, but one may doubt that the operation was responsible. It was in 1934 also that he attended a theater convention in Rome, where he spoke on a familiar theme, the achievement of the Abbey, to an audience of theater worthies that included Maeterlinck, Gordon Craig, and Pirandello.

The last few years of Yeats's life saw him involved in a variety of undertakings: he worked with Shri Purohit Swami on a translation of the *Upanishads*, edited *The Oxford Book of Modern Verse* (1936) (he rejoiced that "in spite of universal denunciation from the right and left, 15,000 have been sold"), undertook a series of five broadcasts on poetry for the B.B.C., issued the revised version of *A Vision* (1937), published *On the Boiler* (1939) and, in his last public attendance, appeared for the opening night of what some people think is his finest play, *Purgatory* (1939).[20] Most remarkable of all, he wrote the poems collected as *Last Poems (1936–1939)*, an astonishingly rich and varied body of poetry that contains such magnificent poems as "The Circus Animals' Desertion," a moving account of his poetic and dramatic career that concludes with a painful affirmation of art and life—"I must lie down where all the ladders start,/In the foul rag-and-bone shop of the heart." This last volume of Yeats's poems represents an interesting opposition to his first: "The last poems stand in a deliberate poise against the first. Instead of withdrawal to the dream we have withdrawal to the mountain. Instead of the aesthete's loneliness there is the loneliness of the man deserted by the circus animals [his poetic symbols]. Instead of life disdained we have life raged against but also eagerly accepted." [21]

Two days before he died at Cap Martin, on the French Riviera, on January 28, 1939, Yeats was engrossed in completing *The Death of Cuchulain*. The outbreak of the war prevented his burial in County Sligo until 1948, when his body was brought back to Ireland by the Irish navy. He is buried in Drumcliff churchyard, in the shadow of Ben Bulben, near the rectory in which his great-grandfather lived. The plain headstone bears the epitaph he wrote for himself in "Under Ben Bulben,"

> Cast a cold eye
> On life, on death.
> Horseman, pass by!

But a more fitting and moving epitaph than this recommendation of stoic arrogance (for Yeats himself never responded to life or death with "a cold eye") might be the last lines of "The Municipal Gallery Revisited" (1937), in which the old poet contemplates the portraits of his dead friends, and concludes by addressing the reader:

> You that would judge me, do not judge alone
> This book or that, come to this hallowed place
> Where my friends' portraits hang and look
>   thereon;
> Ireland's history in their lineaments trace;
> Think where man's glory most begins and ends,
> And say my glory was I had such friends.

II. YEATS AND THE
ABBEY THEATRE

When William Butler Yeats was awarded the Nobel
Prize for Literature in 1923, he seems to have considered that it had been granted him for his work in
the theater as much as or more than for his poetry.
In his lecture to the Swedish Royal Academy, Yeats
emphasized his artistic identity as a dramatist, and the
way in which that identity was associated with the
collective enterprise of the Irish dramatic movement:

> I have chosen as my theme the Irish Dramatic
> Movement . . . Perhaps the English committees
> would never have sent you my name if I had
> written no plays, no dramatic criticism, if my lyric
> poetry had not a quality of speech practised upon
> the stage, perhaps even—though this could be no
> portion of their deliberate thought—if it were not
> in some degree the symbol of a movement.[1]

Yeats was, indeed, responsible in large measure for
initiating the Irish dramatic movement and founding Ireland's national theater. The large body of literature in the Irish language that inspired the literary revival in Yeats's day did not contain any plays
—drama simply did not have a place in the native
Irish tradition. Moreover, the famous playwrights and
actors Ireland had produced since the eighteenth

century had worked exclusively for the English stage, so that the Irish theater can scarcely be said to have existed before Yeats.

The founding and administration of the Irish national theater, and the writing of plays for it, was not, of course, the work of one man, as Yeats gracefully acknowledged when he received the Nobel Prize:

> When your king gave me medal and diploma, two forms should have stood, one at either side of me, an old woman sinking into the infirmity of age and a young man's ghost. I think that when Lady Gregory's name and John Synge's name are spoken by future generations, my name, if remembered, will come up in the talk, and that if my name is spoken first their names will come in their turn because of the years we worked together.[2]

Yeats first discussed the possibility of starting a theater with Lady Gregory and Edward Martyn in 1897, although the first productions of what they named the Irish Literary Theatre did not take place until 1899. Augusta Gregory, the remarkable woman who was to be Yeats's patron and intimate friend for the rest of her life, provided much of the tenacity of purpose and talent for getting things done that brought the Irish theater into existence and sustained it in difficult times. Edward Martyn, like Lady Gregory a well-to-do Galway landowner, underwrote the cost of the Irish Literary Theatre's first productions; his devotion to the Ibsenesque drama, however, soon resulted in his parting from Yeats and Lady Gregory.

The discussions that led to the founding of the Irish Literary Theatre took place at the same time as the talks between Stanislavsky and Nemirovich-Danchenko that led to the founding of the Moscow Art Theater. Like its Russian counterpart, the Irish theater was inspired in part by reaction against the mechanical and extravagant conventions, the narrow and trivial theatricality that characterized the nineteenth-century theater. In *Samhain* (1903), a journal in which Yeats discussed the aims and accomplishments of the Irish theater, we find him roundly declaring, "I think the theater must be reformed in its plays, its speaking, its acting, and its scenery. That is to say, I think there is nothing good about it at present." [3]

Yeats's condemnation was a general one, not limited to the Irish theater, but there was a good deal of justification in what may seem, at first sight, too categorical a rejection of the theater of his day. Most of the nineteenth century was, indeed, a barren one for serious drama in the English-speaking world: the plays of Wordsworth, Byron, Shelley, Browning, Arnold, and Tennyson were closet dramas, designed to be read rather than performed. Popular entertainments, however, made the theater, particularly in the second half of the nineteenth century, a very profitable business—melodrama, farce, spectacle, burlesque, and musical comedies dominated the stage.

The most prolific and popular of the manufacturers of melodrama and farce in the nineteenth century was an Irishman with the improbable name of Dion Boucicault (1822–1890), who based many of his approximately one hundred and fifty plays (his playwriting career spans a period of fifty years) on other people's novels. Boucicault's plays are often revived at the Abbey, invariably with great success. The technical virtuosity and polish of such plays as *The Shaughraun* compel admiration, and it is not altogether surprising that Boucicault is reputed to have made half a million dollars from this one play. Then again, one cannot see a production of a Boucicault play and not realize the extent of his influence on better-known and more serious Irish playwrights such as John Millington Synge, George Bernard Shaw, Sean O'Casey, and Brendan Behan.

Boucicault was not alone in so often using novels as the basis for his plays; the most popular play in nineteenth-century America was a dramatic adaptation of Harriet Beecher Stowe's novel, *Uncle Tom's Cabin,* and in England, dramatic renderings of Dickens's novels were reckoned to be serious drama. Even the best drama was considered to need spectacular effects in order to captivate the audience. Shakespeare's plays in particular were performed in lavish and ingenious productions, with elaborate stage sets.

A notable exception to the general dearth of serious dramatists in the nineteenth century was the great Norwegian playwright, Henrik Ibsen, whose controversial social plays *A Doll's House* and *Ghosts* dominated the serious theater in England in the 1890s and influenced many British playwrights including George Bernard Shaw and Arthur Wing Pinero. Yeats acknowledged that Ibsen was "the one great master the modern stage has produced," but Yeats's own interest in the theater was antithetical to Ibsen's realism.[4] He disliked what seemed to him the mere reflection of the surface of commonplace, middle-class life and its problems, and aspired instead to a form of drama that was symbolic in technique, heroic in subject matter, and spiritual in its effect upon the audience. Synge shared Yeats's aversion to Ibsen's plays, which he condemned in his preface to *The Playboy of the Western World* as being capable only of portraying "the reality of life in joyless and pallid words."

The inclusion of the word "literary" in the title of the Irish Literary Theatre carried overtones of bookishness of which Yeats was well aware, and he realized that his emphasis on restoring poetry to the

drama could be taken for an essential misunderstanding of the nature of dramatic experience. But what
Yeats hoped for was to produce plays that were like
those of the Elizabethan and Jacobean period in being simultaneously good literature and good theater,
eminently readable and eminently dramatic. "We do
not think," he proclaimed, "that a play can be worth
acting and not worth reading." [5] Moreover, the Irish
Literary Theatre was conceived of as a national
theater, as an institution which would play a leading
role in developing Ireland's cultural identity; it
would express the Irish character and "bring upon
the stage the deeper thoughts and emotions of Ireland." [6] Yeats and Lady Gregory intended that the
dramatists who wrote for this theater would draw on
Irish folklore and myth as the material for their
plays.

There were those involved in the founding of the
Irish Literary Theatre who did not share Yeats's desire for a poetic drama based on Irish myth, even if
they believed in the cause of a national theater and
the need for reforming methods of theatrical production. Edward Martyn and George Moore, whom Yeats
described as "cousins and inseparable friends, bound
one to the other by mutual contempt," and whose
relationship he portrayed in his play, *The Cat and
the Moon,* were uneasy with the romantic ideals of
Yeats and Lady Gregory, preferring instead the realism of Ibsen.[7]

Edward Martyn was an acute drama critic, and in
these early days of the Irish dramatic movement, knew
much more about the theater than did Yeats and
Lady Gregory. "He had studied Ibsen's works with the
greatest care, and followed his career with the closest
attention, getting, perhaps, closer to the mood and
spirit of Ibsen than any of his contemporaries who
were writing plays. He had known the Théâtre Libre

in Paris, the Freie Bühne in Berlin, and the Independent Theatre in London, following their work with the closest attention, as in these experimental theatres he saw the only hope for the literary drama." [8]

Martyn's money launched the Irish Literary Theatre, and his Ibsenesque drama of ideas, *The Heather Field,* playing with Yeats's *The Countess Cathleen,* was well-received as the first production of the theater in Dublin's Antient Concert Rooms in 1899. Martyn also differed from Yeats and Lady Gregory in religious persuasion; he was a devout Catholic and caused some uneasiness because he threatened to withdraw his financial support when it appeared that *The Countess Cathleen* would offend Catholic opinion by its heretical tendencies.

George Moore was a well-known realistic novelist, and unlike Yeats and Lady Gregory, he did have some practical experience of the stage. His play, *The Strike at Arlingford,* was produced at the London Independent Theatre (where Ibsen had first been produced in England) in 1894, and he had directed other plays at that theater. He had also seen productions at the innovative Théâtre Libre when he lived in Paris. Thus Moore was able to be of great help to the Irish Literary Theatre, especially in the areas of directing and publicity. As Yeats acknowledged, "I doubt if it [our work] could have been done at all without his knowledge of the stage." [9]

For the three years of its existence, the Irish Literary Theatre strained to accommodate both the symbolic-poetic and the realistic in the seven plays it produced. The collaboration between Yeats and Moore on *Diarmuid and Grania,* produced in 1901, only demonstrated that the two philosophies were incompatible, and for all practical purposes terminated George Moore's connection with the Irish dramatic movement. By this time, too, Edward Martyn had grown unwilling to subsidize a company dominated by Yeats and reluctant to accommodate his plays or other Ibsenesque drama. Consequently, he too ceased his association with the Irish Literary Theatre. Martyn later played a prominent role in establishing several competitors to the Abbey Theatre, one of which, the Irish Theatre Company, produced for the first time in Ireland the works of the great continental dramatists, Ibsen, Chekhov, and Strindberg. Martyn's own promise as a playwright was unfortunately not realized in his work after he left the Irish Literary Theatre.

Yeats was thus given a clear field to shape the policy of what was to become the Irish national theater. Ironically, neither his own advocacy of the verse play based on Irish heroic myth nor Martyn's commitment to the realistic drama of ideas was of determining influence in the development of the Irish theater. Along with the unsuccessful *Diarmuid and Grania,* the Irish Literary Theatre produced Douglas Hyde's *Casadh an tSugain (The Twisting of the Rope),* the first play in Irish to be produced in a theater (and very possibly the first play ever to have been written in Irish). Hyde's seminal play showed the possibilities not so much for drama written in Irish as for drama made from the folk tradition. There can be little doubt that Hyde's play influenced Synge, and "awoke him to the possibilities of the material of the peasant play." [10] It was the realistic-poetic peasant play, at its best in the works of Synge, which was to form the staple of the national theater's productions after it had found a home at the Abbey. Even Yeats, committed to the medium of verse and the subject matter of heroic myth, wrote in collaboration with Lady Gregory the prose folk dramas *Cathleen Ni Houlihan* and *The Pot of Broth,* both of which were produced in 1902 and were extremely popular.

Hyde's play had been directed by William Fay; William and his brother Frank were active in amateur dramatics in Dublin in the early 1890s, and had founded an Irish school of acting some years before the Irish Literary Theatre got under way. Yeats reacted with enthusiasm to a production of a mediocre historical play by their troupe, the Irish National Dramatic Company: "I came away with my head on fire. I wanted to hear my own *On Baile's Strand,* to hear Greek tragedy spoken with a Dublin accent." [11] Though the Fays were amateurs, they had gained a great deal of practical experience of the stage and had read about the productions of the Norwegian National Theater in Bergen, the Independent Theater in London, and the Théâtre Libre in Paris. When the Fays' group joined with the Irish Literary Theatre in 1903 to form the Irish National Theatre Society, the effect of their theatrical expertise on Yeats's work was immediate: the dramatic structure of *The King's Threshold* shows how much Yeats had learned from the Fays. For some years it seemed that the movement had found in William Fay a stage manager who practiced the economy and restraint about which Yeats theorized, and in Frank Fay, a rare actor who spoke verse as Yeats wanted it spoken. The Fays, moreover, brought with them a considerable number of very talented and dedicated Irish actors, such as Maire Nic Shiubhlaigh, Sara Allgood, and Maire O'Neill. The Irish Literary Theatre had employed English actors, but the Fays were committed to training Irish actors, and capitalized on their amateur qualities to evolve a distinctive style of acting that became identifiably that of the Abbey players. This style was essentially simple and natural, a rejection of the histrionic manner of nineteenth-century acting.

Yeats's emphasis on the importance of speech (he wanted "to restore words to their sovereignty" in the drama), and his insistence on the need to reduce gesture and busyness on the stage and to simplify stage design, seem genuinely to have coincided with William Fay's own convictions.[12] They coincided, too, in a very practical way with the reluctance of the amateur actors to use much gesture and with the exigencies of stage production when resources were extremely limited. So, with the genius of common sense, the Abbey management cultivated the natural strengths of their actors, as Lady Gregory pointed out in a newspaper interview when she was accompanying the Abbey players on tour in the United States in 1911:

> When I saw the Sicilian players I was immensely impressed with one salient point, the perfection of gesture. Gesture to the Latin race is as natural as breathing. Our people do not gesture and to try and make them would be foolish. The material we have is the voice. The Irish people have beautiful rhythmic voices, and we have made these our component of value.[13]

The conviction with which Yeats believed in the precedence that speech must take over gesture and the personality of the actor threatened to lead him into comical excesses when he involved himself in directing:

> I . . . had once asked a dramatic company to let me rehearse them in barrels that they might forget gesture and have their minds free to think of speech for a while. The barrels, I thought, might be on castors, so that I could shove them about with a pole when the action required it.[14]

This radical notion was not put into practice (perhaps the actors objected), but Yeats always insisted on a minimum of movement on the stage: in *Samhain* he stipulates that actors should move "slowly and quietly, and not very much, and there should be something in their movements decorative and rhythmical as if they were paintings on a frieze." [15] It is clear that as early as 1904 Yeats was thinking in terms of a stage technique that anticipated, by almost a decade, his first encounter with the stylized Japanese Noh plays.

Yeats was determined that his plays should work on the stage, and always rewrote them after he had seen them performed. This was made possible because the Abbey kept the costs of production low and also functioned very much as a theater workshop, where playwrights were encouraged to make changes in the light of an actual performance. Lady Gregory pointed out its advantages: "It is one value of our theatre . . . that we are able to put on a new play without great expense. . . . There is no kind of teaching that will do so much for the playwright. The most experienced dramatist cannot prophesy how a play will go until he has seen it on the stage. . . . Almost always we change a play very much after it has been performed." [16]

The cooperative nature of the Irish dramatic movement, especially in the early days, encouraged collaboration between playwrights. Yeats and Lady Gregory collaborated very successfully, notably in the making of *The Pot of Broth* and *Cathleen Ni Houlihan;* Lady Gregory and Douglas Hyde, Edward Martyn and George Moore, George Moore and Yeats were also coauthors with varying degrees of success. The most extraordinary form that collaboration took was in George Moore's rewriting of Martyn's third play, *The Tale of a Town*. Martyn's version was unequivocally rejected by Yeats, Lady Gregory, and

Moore as being disastrously bad (Moore said that Yeats behaved toward Martyn like Torquemada denouncing a heretic), but Moore's rewriting of it as *The Bending of the Bough* gave the movement one of its most popular plays.

The Abbey was not only a workshop for Yeats and other Irish dramatists; it also helped generate a body of drama. Potential playwrights were encouraged to write because they knew there was a real possibility of seeing their work tried out on the stage. The mere existence of the Abbey Theatre thus helped to beget Irish drama; certainly early dramatists, such as Lennox Robinson, T. C. Murray, George Fitzmaurice, and St. John Ervine, as Lady Gregory points out in *Our Irish Theatre,* did not start to write plays before seeing a performance at the Abbey.[17] And in the first fifty years of the Abbey's existence, it has been estimated, 384 of the 449 plays produced "might be classified as having been written for the Abbey or as having been inspired by it." [18]

Yeats's emphasis on speech as the essence of dramatic art was complemented by the ideas and practice of Lady Gregory and Synge, whose plays are distinguished by a poetic prose based on peasant speech. Synge and Lady Gregory had learned Irish and were sensitive to the constructions and idioms of English as it was spoken along the western coast of Ireland, by those whose first language was Irish. In addition, both were doubtlessly influenced by the translations from Irish poetry of Douglas Hyde, president of the Gaelic League. The language of their plays is, consequently, a stylized version of the energetic and colorful peasant speech spoken in the remote areas of Ireland, a speech that retained characteristics both of the Irish language and of Elizabethan English. The natural geographic isolation of remote areas resulted in the persistence into the twentieth century of traces of

English as it was first spoken widely in Ireland, that is, during the sixteenth and seventeenth centuries. The poetic prose that became the hallmark of Synge's dialogue and justified his assertion, in the preface to *The Playboy of the Western World*, that "in a good play, every speech should be as fully flavored as a nut or apple," was based on the peasant speech of Kerry and Mayo. The dialect of Lady Gregory's plays, called Kiltartan after the area around her home in Galway, seems self-consciously quaint and extravagant by comparison with Synge's language. At any rate, both writers conceived of Irish dialect as beautiful and poetic—before this, dialect had been used for purely comic purposes, to get a laugh at the expense of the Irish.

In 1903 the first plays by Lady Gregory and Synge were staged by the Irish National Theatre Society, in Molesworth Hall, Dublin. Lady Gregory had collaborated earlier with Yeats on several plays and had done a great deal of practical work in the theater involving management and directing. She started to write her own plays, one-act comedies that were to provide a balance to the poetic dramas of Yeats and to fill out the evening's entertainment (since Yeats's plays were also short). It turned out that Lady Gregory had considerable talent and of the more than thirty plays she wrote, several were favorites in the offerings of the Abbey for many years to come. Her best plays are unsophisticated one-act peasant comedies such as *Spreading the News* (1904), *Hyacinth Halvey* (1906), and *The Workhouse Ward* (1908). Lady Gregory's most famous and popular play was *The Rising of the Moon* (1907). In this play, a Dublin policeman, after conversing and singing with a ballad singer, realizes that the singer is the rebel on the run he has been alerted to watch out for; yet, stirred by his own sense of himself as an Irishman, he allows him to go free.

It is an important aspect of Yeats's greatness that he acted as a catalyst for the Irish dramatic movement, that "he drew into creative activity" not only Lady Gregory, but also John Millington Synge.[19] As early as 1896, Yeats had advised Synge to give up writing criticism, and to seek inspiration not in Paris, where Synge was living at the time, but in the remote and primitive Aran islands off the western coast of Ireland. When Synge's *The Shadow of the Glen* and *Riders to the Sea* were performed in 1903 and 1904 respectively, it was not generally apparent that the Irish dramatic movement had found a great dramatist. Nor could anyone have foreseen that it would be Synge's blend of the poetic and the realistic that would most influence the plays written by later Abbey playwrights. Synge's plays also brought out the best in such actors and actresses as Sara Allgood, Maire O'Neill, Maire Nic Shiubhlaigh, and the Fays. The international appeal of Synge's plays gives an added indication of his dramatic genius: his plays, in particular his masterpiece *The Playboy of the Western World* (1907), have been staged not only in Britain and America, but also in many continental European countries, as well as in Syria and Lebanon and Japan.

In 1904, Annie Horniman, a wealthy English admirer of Yeats who shared his interest in the theater, gave the Irish National Theatre Society a home on Abbey Street in central Dublin. The immediate inspiration for Miss Horniman's generosity was a performance in London in 1903 by the Society of several plays that included Yeats's *The Hour-Glass, Cathleen Ni Houlihan,* and *The Pot of Broth.* The fact that the productions were much admired by such influential English critics as A. B. Walker and William Archer, who saw in the stage technique of the Irish players a delightful and welcome change from that which prevailed on the English stage, must have helped Miss

Horniman act on her desire to see Yeats have access
to a theater. There was never any doubt that it was
ultimately for Yeats's sake that Miss Horniman gave to
the Irish National Theatre Society a small operating
subsidy and the rent-free use of what became known
as the Abbey Theatre. The theater was housed, incidentally, in buildings with a checkered past: one part
had previously been a theater and music-hall, another
had been the headquarters for a Fenian organization in the 1860s, and another had belonged to the
city morgue!

Miss Horniman later founded the Gaiety Theatre
in Manchester and helped Lilian Baylis found the Old
Vic in London. She parted company with the Abbey in
1910, when the theater stayed open on the occasion of
Edward VII's death. Though this happened simply
because of the management's confusion at the time,
Miss Horniman, always on the alert for any contami-
nation of Yeats's genius by nationalist influences,
chose to think that it was a political gesture on the
part of the Abbey. Apologies notwithstanding, she
withdrew from her association with the Abbey. She
did so on extremely generous terms, however, hand-
ing over to the National Theatre Society the fully
equipped theater for the nominal sum of £1,000.

Because of the idealism most of its members shared,
the Irish National Theatre Society was organized
on democratic principles, every member having an
equal vote. The predictable result was that the society's organization verged at times on the chaotic.
When the Irish National Theatre Society was incorporated (and put on a professional footing) in 1905,
Yeats, Synge, and Lady Gregory were designated its
board of directors and invested with sole responsibility for all aspects of the theater's existence. All of the
actors in what was now a professional company were
classified as paid employees, and so, too, was the stage

manager, William Fay. Yeats and Fay had argued in the past about who had the right to cast actors in their roles, but it was now clear that the board of directors was to have the last word on casting as well as on all other decisions relating to the theater.

Sensing a loss of idealism in this reorganization of their society, and resentful of the rather autocratic fashion in which it was to be managed, several members resigned some months after the National Theatre Society was incorporated. Those who left to join Edward Martyn in the Theatre of Ireland included playwrights Padraic Colum and Seamus O'Kelly, Maire Nic Shiubhlaigh, one of the group's best actresses, and the popular George Russell, who wrote under the pseudonym AE. In addition to writing plays, Russell was a poet, mystic, economist, painter, and patron of the younger writers of the Irish literary renaissance.

The Fays stayed on at the Abbey, but not for very much longer. Yeats was unhappy with the quality of production of his tragic plays, and despaired of ever seeing them successfully staged. With Miss Horniman's forceful encouragement, Yeats therefore imported a well-known English director, Ben Iden Payne, who was appointed managing director of the Abbey Theatre in 1907, despite the misgivings of Synge and Lady Gregory and everyone else connected with the theater. During the few months Mr. Payne stayed at the Abbey, however, he directed only one play by Yeats, a revival of *Deirdre*. Synge described the production, in a letter to Lady Gregory, as "a bastard literary pantomime." [20]

William Fay was reinstated as stage manager after Payne left, but the board of directors then unreasonably refused his demands. Fay had asked that he be permitted to exercise more authority over the actors (who were in the habit of appealing to the board in any dispute with Fay), and that the theater adopt a more versatile repertory (Yeats agreed with him that the Abbey's growing dependence on peasant plays was ill-advised). Fay, with his brother and other actors, left the Abbey in 1908. The subsequent careers of the Fays were both, unfortunately, characterized by obscurity. Following a tour of the United States, William Fay settled in London as an actor and director; Frank worked with several English companies before returning to Dublin in 1921 to teach elocution and acting.

The Fays had inaugurated at the Abbey an excellent and distinctive tradition of acting that continued long after their departure, but there was an immediate and perceptible drop in the quality of Abbey productions after 1908, when Yeats, Lady Gregory and Synge undertook the practical work of stage management and instruction in acting. In 1910 Yeats appointed Lennox Robinson stage director and manager at the Abbey, characteristically trying to make a virtue out of Robinson's lack of experience in the theater. Like later Yeats appointees, St. John Ervine and F. R. Higgins, Robinson did not prove to have the imaginative daring or the professionalism that the Abbey needed in its directors.

The growth of the Irish national theater was attended by several notorious controversies, though it is difficult for modern audiences to detect those elements in Yeats's *The Countess Cathleen* or Synge's *The Playboy of the Western World* that gave rise to such acrimony. From a detached point of view, it is easy to dismiss the objections to these plays as coming from some unreasonable individuals whose nationalism was so zealous it could not brook the faintest implication that anything Irish was less than perfect, and from others whose religion was so puritanically inclined as to object to any sexual reference, or so dogmatic as to expect plays, even by non-Catholics, to be perfectly orthodox on every point of Catholic doctrine.

Yet one can understand, to some extent, the touchiness of nationalist sentiment at the turn of the century, which of necessity had to assert and demonstrate constantly that the Irish were not only capable of ruling themselves, but were indeed more capable of doing so than the English. And one can appreciate, too, the near-morbid sensitivity of Catholics about references to their religion made by those of a different persuasion, for the Catholic faith had been actively persecuted in Ireland and had been for centuries virtually the only sustaining force in the lives of a deprived and oppressed people. Since Yeats, Lady Gregory and Synge, the administrators and chief playwrights of the national theater, were three Anglo-Irish Protestants—notwithstanding their enlightened nationalism and separation from their class—Catholic and nationalist opinion was all the more ready to take exception to any of the plays they wrote or produced that seemed critical of Catholicism or Ireland.

A controversy was stirred up in anticipation of the first production of the Irish Literary Theatre, Yeats's *The Countess Cathleen,* in 1899; there were riots when Synge's *The Playboy of the Western World* was produced in 1907, and when Sean O'Casey's *The Plough and the Stars* was produced in 1926.

Before *The Countess Cathleen* was performed, a pamphlet, entitled "Souls for Gold! Pseudo-Celtic Drama in Dublin," attacked Yeats and his play, in which the Countess Cathleen sells her soul to the devil to save the starving peasants of Ireland, but is happily not condemned to hell as a result. Yeats was accused of blasphemy, heresy, and pseudo-nationalism. Cardinal Logue, though he had not read the play, said that no Catholic should go to see it. A petition against the play was circulated in the Catholic university of Dublin, and denunciatory articles appeared in the newspapers. As a result of this agitation of public opinion, the audience on the play's opening night was potentially riotous and Yeats felt it necessary to call in the police. In the end, there was merely a good deal of shouting.

Yeats quickly realized the source of the problem: what he had treated as symbols in his play were realities to his audience. The kicking to pieces of a shrine to the Virgin Mary by an Irish peasant (an incident Yeats later omitted from the play), was genuinely offensive to many Irishmen. So, too, was the peasants' selling their souls for gold and food, since so many Irish had starved in the Famine rather than accept the food offered by Protestant religious organizations on condition that they renounce Catholicism.

But if Yeats offended Catholic opinion in *The Countess Cathleen,* he endeared himself to the nationalist cause with the ultra-patriotic *Cathleen Ni Houlihan.* It was Synge, not Yeats, whose plays were to arouse the deepest resentment in Ireland. When Synge's *The Shadow of the Glen* was first produced in 1903, it was immediately attacked for being an insult to Irish womanhood. The plot of the play has sources in the folklore of several countries as well as Ireland; it involves an old husband who pretends to be dead in order to detect his young wife's infidelity and casts her out after her cowardly lover has rejected her. Synge's realistic treatment of his subject addressed a very discernible social ill in rural Ireland, the loveless marriage, but his critics saw only a libel on the virtue of Irishwomen. Because of the play, Maud Gonne dissociated herself from the Irish National Theatre Society, and two of its leading actors, Dudley Digges and Maire Quinn, resigned. The play's performance was greeted with boos and hisses.

In such circumstances, it was wise of Yeats and Lady

Gregory not to produce Synge's *The Tinker's Wedding*
for fear that its drunken priest would offend Catholic
opinion. Yeats was probably right to feel that it would
have been dangerous to stage the play; indeed, it was
not performed at the Abbey until 1971. But while
Yeats and Lady Gregory had objected to some of the
language of Synge's *The Playboy of the Western
World,* and had insisted on cuts being made before the
play's opening, on Saturday, January 26, 1907, they
were nonetheless unprepared for the storm of protest
that it elicited. Indeed, all seemed to go well for the
first act, and Lady Gregory cabled Yeats, who was lecturing in Scotland, "Play great success." But she had
to send another cable very shortly afterward: "Audience broke up in disorder at the word 'shift'." [21] The
modern theatergoer will find this prudishness incomprehensible; a "shift" was a chemise, a lady's shirt-like
undergarment, and certainly not sexually explicit by
today's standards. Yet as Lady Gregory tells us, even
the newspaper accounts "followed the example of
some lady from the country, who wrote saying the
word omitted but understood was one she would blush
to use even when she was alone." [22] Of course, a widespread distaste for "coarseness" prevailed in many
other countries as well as Ireland at the turn of the
century: England's pride in her greatest dramatist did
not save the works of Shakespeare from careful expur-
gation before they were considered fit for the stage.

On the second night of *The Playboy of the Western
World*'s performance there was organized disruption.
About forty men created such a disturbance by boo-
ing, hissing, and blowing trumpets that the play could
not be heard after the first act. (Yeats satirized their
behavior, which he saw as typical of the pig-headed
unreasonableness of so many people in the Ireland of
his day, in his play *The Green Helmet.*) This attempt
to hoot the play off the stage persisted for a week;

every evening the protesters attempted to drown out
the play, there were scuffles, and many arrests by the
police who were present in force both inside and outside the theater. It is interesting that *The Playboy of
the Western World* aroused such passions despite the
numerous cuts that had been made prior to its performance; indeed, the full text of the play was never
used by the Abbey while Lady Gregory and Yeats were
on the board of directors, even when the company was
later touring Britain and the United States.

The language of the play, even after it had been
cut, was thought wild and blasphemous, in addition to
being obscene in its mention of the unmentionable
shift. But most of all, the play was considered a slan-
der on the Irish because it portrayed them as lovers of
violence. The peasants in Synge's play make much of a
man they think has murdered his father. It was almost
inevitable, in the political atmosphere of the time,
that the peasants' attitude would be interpreted as
typical of Irish national characteristics. Determined to
foster the independence and pride of their race, the
Irish nationalists were unduly sensitive to anything
that could be interpreted as a slur on the national
character. There is, indeed, an element in Synge's play
of satiric attack on Irish Catholic idealism; the fear of
the nationalists that the play could be interpreted as
showing an Irish tendency to glorify the criminal has
some basis. As recently as 1975, a performance of *The
Playboy of the Western World* in London inspired
some English reviewers to connect the Irish Republican Army's bombing campaign in England with
what they saw as a theme of the play: Irish admiration
for lawless violence.

Yeats and Lady Gregory showed admirable courage,
integrity, and loyalty to Synge during the controversy
aroused by his play. Their reward was a resounding
moral victory by the end of that first stormy week's

run of *The Playboy of the Western World.* By insisting on its performance, Yeats and Lady Gregory had
allowed the play itself to vindicate their belief in
Synge's dramatic genius, and had won an important
battle against what Lady Gregory called "mob censorship." Yeats presided over a public discussion in the
Abbey of Synge's play, in which he interpreted and
defended it with an eloquence and conviction that
compelled admiration from a hostile audience. The
victory cost the Abbey dearly, however, for audiences
dropped alarmingly for some considerable time afterward.

In 1911, the redoubtable Lady Gregory accompanied
the Abbey players at a week's notice on a tour of the
United States, where Irish organizations such as Clan
na Gael tried to drive *The Playboy of the Western
World* off the stage, for the same mixture of reasons
political clubs in Ireland had opposed it. Lady Gregory's defense of Synge's play was all the more admirable since she herself disliked it. She wrote from America to her nephew Sir Hugh Lane: "If you knew how I
hate the *Playboy* that I go on fighting for!" [23] *The
Playboy of the Western World* was successfully produced in Boston, Providence, Washington, New York,
Philadelphia, and Chicago despite the disturbances
that accompanied its performance.

In Chicago, Lady Gregory actually received a letter
threatening her with death (she scornfully refused to
take it seriously because the sketch of a gun in the
letter showed, she said, the sender's ignorance of fire-
arms). In Philadelphia, the entire cast was arrested under a municipal law forbidding "immoral or indecent
plays," following a complaint made by a liquor dealer.
When defense lawyer John Quinn, the most dedicated
American friend and patron of the Irish literary and
dramatic movement, asked a prosecution witness if
anything immoral had taken place on stage, he replied

"Not while the curtain was up!" [24] The Abbey players were acquitted. In New York City, Lady Gregory's
friend, ex-president Theodore Roosevelt, accompanied
her to a production of *The Playboy of the Western
World* and her own *Gaol Gate*. There were scuffles
during both plays, but Roosevelt's presence lent prestige and moral support to the Abbey's cause. The up-
shot of all of this was to make the accomplishment of
the Irish dramatic movement familiar and popular in
America. The Abbey's victory over "mob censorship"
was consolidated by its appeal to a wider audience
than Ireland, and by the establishment of Synge, only
a few years after his premature death in 1909, as a
major international playwright.

Eugene O'Neill, "the father of American drama,"
was an enthusiastic member of the audience many
times when the Abbey players came to New York during their American tour of 1911, and later acknowledged their influence on his own work: "It was seeing
the Irish Players that gave me a glimpse of my opportunity. I went to see everything they did. I thought
then and I still think that they demonstrate the possibilities of naturalistic acting better than any other
company." [25] It is very likely that the example of
the Abbey was influential in the founding of the Prov-
incetown Players Theater, which performed O'Neill's
first successful play and in the founding, too, of several small theaters based on principles similar to those
of the Abbey, such as the Chicago Art Theater. "The
full consequences of this Abbey Theatre tour of
North America would have astounded even the visionary mind of Yeats. From it sprang a major impe-
tus for the amateur Little Theatre Movement across
the United States and Canada, which has since evolved
into a system of professional regional theatres." [26] So
the conception and technique of the Abbey Theatre,
coupled with that of the Théâtre Libre and the Mos-

cow Art Theater, served as an example to inspire and shape the character of the modern theater in North America.

Yeats and Lady Gregory also stood firm in opposing the attempt of Dublin Castle, the seat of the English administration in Ireland, to prevent the Abbey from performing *The Shewing-Up of Blanco Posnet* by George Bernard Shaw in 1909. The Lord Chamberlain, the British official responsible for theater censorship, had already vetoed the production of Shaw's play in England; he had no jurisdiction in Ireland, but the authorities at Dublin Castle forbade the play's performance on the grounds of its blasphemous tendencies. They threatened to revoke the Abbey's patent (the license that allowed it to perform plays in Ireland), which would have been a disastrous blow for the Irish dramatic movement. *Blanco Posnet* was performed for a large and appreciative audience despite official bullying and cajoling, Yeats and Lady Gregory having remained unintimidated and unimpressed even after being summoned to an interview with the head of the English administration, the Lord Lieutenant. This defiance, which Dublin Castle did its best to ignore, endeared the Abbey, for a time anyway, to the Irish nationalists.

The Abbey Theatre had not been in existence for more than five or six years before it became apparent that one type of play was to dominate its repertoire. It was the realistic peasant or folk play, whose dialogue is in some sense poetic (often a colorful and imaginative speech based on dialect), the sort of play that derived ultimately from the influence of Synge and Lady Gregory rather than Yeats. Yeats despondently came to realize that he had founded a realistic theater despite his intentions, a theater in which his own symbolic verse plays seemed anomalous and bizarre. In an open letter to Lady Gregory, Yeats acknowledged that "we did not set out to create this sort of theatre, and its success has been to me a discouragement and a defeat." [27]

Lady Gregory's main interest in establishing and maintaining the theater had always been the staging of Yeats's verse plays, as she insisted in *Our Irish Theatre*: "The plays that I have cared for most of all though, and for love of which I took up this work, are those verse ones by Mr. Yeats, *The Countess Cathleen* with which we began, *The Shadowy Waters*, *The King's Threshold*, and the rest. . . . I feel verse is, more than any prose can be, the apex of the flame, the point of the diamond." [28] But the realistic peasant play was popular, and the policy of Yeats and Lady Gregory as members of the board of directors of the Abbey diverged sharply from their theory when it came to the perennial problem of filling seats in the theater:

> . . . the only new play by Yeats produced at the Abbey between 1908 and 1919 was *The Golden Helmet* (and its revision, *The Green Helmet*); when *The Player Queen* was finally produced late in 1919 it had already received its premiere by the Stage Society in London. The Abbey instead became a business, and Yeats was determined to make it succeed. "I have often failed as a poet but not yet as a businessman", he wrote to Olivia Shakespeare towards the end of his life. The Abbey in its later form owes its life as much to that determination shared by Yeats and Lady Gregory, long after it had ceased to be the personal venture they had planned, as to the playwrights who carried it off on another path.[29]

Among the playwrights who gave the Abbey the type of play that came to characterize its repertoire, in addition to Synge and Lady Gregory, were Padraic

Colum, Seamus O'Kelly, William Boyle, George Fitzmaurice, and T. C. Murray, and, after 1916, Lennox
Robinson, W. F. Casey, St. John Ervine, Rutherford
Mayne, George Shiels, and, of course, Sean O'Casey.
Needless to say, there are considerable differences
among the works of these playwrights—O'Casey's plays,
for instance, deal with the Dublin poor in the setting
of the Troubles rather than with rural society—yet
they all have more in common with each other in
their basically realistic orientation than any of them
have with the symbolic verse drama of Yeats. These
playwrights and many others have created a tradition
of realistic Irish drama that by now spans more than
half a century and mirrors the social process of modern
Ireland in taking as its subject matter the role of land,
politics, marriage, and money in the lives of the people.

It is interesting and amusing to speculate about the
extent to which the subject matter and technique of
one of the greatest of modern playwrights, Samuel
Beckett (born and raised in Dublin), must have been
inspired by reaction against the realistic tradition of
the Abbey. The protagonist of Beckett's novel *Murphy*
(1938), derisively requires in his last will and testament
that

> "With regard to the disposal of these my body,
> mind and soul, I desire that they be burnt and
> placed in a paper bag and brought to the Abbey
> Theatre, Lr. Abbey Street, Dublin, and without
> pause into what the great and good Lord Chester-
> field calls the necessary house, where their hap-
> piest hours have been spent, on the right as one
> goes down into the pit, and I desire that the
> chain be there pulled upon them, if possible
> during the performance of a piece, the whole to
> be executed without ceremony or show of grief." [30]

Yeats was acutely aware that the sort of plays he

himself was interested in writing would never appeal very strongly to Abbey audiences, and he character- istically made an aristocratic virtue out of their lack of popularity:

> I want to create for myself an unpopular theatre and an audience like a secret society where admis- sion is by favour and never to many. Perhaps I shall never create it, for you [Lady Gregory] and I and Synge have had to dig the stone for our statue and I am aghast at the sight of a new quarry, and besides I want so much—an audience of fifty, a room worthy of it (some great dining- room or drawing-room), half a dozen young men and women who can dance and speak verse or play drum and flute and zither, and all the while, instead of a profession, I but offer them "an accomplishment." . . . I seek, not a theatre but the theatre's anti-self. . . .[31]

Practice in this case had preceded theory, for as early as 1916, three years before Yeats made this statement, *At the Hawk's Well* was being staged in London in Lady Cunard's drawing-room. The elitism of Yeats's attitude at this stage of his career may be partly at- tributed to the defensiveness he undoubtedly felt about the lack of popular appeal of his verse dramas.

Despite the disappointment of his personal ideals for the Abbey, Yeats was nevertheless determined that it should flourish as Ireland's national theater. Partly as a result of his influence and energetic lobbying, the Abbey was subsidized in 1924 by the Irish government, making it the first theater in the English-speaking world to be directly funded by the state. (The Dublin Gate Theatre, which, under the management of Hil- ton Edwards and Michael MacLiammoir, dominated Irish theater in the 1930s, has in recent years also been the recipient of a government subsidy.)

The Abbey burned down in 1951, but excellent new facilities were built on the same site by the Irish government in 1966. Ironically enough, the shape of the new theater would seem to be close to the ideal Yeats had dreamed of in 1901:

> Were our theatres of the shape of a half-closed fan, like Wagner's theatre, where the audience sit on seats that rise towards the broad end while the play is played at the narrow end, their pictures could be composed for eyes at a small number of points of view, instead of for eyes at many points of view, above and below and at the sides, and what is no better than a trade might become an art.[32]

Like so many theaters that have been founded with a deliberately innovative aim, the Abbey has often been accused, sometimes justifiably, of having lost the spirit and the technical excellence of its early days. It was almost predictable that the Abbey's tour of the United States in 1976, the first in thirty-eight years, would disappoint those who expected to encounter the legendary charisma associated with the early productions of the Irish national theater. One drama critic in particular gave voice to this sense of disappointment when he saw the Abbey's production of O'Casey's *The Plough and the Stars*, which was presented at the Brooklyn Academy of Music in November, 1976:

> The Abbey players who created *The Plough and the Stars* are mostly just as dead as those precursors of the Comédie Française who first performed the plays of Molière. And bequeathing a theatrical tradition is rather like bequeathing a cheese: No matter how hard you try to keep it fresh, it does

tend to go bad after a while, and nothing is worse
to have around the house than an old smelly
tradition. Better to throw it out and start again.[33]

This kind of radical critique of the modern Abbey is
one that many Irish drama critics have articulated
over the years, but it would seem to have been most
appropriate during the 1940s and 1950s, when the theater did seem distinctly moribund. For the last fifteen
years or so of its existence, however, the Abbey has
maintained consistent standards of excellence in acting and production, and given little cause for the al-
legation that it is clinging to an outworn tradition.
More often than not, the Abbey Theatre demonstrates
that it is very much alive and well, and not some
moldy relic of its former self.

The Abbey has remained true to the ideals of its
founders in that it is both a national and a popular
theater, committed to producing drama by Irish authors and ensuring that the average citizen can afford
to frequent the theater. (Admission prices to the Abbey and the other Dublin theaters are relatively cheap
even by Irish standards. They are no more expensive,
and often cheaper, than the cost of admission to the
movies, which makes the theater in Ireland popular
in a way that is rare in the United States.) And finally,
despite the Abbey's early disagreement with the Irish
nationalists over Synge's work, it remains a potent
example for countries concerned with inculcating in
their citizens a strong sense of national identity. Since
about 1960, the Abbey has been much admired in
Egypt, Syria, and Lebanon as a theater that, in helping to make the people aware of their cultural identity, provided an invaluable complement to the political struggle for nationhood.[34]

From the point of view of one who admires Yeats's
plays, what is to be regretted about the enterprise of

the Irish national theater is that Yeats was not able to find in it the theater he needed for his drama. "Yeats . . . was never to have a company of Irish actors capable of adequately interpreting his plays. Obviously, what he needed most was a literate man of the theatre, such as Stanislavsky or Lugné-Poe, to work side by side with him as both a stage director and acting teacher. Along with this he needed a school or conservatory of the theatre to educate and train theatre artists possessing the profound qualities of mind and spirit, talent and technique essential for interpreters of his plays." [35]

From the perspective of one who has in mind the best interests of the Irish national theater, what is to be regretted is that there was such a wide gap between Yeats's and Lady Gregory's ideas about what a national theater should be, and their practice as administrators of the Abbey. If there was no room at the Abbey for Yeats's plays, he and Lady Gregory need not have gone so far in the opposite direction of seeking to make it a financial success by relying on the peasant play. There were a number of dramatists who were clearly far superior to the general run of Abbey playwrights during Yeats's lifetime, who received much less attention and encouragement than they deserved from both Yeats and Lady Gregory.

The experimental, expressionist dramas written by George Fitzmaurice (*The Magic Glasses*, 1913) and Sean O'Casey (*The Silver Tassie*, 1928), ended the association of these dramatists with the Abbey Theatre —the board of directors did not approve of the plays, and the Irish theater lost the allegiance of two excellent playwrights. Then again, the treatment of Denis Johnston was somehow symptomatic of the management's attitude; one of his manuscripts was returned from the Abbey with those words scrawled on its cover (indicating that Lady Gregory had rejected the play) which he later adopted as the play's title—*The Old Lady Says No.*

Yeats's determination to maintain autocratic control of the Abbey, especially in its early years, no doubt impaired the achievement of the Irish national theater; certainly the departure of William Fay was ultimately occasioned by Yeats's need to maintain power over all aspects of the theater's operation. And Yeats and Lady Gregory were also myopic in not permitting the production of experimental works by playwrights who had proved their worth in more conventional forms of the drama.

Nonetheless, one must admire Yeats for his part in founding and administering the Abbey Theatre. While it is true that he was moved to do so partly because he wanted a theater in which to stage his own plays, he was motivated much more strongly by the desire to create a national theater for Ireland. And, when it became apparent that the national theater was to have a different sort of identity than the one he had hoped for, he selflessly devoted innumerable hours of his long life to the tedious business of theater management. He had many collaborators along the way, as he was the first to acknowledge, but it was Yeats's vision and determination that played the crucial role in bringing into being and fostering the growth of Ireland's national theater.

III. PRELUDE TO PLAYWRITING

> I had begun to write poetry in imitation of Shelley
> and of Edmund Spenser, play after play—for my
> father exalted dramatic poetry above all other
> kinds—and I invented fantastic and incoherent
> plots. My lines but seldom scanned, for I could
> not understand the prosody in the books, although
> there were many lines that taken by themselves
> had music. I spoke them slowly as I wrote, and
> only discovered when I read them to somebody
> else that there was no common music, no prosody.[1]

Yeats has described very clearly, in the above quo-
tation, the shortcomings of the four early "dramatic
poems" (to use the subtitle of *The Seeker*) which are
included in the *Variorum* text of the plays. These
works can be broadly characterized as juvenilia (Yeats
was, in fact, only nineteen at the time of their composition), and more as verse than drama. The plots are
improbable and obscurely allegorical; moreover, the
verse is not only un-dramatic but archaic and derivative. But these are Yeats's first works in what was intended to be a dramatic form, and they are therefore
of interest to the student of Yeats's drama.

What is there in these four works that anticipates
the later drama? At first sight, not very much. Like the
poetry with which they are contemporaneous, these
plays seem merely to exalt a visionary dream-world
at the expense of the real world. The conflict between

these two realms is potentially dramatic, however, and Yeats was able to give several of his later plays a dramatic structure based on this conflict. The structure of *The Countess Cathleen, Cathleen Ni Houlihan, The Land of Heart's Desire, The King's Threshold* and other, later plays can be traced to the muted dialectic of these early pieces.

The Island of Statues, subtitled *An Arcadian Faery Tale—in Two Acts,* operates at several removes from everyday reality. That is, the 'normal' world of the play is Arcadia, an idyllic realm peopled by shepherds and shepherdesses; the play opens with a motif of classical pastoral—a singing contest between two shepherds. Yeats also follows tradition in portraying his Arcadia as an idealized version of everyday life in which love and music and leisure hold sway. Yeats's Arcadia, then, does not involve a transcendence of mortal cares, or an ideal, spiritual reality, as does the other realm of existence in the play. This other realm takes the form of an island ruled by an enchantress, on which grows a flower that brings to the wearer truth, wisdom, and "long years of youth/Beyond a mortal's years." But the island is full of the petrified forms of those who have failed to select the right flower from among the profusion that grows on the island, and have consequently been turned into statues by the enchantress.

The shepherdess Naschina, weary of Arcadia, longs for some courageous man to undertake a dangerous quest to prove his love for her. Her lover, Almintor, therefore seeks for the magic flower on the Island of Statues, but in vain: he, too, is turned to stone. Naschina is stricken with remorse and sets off for the island, disguised as a shepherd boy. She finds out from the enchantress, who seems to fall in love with her, that the only person who can pluck the magic flower is a shepherdess for whom someone has died. (Two shepherds have fought each other and died in an attempt to prove to Naschina the seriousness of their love for her.) Naschina thus is "mightier now by far" than the enchantress, and compels her to identify the magic flower, which she plucks and thereby awakens Almintor and the other statues from their stony sleep. The awakened sleepers (with the exception of Almintor) soon come to the melancholy realization that the noble causes of their quests have long since perished, and that they themselves must continue to exist outside time, and without human love. They determine to go on living on the island with Almintor and Naschina as king and queen.

The Island of Statues embodies what is characteristic of the early Yeats—a muted theme of conflict, between the everyday world (in this play an Arcadia that represents the best of the real world) and an amorphously ideal realm (of magic, beauty, art, and eternity). There is a complicating sense, too, in this play, that the joys of ordinary human love and friendship are spoiled by the pursuit of the ideal. Naschina's triumph is, we are made to feel, something of a Pyrrhic victory. This, too, is characteristic of the early Yeats. F. R. Leavis makes this point about the early poetry in general:

> . . . everywhere there is a recognition, implicit in the shifting cloudy unseizableness of the imagery, that this 'reality' [i.e., of the ideal world] must be illusory, and that even if it could be reached it would leave human longing unslaked. And this recognition is subtly turned into a strength: it validates, as it were, the idealizing fanaticism of the poetry and counterpoises the obsession with the transcendental. . . .[2]

The Island of Statues also reveals Yeats's fascination with heroic female characters. It is Naschina, after all, who successfully completes the dangerous quest of the play. The destructive cost of accomplishing the quest, which Yeats is conscious of in all the poems and plays that involve the pursuit of the ideal, is reflected in the ominously suggestive stage directions of the play's last lines, which suggest the loss of humanity on the part of the protagonist and the other seekers after the ideal: in the light of the rising moon, "Naschina is standing, shadowless." Yeats himself could later manage only faint praise for the play: "I am sure the 'Island' is good of its kind." [3]

The Seeker is subtitled *A Dramatic Poem—In Two Scenes,* and is only eighty-one lines long. In the first of the play's scenes, three shepherds in "a woodland valley at evening" encounter an old knight who tells them he has been wandering, "dream-led," for sixty years. But now he is sure that his journeying is near an end, for he has been led to this valley by a mysterious voice. The shepherds vainly try to prevent him from following the voice to its source in the nearby enchanted woods. The second scene is set in a ruined palace in the forest. The floors are covered with dried leaves, which the knight presses to his breast as he kneels before "a motionless Figure," begging it to speak, recognizing this "visionary one" as the origin of the voice that has obsessed him since childhood and made him wander on his lifelong quest, bereft of ordinary human joy and love. The light suddenly reveals this figure to be a bearded witch, called Infamy. The knight is appalled, and attempts to reject her—"I sought thee not," he exclaims in horror, but the figure insists "Lover, the voice that summoned thee was mine." When the figure holds up a mirror that reflects the knight, he falls and dies.

That the obsession with a visionary quest may lead only to sterility and death, and may ultimately be heroism *manqué,* is a theme of Yeats's poetry, but

more importantly in this context, of a later very successful play, *At the Hawk's Well*. The old man of
that play, who has wasted his life by the side of a dry
well, waiting vainly for the magical waters to flow, is
reminiscent of the old knight of *The Seeker*. The dry
leaves in both plays are used as symbols of spiritual
aridity, and the sibylline females who guard the holy
places are comparably sinister and destructive. As a
play, there is not much to *The Seeker*, but it is an
interesting foreshadowing of one of Yeats's more important and successful plays.

Mosada is surely the most entertaining of these four
plays. The play is set in Spain during the Inquisition. It is a brief play (of 134 lines) in three scenes. In
the first scene, Mosada, described as "a Moorish lady,"
plaintively remembers how her Christian lover Gomez
left her three years ago, because "I and all my people
were accurst/Of his sad God." She burns herbs on a
dish, and summons the lame boy, Cola, from the
street to look into the smoke (as into a crystal ball),
and tell her the whereabouts of Gomez. Cola refuses
to participate in this magic, for the "great monk
Ebremar" has told him it is a sin. In fact, Cola has, it
turns out, betrayed Mosada to the officers of the Inquisition, who now enter and arrest the girl, telling
her that she will be burned at the stake, apparently
more on account of her practice of magic than because
of her heretical allegiance to the Islamic religion.

The second scene takes place in "the building of the
Inquisition of Granada," which is lighted by a stained-
glass window. Monks and inquisitors discuss Mosada.
One of the group is sympathetic to the girl and begs
Ebremar, who is "bright-eyed, and hollow-cheeked
from fasting," to spare her life. Ebremar is adamant
that she must die, and prays to God to fill him with
rage to punish heathen and heretic.

The last scene takes place in Mosada's cell at dawn.

She poignantly remembers her home and family as the men in the square outside her cell prepare for her execution, then swallows poison from her ring. Before losing consciousness, she thinks of the delightful possibility of being united with her lover in death. Ebremar comes in to urge Mosada to repent of her sin because her death is imminent, recognizes the unconscious girl as his former love, and thereby reveals himself to the audience as Gomez. He rouses Mosada, and, apparently undergoing a radical change of heart, promises to run away with her. Mosada is happy at first, but her mind wanders to the past, and she dies remembering only Gomez's desertion. Gomez bitterly reverts to his identity as Ebremar, the inquisitor, and exits with the intention of persuading other imprisoned sinners of the need to confess their wrongdoing.

This interesting, rather operatic play pits love, life, and magic against hatred, death, and the institution of religion at its least sympathetic. There can be little doubt where the audience's allegiance is supposed to lie. The simple and brief play is, however, possessed of a certain force: the clarity and relative convincingness with which the opposing forces are portrayed, and the evocative images of the uncluttered verse (for example, in the passage where Mosada remembers her home), make the play much more appealing than its companion-pieces.

Time and the Witch Vivien is extremely short, a mere sixty-nine lines, in fact. According to Ellmann, the play was "rehearsed and possibly presented by Yeats and a group of his friends at the home of a Judge Wright on Howth." [4] The witch Vivien, in a "marble-flagged, pillared room," admires herself in the water of a fountain in the center of the room, and congratulates herself on being an unequalled magician. Time enters, dressed as a pedlar and per-

haps rather over-equipped with the tools of his trade
—a scythe, a black bag, and an hour-glass. Vivien
challenges him to a game. First they play at dice, and
of course Vivien loses (she points out that "Time always plays/With loaded dice"), just as she loses the
second game, a game of chess. Defeat in this game, as
Time reminds her, means death, and Vivien dies when
checkmated, reflecting ironically on the luck and skill
of Time.

Time and the Witch Vivien can hardly be taken
seriously as a play. Vivien's pride in her beauty and
secret knowledge is barely stated, so that the Faustian
motif of man attempting to transcend mortality is only
hinted at in the play. The encounter between Vivien
and Time lacks any compelling dramatic motivation.
But the vaguely medieval ambience, evident in the
personification of Time (he has a whiter beard "than
Merlin," King Arthur's magician), and more importantly in the nature of the play's action, anticipates
the most medieval of Yeats's morality plays, *The
Hour Glass*. In that play, though, the protagonist's
intellectual pride and the existence of the spiritual
realm of existence that he denies are portrayed much
more convincingly.

That three of the four dramatic poems have female
protagonists, and at least two were inspired by Yeats's
first love, is indicative of the extraordinary role of
women in the development of Yeats's drama from its
beginnings. Women with whom he was emotionally involved are demonstrably his muses, frequently provid-
ing the inspiration that leads to the conception and
writing of the plays. Occasionally Yeats also intends
them actually to take part in the drama, to play the
theatrical roles of the strong-minded women who
dominate the action of many of his plays. Women are
also partly responsible for helping Yeats to realize his
distinctive identity as an Irish dramatist, and largely

responsible for the practical help that enabled him to have access to a theater.

Thus, the young Yeats wrote *Time and the Witch Vivien* and *The Island of Statues* for Laura Armstrong: "The part of the enchantress in both poems was written for her," he wrote to Katharine Tynan.[5] The latter first urged him "to write a play about Ireland," and Maud Gonne suggested the possibility of having *The Countess Cathleen* put on by amateurs in Dublin.[6] Maud Gonne was also, of course, the source of inspiration and the subject of many of Yeats's poems and plays. Yeats was, in the early years of his career, discovering his Irishness (with some help from his friends), realizing that Irish myth and legend were to provide him with his subject matter (none of the four dramatic poems is, in any way, Irish), and becoming aware that Ireland was to provide him with an audience and a theater. Lady Gregory's translations opened up to him the storehouse of Irish myth and legend, and her practical help, along with that of Miss Annie Horniman and others, enabled him to have a theater more or less at his disposal. The English actress, Florence Farr, staged the first of Yeats's plays to be performed in a public theater (*The Land of Heart's Desire*, in the Avenue Theatre, London, in 1894), and her speaking technique reinforced his commitment to the tradition of the poetic drama.

It should go without saying that there were many other influences at work on Yeats during the years he was discovering the nature of his genius, and other individuals who helped him find his characteristic strength as a dramatist. But there can be little doubt, either, of the extent to which women nourished Yeats's genius, inspired so much of his work, and helped him realize his dreams of founding a theater.

The plays written during the first mature phase of Yeats's playwriting, that is, the fifteen years or so subsequent to the writing of the four dramatic poems discussed above, illustrate the way cultural and social influences, as well as the influences of his friends, had coalesced in Yeats's life and art in a very creative and productive fashion. The grounding of the plays of this period in Irish life, their shaping by actual theatrical performance, the emergence in them of genuine dramatic structure, the achievement of the verse—all this makes the early plays of the mature Yeats accomplishments of a different order than the dramatic poems. The dramatic poems are, by comparison, distinctly literary in inspiration and achievement.

Yet the same assertion of the superiority of the ideal to the real as in the four poems can be seen in *The King's Threshold* and *On Baile's Strand,* and the same prominence of heroic female characters can be seen in *The Land of Heart's Desire, The Countess Cathleen,* and *Cathleen Ni Houlihan.* These later plays, as well as *The Unicorn From the Stars* and *The Hour Glass,* retain, too, the same allegorical coloring as the dramatic poems. *The Island of Statues, The Seeker, Mosada,* and *Time and the Witch Vivien,* then, anticipate thematically Yeats's later plays and demonstrate Yeats's commitment, from the very beginning of his career, to the poetic drama. They demonstrate, too, that remarkable unity of Yeats's artistic vision to which Harold Bloom draws our attention: "Yeats, in later life, writing about Shelley, said that a man's mind at twenty contains everything of importance it will ever possess. Whatever we think of this as a general principle, it does seem relevant to Yeats himself." [7]

IV. FOLK AND MORALITY PLAYS

The seven plays discussed in this category include Yeats's earliest contributions to the repertoire of the Irish national theater. With the possible exception of *The Unicorn from the Stars,* all have sources in Irish folklore. All are set in Ireland, and those that are not composed in verse employ the Kiltartan dialect, a poetic prose patented by Lady Gregory. Indeed, it is almost certain that Lady Gregory's interest in folk plays influenced all of Yeats's plays up until 1916, by which time he had fastened on the Japanese Noh play as a model for his drama.

These consciously Irish plays belong, therefore, in their subject matter and tone, to the ambience of the Irish cultural renaissance, and helped set the model for the peasant drama that was to be identified with the Abbey Theatre. The political implications of two of these plays, *The Countess Cathleen* and *Cathleen Ni Houlihan,* provoked, respectively, the ardent disapproval and approval of Irish nationalists and stamped Yeats and his theater as being politically controversial. Yeats's relationship with Maud Gonne, one of the most radical and certainly the most beautiful of the Irish nationalists, is reflected in the political and romantic implications of these two plays in particular.

A further distinguishing characteristic of these early works is that they are all morality plays. *The Hour-Glass,* subtitled "a morality," is most obviously like a medieval morality in subject and structure, but all are essentially dramatic allegories that seek to demonstrate the superiority of the spiritual over the material world. Only in *The Hour-Glass* and *The Countess Cathleen,* however, can these spiritual values be described, even loosely, as Christian ones. In the other plays, the transcendent realities assume the form of a fervid nationalism (in *Cathleen Ni Houlihan*), a pagan (as opposed to a Christian) otherworld (in *The Land of Heart's Desire*), and a new order anticipated through mystical symbolism in *The Unicorn from the Stars* and *The Shadowy Waters*). The rejection of worldliness for a variety of spiritual realities in all these plays was part of a constant attempt by Yeats to educate the imagination and conscience of his countrymen. It is surely a mistake to equate the simplicity of these folk and morality plays with quaintness or naïveté, for they share with his later Abbey plays the dramatic conflict between two opposing world views. Moreover, they also share an important structural element with the Noh plays, as Peter Ure points out:

> The Noh plays, with which much of his work has structural affinity, helped Yeats to strengthen and define the climactic moments of revelation and spiritual enlightenment, but such moments are characteristically present in plays written long before he had heard of the Noh; indeed, a list of them would include all the early plays—*Cathleen Ni Houlihan* itself, long his most famous and popular piece, is one of the best examples.[1]

1. *The Countess Cathleen* (1892)

Like so many of Yeats's plays, *The Countess Cathleen* is set in early Ireland, when pagan beliefs

Above, Mary, the Countess Cathleen, Oona, and Aleel in *The Countess Cathleen. Below,* Seamus, Teigue, and Mary. An Abbey Theatre Production.

THE ABBEY THEATRE; DERMOT BARRY

existed side by side with Christianity. The first of this episodic play's five scenes is set in the cottage of Mary, Shemus, and their son Teigue. The land is famine-stricken, baleful horned owls inhabit the woods, and there is hardly any food left in the cottage. Mary has faith that God will provide, but Shemus and Teigue say that either God has fallen asleep and cannot hear the people's prayers, or that His kitchen is bare and He cannot provide for them. The Countess Cathleen, accompanied by her old nurse Oona and the poet Aleel, stops at the cottage to find her way back through the woods to her castle. After she leaves, two devils materialize in the shape of Eastern merchants. They proclaim that they are willing to buy souls for gold and pay Shemus and Teigue to announce this news at every crossroads.

When Shemus and Teigue tell Cathleen about the merchants' offer in the second scene, she determines to sell all she owns to save the souls of her people. In the third scene, Cathleen is praying in her oratory when Aleel enters and vainly beseeches her to go with him to the hills and live "Among the sounds of music and the light/Of waters, till the evil days are done." When the theft of Cathleen's riches by the merchants is discovered, making the plight of the peasants apparently hopeless, Cathleen has "a strange thought" that she reveals to no one. She conceives of selling her own soul to the demons, who will pay enough money for the soul of this "saint with the sapphire eyes" to enable her to save the people.

The very brief fourth scene, set in the woods near the castle, contrasts the peasants' discussion of the virtues of gold with Aleel's beautiful but forlorn love song. In the next and last scene, the peasants crowd into Shemus's house, where the merchants have set up shop to buy souls. Mary lies on a bed, mortally ill because, in her son's words, "She would not eat/One crumb of bread bought with our masters' money/But lived on nettles, dock, and dandelion." The bartering over souls is quite humorous, for the merchants are aware of the lack of virtue in the souls they buy and offer an insultingly low price for them. Cathleen enters and offers to sell her soul if the merchants in return will give enough to feed the peasants until the famine has passed, and if they will set free the souls they have already bought. The merchants readily agree.

There is a great storm and darkness descends as Cathleen dies—"When she signed,/Her heart began to break." Angels appear, and Aleel seizes one of them, demanding to know the fate of Cathleen. He is told that she is in heaven, for God "Looks always on the motive, not the deed."

The play is based on a tale in Yeats's book *Fairy and Folk Tales of the Irish Peasantry* (1888), though there is no mention in that tale of Aleel, Mary, Shemus or Teigue, and no indication that Cathleen has gone to heaven. The date of 1892 provided in *Collected Plays* is somewhat misleading, for though the play was first written then ("before I knew anything of the theatre," as Yeats said), the version included in *Collected Plays* is the fifth and final revision of the play.[2] The main objective of the revisions was to give more prominence to the role of Aleel, and to improve the play's dramatic structure in the light of the performance of *The Land of Heart's Desire* in 1894. The play that premiered in The Antient Concert Rooms, Dublin, on May 8, 1899, was Yeats's third version of *The Countess Cathleen*. It took, according to Yeats, just over one hour to perform without intermissions. Though Yeats was aware that the play remained rather static despite the revisions, he was always fond of it, saying that it gave him "more pleasure in the memory than any of my plays." [3] He remembered with pleasure, too, the performance of his friend Florence Farr in the role of Aleel because she spoke his verse in a delightful musical chant.

The Countess Cathleen is intended to be allegorical rather than realistic, though those who took violent exception to the play clearly did not think so. The setting of *The Countess Cathleen* in Ireland's early history, rather than at the time of the Great Famine in the nineteenth century, suggests the symbolic nature of the play. The famine in the play symbolizes the spiritual deprivation of modern Ireland and the materialism which seemed to Yeats to have infected so much of Irish society. The eagerness of Shemus and Teigue to barter what they consider a mere vapor is, it seems, Yeats's comment on the philistinism and materialism of modern Ireland, and the noble and redemptive self-sacrifice of the Countess his object lesson in idealism for his contemporaries.

The play is a personal as well as a social allegory. It is dedicated to Maud Gonne, and there is an obvious parallel between the heroic self-sacrifice of Cathleen and the stern commitment of Maud Gonne to the revolutionary cause in Ireland. Cathleen's saintly devotion to her peasants is to be compared and contrasted with Maud Gonne's activism, in the early part of her revolutionary career, on behalf of the Irish peasants who were still being evicted and otherwise oppressed by landlords and their agents in Donegal. The poet Aleel corresponds to Yeats, who was deeply impressed by Maud Gonne's social and political engagement, and who in the early years of their relationship, at least, regretted bitterly that he could only offer her a love and art that were not socially or politically motivated.

The play, then, has two rather distinct aspects. First, it functions as a morality play, recommending to its

audience the spiritual idealism of the Countess as opposed to the cupidity of the peasants. Second, it operates as a personal allegory familiar to the reader of
Yeats's early poetry, in which there is a battle between
the conflicting claims of social and political responsibility (assumed here by Cathleen), and love and art
(represented by Aleel).

Both the static quality of *The Countess Cathleen*
and the fineness of its blank verse (which, as in *The
Land of Heart's Desire,* tends to be lyrical rather than
dramatic) are captured in Yeats's description of it as
"a piece of tapestry." [4] Yeats was soon to realize, too,
that his dramatic strength was not best expressed in a
conventional full-length play, but rather in a compressed and tightly unified structure. Joseph Holloway, a devotee of Irish theater and the architect who
designed the Abbey Theatre, was present at the play's
premiere. Holloway was somewhat dubious about the
effect created by the measured chant of the verse as it
was spoken on that occasion, but he was later inspired
to observe that "a Yeats play is like a symphony in
which the voices are the instruments employed, and
if one or more is harsh or over-loudly employed the
harmony is slain." [5] *The Countess Cathleen* was performed in Frankfurt in 1934, the occasion being
marked by the granting to Yeats of the Goethe
Award. It was also played in Cologne after the war,
very much in the manner of a romantic fairy tale.[6]

2. *The Land of Heart's Desire* (1894)

The play takes place "at a remote time" in
Ireland's past, in the western county of Sligo, where
Yeats had spent the happiest times of his childhood
and youth, and where he first encountered Irish peasant life and folklore. The set for this first of Yeats's

plays to be performed on the stage—the living room of a cottage, with an open-hearthed fireplace, a table and benches in an alcove, and a crucifix on the wall —was to become very familiar to the Irish theatergoer in years to come, when the peasant play would dominate the Abbey's offerings.

Mary Bruin, newly married to Shawn, the son of Maurteen and Bridget, is the subject of conversation as she stands by the door engrossed in a book about fairyland. When Mary looks up, she can see into the woods. Bridget complains crossly of Mary's unwillingness to help with the household chores, and Maurteen gently reproaches Mary by telling her that if he had read or written books, he could not have accumulated the legacy he plans to bequeath to her and Shawn. Father Hart tries to reassure Mary and her husband's parents that her restlessness is common in young women. Like all the others, she will grow out of it and be glad to be "minding children, working at the churn,/And gossiping of weddings and of wakes."

Mary gives the unlucky gifts of milk and fire to an old man and woman who come to the door on this the unluckiest night of the year, May Eve. The fairies will have power over the house because of what she has done, and Bridget scolds her. Mary calls to the fairies to take her out of this dull house, exclaiming that she is weary of them all—Maurteen, Father Hart, Bridget, and even her new husband. Shawn's gentle rejoinder makes her instantly regret her outburst, and she speaks tenderly of her love for him.

A voice is heard singing in the woods. It belongs to a young girl whom Maurteen unthinkingly brings into the cottage out of the cold. When the child sings and dances we realize that she is a fairy who has come to take Mary with her to the Land of Heart's Desire. Mary is torn between her desire to go with the fairy child and to remain with the husband she loves. She dies and the child leaves, presumably taking Mary's body and soul with her, for Bridget calls what remains an image, "a drift of leaves, / Or bole of an ash-tree changed into her image." Outside there is the sound of singing and dancing, and among the figures seen in the woods is a white bird, a fairy metamorphosis of Mary.

The Land of Heart's Desire was produced at the Avenue Theatre, London, as a curtain raiser for John Todhunter's *A Comedy of Sighs!* on March 29, 1894. From a poster designed by Aubrey Beardsley that advertised the play, it seems that it would have lasted about a half hour. The play was well-received and ran for six weeks. In 1901 the play was taken on tour in the United States by Mrs. Sarah Cowell Le Moyne. It played in Philadelphia, Pittsburgh, and Chicago on a double bill with Robert Browning's poetic drama *In a Balcony*. The reviews generally acknowledged that Yeats's play was refreshingly different from the usual run of theater entertainment, but the praise for this "beautiful," "pretty," and "quaint" piece was typically qualified by such terms as "literary" and "weird."

The play was written, according to Yeats's account, when Florence Farr asked him for a one-act play in which her eight-year-old niece, Dorothy Paget, could make her stage debut. So it comes that *The Land of Heart's Desire* is dedicated to Florence Farr, was staged by her, and the part of the fairy child was acted by Dorothy Paget. Yeats noted approvingly the restrained style of a later production by Lennox Robinson, who "kept all the players except the fairy child as still and statuesque as possible, so that the blank verse where there is so little animation seemed their natural utterance." [7]

The Land of Heart's Desire has only the most gen-

eralized source in the many Irish folk tales about
changelings. Inherent in these tales for Yeats was the
struggle between contrary impulses toward worldly responsibility and other-worldly freedom, a conflict
which is a major theme in Yeats's early life and work.
Yeats experienced this sort of struggle in terms of the
dialectic between a life of social, more or less conventional responsibilities, and a life dedicated to art.
(For works with a dialectic similar to *The Land of
Heart's Desire,* see, among others of Yeats's poems,
"The Man Who Dreamed of Faeryland" and "The
Stolen Child.") In *The Land of Heart's Desire,* what
Mary's life holds in store for her as the wife of Shawn
Bruin is predictable. It is against these commonplace
responsibilities, approved by the Church as Christian
duties, that she rebels—a life of working her fingers to
the bone, like Bridget; of growing into Maurteen's
worldly wisdom that accumulates land and gold; of
contenting herself with ordinary rural chores and
pleasures, like the neighbor women. Even her love
for Shawn is experienced as a kind of drowsy imprisonment. What she reads of in the book, and what
the fairy child epitomizes, is an existence that is the
antithesis of these responsibilities, a pagan life of
amoral joy in the Celtic Tir na nOg, the land of the
ever-young, where youth and beauty, love and joy are
eternal.

The play is made dramatically worthwhile by
Yeats's characteristic refusal to allow this struggle to
be a black-and-white contest between opposites. He
injects a meaningful complication into both attitudes
that helps make the play psychologically more convincing than it might otherwise be. Thus the life represented by Bridget, Maurteen, and Father Hart is by
no means felt to be drably materialistic or grimly repressive: real beauty and warmth radiate from their

tranquil domesticity, and their attitude to Mary and Shawn is basically loving and compassionate. Ironically, Father Hart's gentle nature is ultimately responsible for Mary's death. His removal of the crucifix when the fairy child shows her fear of it renders him powerless to thwart her influence on Mary. Even Bridget, who complains bitterly of Mary's lack of interest in household work, is moved to gentleness and sympathy by the plight of the cold and lost child the fairy seems to be. Most of all, though, Shawn's evident love for Mary and hers for him make the world of responsibilities something that Mary can reject only with very mixed feelings.

Likewise, the world of fairyland is not wholly attractive. As the warm and loving qualities of the Bruins qualify the dullness and mediocrity of their lives, so a certain coldness and ominousness qualify the eternal and beautiful aspects of fairyland. Mary dies apparently still hesitating between the two worlds, aware simultaneously of the attractions and limitations of both, and torn between them. *The Land of Heart's Desire* is an engaging mixture of a folk play that is particularly charming in its representation of peasant life, and a morality play that approvingly emphasizes Mary's efforts to transcend her life on earth for a spiritual existence. The blank verse of the play is often beautiful and memorable, but remains essentially lyric rather than dramatic in nature, as in Mary's expression of weariness with Maurteen, Father Hart, Bridget, and Shawn:

> ". . . I am right weary of four tongues:
> A tongue that is too crafty and too wise,
> A tongue that is too godly and too grave,
> A tongue that is more bitter than the tide,
> And a kind tongue too full of drowsy love,
> Of drowsy love and my captivity."

3. *Cathleen Ni Houlihan* (1902)

This most patriotic of Yeats's plays takes place near the town of Killala in the western county of Mayo, where French forces landed to aid the Irish rebellion of 1798. The setting is the interior of a cottage; its inhabitants, the Gillanes, are preoccupied with the marriage the next day of their son Michael to Delia Cahel. Michael's brother Patrick, a boy of twelve, speculates about the noise of cheering coming from the town, and comments on the slow progress of an old woman whom he sees through the window, coming down the road and stopping at a neighbor's farm. His parents dismiss his recollection of the folk tale "about the strange woman that goes through the country whatever time there's a war or trouble coming." Michael comes in with his future wife's dowry, and his father exultantly spills the hundred pounds out of the bag, exclaiming that now he will be able to buy and stock the ten acres of land up for sale after a neighbor's death. When cheering is heard again from the direction of town, Michael sends Patrick into town to find out the reason for it.

Michael sees the old woman coming up the path to their cottage, and feels some foreboding as she looks at him through the window; his father is anxious about admitting a stranger when there is so much money in the house. The old woman is, nonetheless, offered traditional hospitality, and is soon sitting by the fire and telling the Gillanes of her perpetual wandering since she was dispossessed of her land and house. She sings a beautiful lament for "yellow-haired Donough," hanged by the British. When she says that Donough and many others have died for love of her, Peter and Bridget begin to think that her wits are astray. Michael, however, is more and more interested in what the old woman has to say, and sits down beside her on the hearth as she tells the tragic story of the many lovers who died for her. Peter offers her a shilling to get her to leave, and is bewildered when she refuses the money. The old woman gets up, telling Michael she must go to meet her friends who are gathering to help her. Michael offers to go with her, but Bridget reminds him that his first thoughts should be of the young woman who is coming into the house, his future wife. The old woman reveals that her name is Cathleen, the daughter of Houlihan, sometimes called the Poor Old Woman, and sings a song forbidding mourning for those who will die for her on the next day, because they will be remembered forever by the people of Ireland. When Michael asks if he can be of service, she warns him as she leaves:

> "It is a hard service they take that help me. Many that are red-cheeked now will be pale-cheeked; many that have been free to walk the hills and the bogs and the rushes will be sent to walk hard streets in far countries; many a good plan will be broken; many that have gathered money will not stay to spend it; many a child will be born and there will be no father at its christening to give it a name. They that have red cheeks will have pale cheeks for my sake, and for all that, they will think they are well paid."

Bridget is alarmed at Michael's strange appearance, and she tries to bring him back to himself by putting his wedding clothes on his arm and telling him to try them on. Cheering is heard outside, as a crowd of neighbors arrives with Patrick and Delia; they announce that the French have landed at Killala to help the Irish fight against England. Michael drops the wedding suit and at first seems not to recognize Delia;

then as she embraces him, he seems willing to stay with her. But the old woman's voice is heard outside promising immortality for her lovers, and Michael rushes out. When Peter asks Patrick if he saw an old woman going down the path, the boy replies, "I did not, but I saw a young girl, and she had the walk of a queen."

Cathleen Ni Houlihan was first performed by the Irish National Dramatic Company (the Fays' group) at St. Teresa's Hall in Clarendon Street, Dublin, on April 2, 1902. This one-act play was immediately recognized as extremely effective theater and an explosive piece of nationalist propaganda. The metamorphosis of the stooped old woman into a queenly girl was a powerful traditional symbol of nationalist hopes that was all the more inspiring for the casting of Maud Gonne in the title role. Stephen Gwynn, critic of Irish literature and drama, was in the audience and recalls the play's tremendous impact:

> The effect of Cathleen Ni Houlihan on me was that I went home asking myself if such plays should be produced unless one was prepared for people to go out to shoot and be shot. Yeats was not alone responsible: no doubt Lady Gregory had helped him to get the peasant speech so perfect; but, above all, Maud Gonne's impersonation had stirred the audience as I have never seen audience stirred.[8]

The *Irish Independent* denied that there was any dramatic impersonation of the role of Cathleen, and insisted that Maud Gonne was simply and seditiously herself, "the well-known political agitator."[9] It may not have been entirely coincidental that the company was required to leave the hall at the end of the week's performance.

In Yeats's own account of the play, which appeared

(before its premiere) appropriately in the nationalist newspaper *The United Irishman,* he acknowledged the play's overtly political theme: "my subject is Ireland and its struggle for independence." [10] A great deal of the inspiration for the play doubtless came from Yeats's involvement with Maud Gonne when they organized centennial celebrations to mark the 1798 rebellion. While the rebellion was savagely suppressed by the British, it had long been considered a glorious failure, synonymous with a re-awakening of pride in Irish nationality and with the ideal of self-sacrifice for this cause.

Whether one calls her Cathleen Ni Houlihan or the Poor Old Woman, this personification of Ireland's oppression who calls on the young men of Ireland to rid her house of strangers and win back her four green fields (the traditional four provinces of Ireland) is a potent figure in Irish folk belief. The actual plot came to Yeats "in a dream almost as distinct as a vision." [11] There can be little doubt that Yeats's treatment of the legend added fuel to the fire of Irish nationalism, and contributed in particular to the self-sacrificial mentality of the 1916 insurrection. Interestingly enough, a performance of this patriotic play was scheduled coincidentally for Easter Monday, 1916!

The conflict that is the play's action is extreme and compelling. It stems from Michael's having to choose between the uncompromising idealism that lays claim on him (Cathleen Ni Houlihan's assertions that her claims take precedence over all mundane considerations recall the demands Christ made on his followers), and the commonplace though far-from-trivial happiness of love, marriage, and work. The play's success derives from the simple dramatic force of this conflict. The claims of exalted idealism on poor people preoccupied with life's normal joys and woes makes for very successful theater, as Sean O'Casey also realized in his best plays. One critic describes Cathleen Ni Houlihan as "a small masterpiece, with far more of dramatic substance than some of its successors." [12] While Yeats pointed out that the play's significance should not be limited to Ireland's struggle for independence, but should include the struggle of "every other ideal cause . . . against all that we mean when we say 'the world'," there can be little doubt that the circumstances in which Yeats clothed this conflict in *Cathleen Ni Houlihan* made the play overwhelmingly popular with Irish audiences.[13] It was not until the Easter Rising of 1916 that Yeats fully realized how much he had contributed to the ideal of political martyrdom that inspired the leaders of the insurrection.

The first performance of this play, Yeats records, provided the beginnings of an identifiable style of acting for the Abbey Theatre: "This was the first play of our Irish School of folk-drama, and in it that way of quiet movement and careful speech which has given our players some little fame first showed itself, arising partly out of deliberate opinion and partly out of the ignorance of the players." [14] The language of the play, Yeats's first prose drama, shows few of the linguistic extravagances one might expect to afflict the dialogue from the information that Lady Gregory helped Yeats write it. Indeed, Yeats was able to use a chastened Kiltartan dialect for serious purposes, though dialect had hitherto been used on the Irish stage only for comic purposes—which may explain the laughter that greeted the beginning of the play at its first performance.

4. The Pot of Broth (1904)

This play is based on a folk tale common to many countries besides Ireland. A tramp enters a cottage, and seeing no one is about, looks around the kitchen but finds nothing to eat or drink. John Coneely and his shrewish young wife Sibby are heard outside, chasing a hen which is to be cooked for the dinner of a visiting priest. The tramp realizes whose house he's in; Sibby Coneely, he has heard, is "a slave-driver that would starve the rats, a niggard . . . that would skin a flea for its hide!" Sibby comes in and tells the tramp to leave, for she has nothing for him; but he says he doesn't need anything, for he has his magical stone that turns water into broth. Sibby is both credulous and greedy, and demands to know more about this stone. The tramp obliges, making broth from a pot of boiling water by dropping the stone into it—in addition, that is, to cabbage, onion, ham, and chicken which he borrows briefly from Sibby while flattering her outrageously and telling her preposterous stories about the fairies. After drinking some of the soup, the tramp exchanges his "magical" stone for a chicken, a ham and a bottle of whisky, and leaves Sibby dreaming of getting rich. Sibby's long-suffering husband shakes the tramp's hand, congratulating him on outwitting Sibby, and ironically tells his wife to put the stone in the pot again, for he can see the priest coming for his dinner.

This farce is as much Lady Gregory's work as Yeats's, and he hesitated before including it in his *Collected Plays*. Insofar as the play is Yeats's, it is the only comedy he wrote. Yeats said:

> I hardly know how much of the play is my work, for Lady Gregory helped me as she has helped in every play of mine where there is dialect, and sometimes where there is not. In those first years of the Theatre we all helped one another with plots, ideas, and dialogue, but certainly I was the most indebted as I had no mastery of speech that pur-

ported to be of real life. This play may be more
Lady Gregory's than mine, for I remember once
urging her to include it in her own work, and her
refusing to do so.[15]

The Pot of Broth was first performed on October
30, 1902, in The Antient Concert Rooms, Dublin.
Yeats remembered the play as a trivial thing, of significance only because it introduced William Fay for
the first time as a comedian (he played the tramp),
and because it was "the first comedy, in dialect, of our
movement." [16] But *The Pot of Broth* was, like Yeats's
other early prose play, *Cathleen Ni Houlihan,* extremely popular in Ireland, and in co-authoring it
Yeats contributed to the development of the peasant
comedy that was to be such a staple of the Abbey
repertoire. It is ironical, then, that Yeats unwittingly
encouraged the growth of the peasant play while his
own poetic drama was to be relegated by public in-
difference and antipathy to a minor part of the
Abbey's offerings.

5. *The Unicorn from the Stars* (1908)

In this play, uncharacteristically set in the
nineteenth century, Yeats seeks to dramatize his ambivalent ideas about apocalyptic destruction, a preoccupation of some of his best poetry. Martin Hearne,
the protagonist, is prone to visions and trances, much
to the embarrassment of his uncle, a coachbuilder,
who wishes that his nephew were more interested in
the "real" world of work and the golden coach they
are building for the Lord Lieutenant in Dublin. The
play opens in the interior of his uncle's workshop,
where Martin is in a trance; on being awakened by
Father John, a priest who is sympathetic to the boy,

Martin tells of riding a white unicorn which trampled grapes and wheat, and of being given a command which he cannot remember. One of a group of beggars is apprehended in the workshop trying to steal money, and when he ruefully exclaims "Destruction on us all!" Martin remembers that the command given in his dream was to destroy in order "to bring again, the old disturbed exalted life, the old splendour."

Martin makes a banner with a unicorn on it, which the beggars interpret as a nationalist symbol of Ireland's antagonism to England. Martin tells them that Law and Church must be destroyed, and starts that work by setting fire to the golden coach intended for the Lord Lieutenant. As the third and last act opens, in "a wild, rocky place," the beggars are recalling their plundering and burning of a big house. Martin, who led that attack, is now in another trance, from which he awakens to confess that he had misunderstood the nature of the destruction involved in the command given him in his earlier dream. It is not Law and Church that have to be destroyed, for "The battle we have to fight is fought out in our own mind." The joy of heaven can only be experienced when the self has rejected, intellectually and emotionally, the whole world: "where there is nothing—there is God!" Martin is shot and killed accidentally as the constables who have come to arrest him struggle with the beggars.

This play is one of the less happy examples of collaboration in the Irish dramatic movement. Its history is rather complicated. Yeats and George Moore discussed working together on a play, then quarreled. Moore threatened to use the plot for a novel, but Yeats collaborated with Lady Gregory and Douglas Hyde "to keep George Moore from stealing the plot," as he said, and in two weeks they had turned out the five-act prose play *Where There Is Noth-*

ing.[17] The play was performed at the Royal Court Theatre, London, on June 26, 1904 (it had been published by *The United Irishman* in 1902). Yeats grew to dislike it, however, because he thought its organization haphazard and the hero "arid" and "dominating." With Lady Gregory's help, Yeats started to rework it, but he experienced such difficulty with the prose dialogue, that, as he puts it, "I gave up my scheme to her. The result is a play almost wholly hers in handiwork, which is so much mine in thought that she does not wish to include it in her own works." [18] Yeats evidently thought that the outcome of this collaboration with Lady Gregory, the three-act prose play entitled *The Unicorn from the Stars,* was worthy of inclusion in his *Collected Plays.* It was first performed at the Abbey, November 21, 1907.

Joseph Holloway was present at this first performance of *The Unicorn from the Stars,* and described the play as "dramatically ineffective." He concluded: "It is a mystical and unsatisfying piece of dramatic work . . . presented before a thin house (mostly of friends of the dramatists), and greeted with laughter in the wrong places. The audience was mystified during the first act. . . ." [19]

Yeats's attribution of the play's "handiwork" to Lady Gregory and its idea to himself is manifestly accurate. The dialogue, especially of the low characters, the beggars Johnny Bocach, Paudeen, Biddy Lally, and Nanny, is the often extravagantly "poetic" folk dialect employed by Lady Gregory. When Biddy discovers that the horseshoes she gathered up in the course of looting the big house are not really silver, as the moonlight made them appear to be, she complains in high Kiltartan:

> "The time I will go robbing big houses again it will not be in the light of the full moon I will go

doing it, that does be causing every common thing to shine out as if for a deceit and a mockery. It's not shining at all they are at this time, but duck-yellow and dark."

The Unicorn from the Stars is characteristic of Yeats's thought in its opposition of world and dream, and of his symbolism in its mystical use of the unicorn. The unicorn heralds the end of one cycle of history and the apocalyptic violence that attends the destruction of the old order and the birth of the new. But the joyful destruction which characterizes Martin's nihilism is discernibly Nietzschean in origin. It is in Yeats's later poems, such as "Leda and the Swan," "The Second Coming," "A Prayer for my Daughter," and "Nineteen Hundred and Nineteen," that one finds a complex and profound treatment of the apocalyptic theme.

Yeats's ideas are, unfortunately, not dramatically employed in *The Unicorn from the Stars*. There could have been a dramatic conflict in the play between the idea that a new social order can be created by revolutionary violence, and the opposing idea that it can be achieved only through psychological change within the individual. Instead, the play's protagonist accepts literally the injunction to destroy and acts on it; then, at a very late point in the play, he realizes that he should have interpreted the command metaphorically, and that he has made a terrible mistake. The audience is apt to feel misled and confused by this bathetic resolution of the action. One suspects that Yeats himself is at first sympathetic to Martin's longings, rather like Father John, who decries the spiritual aridity of his society and yearns to change it even if it means great violence ("now it is all work, business, how to live a long time. Ah, if one could change it all in a minute, even by war and violence!").

But then, toward the end of the play, Yeats would seem to be struck, like Martin, with the happy and sober thought that in the rejection of the world, rather than its destruction, we find God.

In addition, the play is made rather perplexing by the amount of esoteric reference to Yeats's private symbology (the title for the play *The Unicorn from the Stars* is, incidentally, a translation of the name Yeats held in the 1890's, in the occult society known as The Order of the Golden Dawn). Another notable shortcoming of the play is the incongruity between the main character and his exalted, visionary concerns, and the uncomprehending beggars, who are self-consciously picturesque and folksy. With a few notable exceptions, neither Yeats's ideas nor Lady Gregory's craft are present in a dramatically impressive fashion in the play, and there is little or no possibility, therefore, of a fruitful engagement between the two.

A production of *The Unicorn from the Stars* caused a furor in Munich in 1940. Because of the actors' ironical interpretation of the play, the audience was convinced that it was being used as a vehicle for an oblique attack on Fascism. As a consequence, the play was banned. It was performed after the war at Cologne and Tubingen; on these occasions *The Unicorn from the Stars* was interpreted as a battle of ideas in dramatic form.[20]

6. *The Shadowy Waters* (1911)

The influence on Yeats's plays of late nineteenth-century European symbolism is most apparent in *The Shadowy Waters*. The setting is a pirate sailing ship at sea. Forgael, "a sea-king of ancient Ireland," sleeps, while his sailors complain that he is crazed and determined to lead them to some mysterious and ominous other world (George Moore amusingly and aptly described Forgael as "the metaphysical pirate"). The sailors plan to kill Forgael while he sleeps, but are prevented by Aibric who is loyal to his master. Yet Aibric admonishes Forgael for following the mysterious birds, souls of the dead from the last ship they plundered, who are leading him westward: "Be satisfied to live like other men, / And drive impossible dreams away." The sailors spot another ship, loaded with spices, as they can tell from the fragrance carried to them by the wind; a king and queen are on the ship's deck, and kiss as the pirates draw near. Aibric leads the sailors on board the ship of spices while Forgael remains at the tiller, musing on the joyful possibility of encountering a "shadowless unearthly woman" whose love will immortalize him.

The sailors return, having slain the king and captured his queen, Dectora. Dectora is contemptuous when Forgael speaks to her of love, and she contemplates suicide; then she encourages the sailors to kill Forgael. But Forgael casts a spell on them by playing his harp, and the sailors go back to the ship they have seized with Aibric. Dectora threatens Forgael with the sword she has taken from Aibric, but is also enchanted by the music. Aibric returns to vainly implore Forgael to reject the death that awaits him if he continues this journey, then rejoins the sailors who are determined to sail homewards on the spice-ship. Forgael asks Dectora to go with Aibric, but she refuses. The severing of the rope binding the two ships together severs all that is worldly from the lives of Dectora and Forgael; she covers him with her hair, for they have determined to "gaze upon this world no longer." The harp begins to burn as, gathering Dectora's hair about him, Forgael proclaims that they have made their own destiny, have realized a dream, and have become immortal: "dreams, / That have had dreams for father, live in us."

The acting version of *The Shadowy Waters* published in Yeats's *Collected Plays* is the result of a great deal of rewriting, and should be distinguished from all other versions, including the one in *Collected Poems*.[21] An early, more heavily and obscurely symbolic version was staged by the Irish National Theatre Society at the Molesworth Hall on January 14, 1904, with the role of Dectora played by Florence Farr. The following year Miss Farr produced the play for the membership of the International Theosophical Congress in London. The symbolist playwright, Maurice Maeterlinck, by this time "the European theatre's sole and tenuous bastion against . . . Ibsenite drama" was in the audience.[22] But Yeats was unhappy with the production; he called it "execrable" (except for Florence Farr's performance), and described *The Shadowy Waters* as "the worst thing I ever did dramatically."[23]

Accordingly, he spent the whole summer of 1905 rewriting it, and by September was content that he had made "a strong play of it." The revision was radical and effective, as Thomas Parkinson explains: "He clarified and strengthened his sense of character, contracted his vocabulary to exclude his most esoteric symbolism, and expanded his vocabulary to include more common language and provide an elucidating context for the symbols he retained."[24] There can be no doubt that *The Shadowy Waters* was much improved because of these extensive changes. Nonetheless, Yeats thought it necessary to make the further, not entirely felicitous, change of introducing a Kiltartanized prose for the sailors' speech before the play's performance at the Abbey on December 8, 1906.

Yeats was pleased by the effect of the dark blues and

greens "with a glimmer of copper here and there" used in the set and costumes of the Abbey's production, which made the players seem "like people in a dream." [25] Indeed, one distinguishing attribute of *The Shadowy Waters* is its dream-like quality. T. S. Eliot commented on its "vague enchanted beauty," a quality typical of this phase of Yeats's development, when he was treating the subjects of Irish legend with the mixture of world-weariness and exaltation of the beautiful which was fashionable at the end of the nineteenth century.[26] Yet, the use of Celtic mythology and folklore in *The Shadowy Waters* is, as Yeats himself described it, "incidental." The important affinities of this play, and to some extent of Yeats's early volume of poems *The Wind Among the Reeds,* are found in Continental symbolist literature—in the plays of Villiers de L'Isle Adam and Maeterlinck, the novels of Huysmans, and the poems of Verlaine and Mallarmé.

The influence of de L'Isle Adam's famous play *Axël* on *The Shadowy Waters* is clearly marked. In the company of Maud Gonne, Yeats had seen a production of *Axël* in Paris in 1894, and wrote an enthusiastic review for a London journal. *Axël* immediately became, as Yeats described it in a letter, one of his "sacred books." Although Yeats had already started to write *The Shadowy Waters* before he saw the production of *Axël,* he was inspired to start over again. If W. Y. Tindall overstates the similarity when he says that Yeats's play is "a translation of *Axël* into nautical terms" (i.e., that Yeats simply changes the setting of Axël's castle for that of Forgael's ship), it does seem evident that *The Shadowy Waters* bears greater resemblance to contemporary symbolist literature than any of Yeat's other plays.[27] Indeed, the atmosphere and psychology of *The Shadowy Waters* are symbolist in a rather dated way. The connotations of the title, the mood which mingles love with violence and death, the connection of poetry with magic, of the poet with the magician in the figure of Forgael, the overtly symbolic use of the sea voyage as an archetype for spiritual discovery, the heroic and exalted sensibilities of hero and heroine, and the death-oriented rejection of the world—all characterize *The Shadowy Waters* as a play shaped very distinctly in the symbolist mode of the late nineteenth century.

7. *The Hour-Glass* (1914)

In structure and theme *The Hour-Glass* is the most medieval and Christian of Yeats's morality plays. When the play opens, the Wise Man's pupils, who have been allowed to choose the subject for the day's lesson, are looking through his book, discussing their teacher's rationalist conviction that there is "no God and no soul." Teigue the Fool comes in begging for a penny and the pupils make him kneel while they rest the big book on his back, as a priest would lay his book on the church lectern.

The action thus far has taken place in front of the stage curtain; now the curtain is drawn back to reveal the Wise Man at his desk, which has an hour-glass upon it. The passage the pupils have chosen for the lesson postulates the existence of a spiritual realm accessible only to those who renounce this world. The Fool claims that he has seen and heard proof of the existence of the spiritual world. The Wise Man ridicules the text as "a monkish thought," yet he is troubled for he has twice dreamed of the passage, and it makes him distrust his materialist philosophy (essentially the Victorian scientific rationalism which Yeats despised). When the pupils leave, the Fool decries the Wise Man's influence: at Carrick-orus, "where the friars used to be fasting and serving the poor, I saw them drinking wine and obeying their wives." The Fool asserts his own belief when he explains to the Wise Man that the shears he carries are needed to cut the black nets that men of evil disposition have spread over the hills to catch angels. The Wise Man reflects that before he brought enlightenment to the area, everyone used to be as silly as the Fool.

An Angel enters, wearing, according to the stage directions, either "a little golden domino and a halo made of metal," or else "a beautiful mask." As the Angel upturns the hour-glass, he tells the Wise Man that he will die in an hour "when the last grain of sand / Has fallen through this glass," and go to Hell, "the place of those who have denied." The Wise Man argues that his disbelief ought to be forgiven, for he had never before encountered any proof of the existence of the spiritual world. The Angel tells the Wise Man that he may be allowed to go to Heaven through Purgatory if he can find one person who believes in the other world before the sand has run out.

The Wise Man appeals in turn to his pupils, his wife, his children, and the Fool, but they all refute his arguments for the existence of Heaven and Hell with his own words, thinking that he is trying to trick them, and fearing his ridicule if they were to agree with him. The truth, his pupils assert, is learned not in dreams or mystical thought, but only through reason, when "the intellect is deliberate and cold, / As it were a polished mirror that reflects / An unchanged world." The Wise Man realizes that "Only in spiritual terror can the Truth / Come through the broken mind." He no longer needs or wants to save his soul, and dies acquiescing in the will of God. The Angel enters with a golden box. The Fool catches the white butterfly that has emerged from the dead man's

Above, the Fool and the Pupils in *The Hour-Glass. Below,* the Fool and the Wise Man. A Project Arts Centre production, Dublin, 1976. Directed by James W. Flannery.

JAMES W. FLANNERY

mouth (obviously his soul) and puts it in the box, which the Angel will open in the Garden of Paradise.

The prose version of this play was first performed in the Molesworth Hall in Dublin on March 14, 1903, by the Irish National Theatre Society, on a double bill with Lady Gregory's *Twenty-Five*. It was extremely well received. Maire Nic Shiubhlaigh was greatly admired as a distinctly pre-Raphaelite Angel, and Dudley Digges and Frank Fay distinguished themselves as, respectively, the Wise Man and the Fool. According to Lennox Robinson, this first version became very popular; Yeats and Lady Gregory considered it successful enough to be one of the plays produced by the Irish National Theatre Society in their weekend performance in London. This production evoked the praise of the London drama critics, and more importantly, perhaps, aroused the interest of Annie Horniman, who was later to give the Irish dramatic movement a permanent home in the Abbey Theatre.

The Hour-Glass was revised four times, most radically in 1912; the 1912 verse and prose text underwent further additional but slight revisions until as late as 1922, before its inclusion in *Collected Plays*. The source for the play was a story Yeats included in his *Fairy and Folk Tales of the Irish Peasantry;* in the play he changed the main character from a priest (perhaps an unlikely profession for a disbeliever) to the Wise Man, and changed the character of a Child to the Fool.

When *The Hour-Glass* was first performed, at least one member of the audience, the critic and writer Wilfrid Scawen Blunt, objected to its strong similarity to a medieval morality play, calling it "a stupid imitation of that dull old morality, *Everyman*." [28] The play does seem very closely modeled on the medieval

Everyman; both plays have in common the announcement to the protagonist that he has a short time to live, his vain application for help to those advocates of a worldliness he had espoused, and his realization of the vanity of trust in the material and of the necessity for belief in the spiritual. But no doubt it was precisely the conventional Christian morality and the more derivative aspects of the play which made it popular with the rest of the audience, and which "converted a music-hall singer and kept him going to mass for six weeks." [29]

Yet while its structure is undeniably based on *Everyman* and its content seems essentially Christian, the play has more modern affinities, too. Especially in its later versions, as Una Ellis-Fermor points out, *The Hour-Glass* is comparable to "the modern symbolic morality, such as the fifth act of Peer Gynt." [30] The struggle between the materialism of the Wise Man and the Fool's belief in the supernatural world is a familiar one in Yeats's other plays. But *The Hour-Glass* differs from these other plays in that the Wise Man's materialism is accorded the status of a philosophical, rationalist belief. And while *The Hour-Glass* is undoubtedly medieval and Christian in form and implication, it would be wrong to interpret the play solely in these terms, for the action of the play, as Yeats tells us, is also "a parable of the conscious and the subconscious life." [31]

In the 1903 version of the play, Yeats had the Wise Man kneel abjectly in front of the Fool as the sand runs out in the hour-glass. But in later versions, in which Yeats is trying to move the play away from its conventional morality, he makes the Wise Man a more sympathetic figure, allowing him a dignified if anguished acceptance of the existence of the spiritual world, which he believes will entail eternal suffering for him. Revision also improved the play by making the Fool a less self-conscious and saintly representative of spirituality.

Yeats was moved to revise *The Hour-Glass* so thoroughly as a result of a 1911 revival of the play (together with *The Countess Cathleen* and *The Land of Heart's Desire*), when he employed the innovative setting, masks and costumes designed by Gordon Craig. The stage setting of 1903 had been dominated in a flat and conventional way by the Wise Man's study, with his desk directly center stage. The 1911 setting was, in contrast, an organic extension of the play's action and content:

> In Craig's new design, the Wise Man's study is only part of the set. The desk, now in profile, is in an alcove at the right front corner, in shadow. From the study, a corridor of screens curves round to the left, disappearing back centre stage into light. This arrangement suggests that the Wise Man's place is at one point of a circular pathway, that his domain of learning is at the dark end of a path moving towards light.[32]

The revisions of *The Hour-Glass* which Yeats undertook after the 1911 revival of the play are significant and interesting. Yeats's experiments with the Craig settings, masks, and costumes increased his understanding of the purely theatrical possibilities for his plays: the use of masks for his characters was to become an essential part of his dramaturgy, and the use of a lyric to close the play became characteristic of his later dance plays. Yeats also refined the character of the Fool, a figure whose symbolic significance is successfully exploited in *On Baile's Strand* and *The Herne's Egg*. The verse of the play was pared of its former "poetic" luxuriance; it is concrete and vivid, and approximates the rhythms of real speech. Most of all, it becomes wholly dramatic, as when the Wise Man fearfully anticipates his imminent damnation:

"Will there be a footfall,
Or will there be a sort of rending sound,
Or else a cracking, as though an iron claw
Had gripped the threshold-stone?"

The version of *The Hour-Glass* published in 1913 in Craig's theatrical journal *The Mask* reveals a significant growth in Yeats's stagecraft, and the quickening of those elements which are to distinguish Yeats's best work for the stage. The play does seem to have a universal appeal if one can go by its stage history. *The Hour-Glass* was translated and produced in Japan by Kaoru Osanai, the founder of the Tsukiji Little Theatre in 1924. It was also produced in Basel, Switzerland, in 1935; on this occasion it was conceived of as an Irish dramatic version of the Faust story. A later production in Essen, Germany, in 1958, staged *The Hour-Glass* as a symbolic play about knowledge and belief.[33]

That *The Hour-Glass* retains its dramatic impact was demonstrated by James Flannery's revival of the play in Dublin. A review in *The Irish Times* registers the play's theatrical possibilities and its moving portrayal of spiritual struggle:

> *The Hour-Glass* has two elements that have wrecked many a play before—child parts and the appearance of a being from another world, in this case an angel. In an evening when the adult actors were almost uniformly good throughout, the children in this play deserve special praise, the pupils for maintaining a spirited argument in Latin, and the two real tinies, Katherine Nealon and Peter Fowler. Patricia McMenamin's angel

was quite astonishing, her costume designed with the rest by Nicola Kozakiewicz, as wonderful and strange as any angel half-imagined. Laurence Foster as Teigue the fool was an alien dressed like an Æ fantasy, half mad, half frighteningly calm, and this strangeness was balanced beautifully by Kate Canning as the Wise Man's wife, heart-scalded between her philosophical husband and her household chores; Peter Dix was genuinely moving as the Faust figure for whom the sands of time are literally running out.[34]

V. HEROIC AND TRAGIC PLAYS

The conflict at the heart of these plays is by and large imagined in terms that make them more dramatic in nature and wider in appeal than are the allegorical folk and morality plays. In these heroic and tragic plays a distinction is made between two different modes of existence: "the basic split . . . is that between the institutional world—tame, limited, calculating, interested in the virtue of fixed character —and the personal world—exuberant, carefree, wild, affirming the values of intense personality." [1] In the folk and morality plays there was only one limited and materialistic world, and the tendency of the protagonist was to withdraw from it into a spiritual realm that of necessity could not be very successfully realized in dramatic terms. The protagonists of *The King's Threshold, On Baile's Strand, Diarmuid and Grania,* and *Deirdre,* on the other hand, are locked in an active struggle with the institutional world; like Shakespeare's *Hamlet* or *Richard II,* they embody radically different values from those the institutional world assumes. The consequences of their struggle, in Yeat's plays as in Shakespeare's, are tragic. The heroic assertion of self-fulfilling human values in the teeth of a highly politicized social system invites disaster; Seanchan, Cuchulain and Deirdre can no more survive in their societies than Hamlet and Richard II in theirs. But the assertion of these values in Yeats's plays is nonetheless heroic, joyous, and triumphant even in the face of death and disaster.

If the content of this group of Yeats's plays reminds us of Elizabethan drama, their compressed and highly unified structure is perhaps reminiscent of Greek tragedy. In the folk and morality plays, Yeats used Irish folklore as a source; his use of myth in the heroic and tragic plays gives to *On Baile's Strand* and *Deirdre* something of the resonance of Greek tragedy. The vaguely Christian settings and the folksy ambience of the morality plays have been left behind. In the pagan world of the heroic and tragic plays, we draw breath in a more rarefied and exalted atmosphere, in a world dominated by a conception of life as noble and tragic. The importance of Irish myth for Yeats's poetry and drama is beyond doubt. The heroic figure of Cuchulain was of enduring fascination for Yeats, as can be seen in the prominence of Cuchulain in so many of Yeats's poems and plays over the entire span, virtually, of his career. Yeats tended to identify with Cuchulain's exalted sense of purpose, his aristocratic refusal to lower himself to the petty considerations of those who surround him, and his moral courage. (Many of Yeats's contemporaries also identified with Cuchulain: for the extreme Irish nationalists led by Padraic Pearse, Cuchulain was a cult figure whose physical courage and martial prowess held up an example of what Irishmen should aspire to in their struggle with England.)

Irish myth was made accessible to Yeats by Lady Gregory's translations of the Cuchulain and Fenian cycles. In a note to a 1907 edition of his plays that includes *On Baile's Strand, The King's Threshold,* and *Deirdre,* Yeats acknowledges the importance of Irish mythology for his plays: "almost every story I have used or person I have spoken of is in one or other of Lady Gregory's *Gods and Fighting Men* and *Cuchulain of Muirthemne*. If my present small audience for poetic drama grows and spreads beyond Dublin, I shall owe it to these two books. . . ." [2]

Yeats's interest in the Greek drama and its influence on his art is attested to by his excellent translations of Sophocles's *King Oedipus* and *Oedipus at Colonus*. In these translations, as one critic points out, Yeats "tightens the already tight structure of Greek tragedy." [3] The fact that Yeats chose to translate *King Oedipus* is also, in part, a reflection of his preoccupation with the relationships between fathers and sons, a preoccupation that dominates his own *On Baile's Strand* and *Purgatory*.

8. *Diarmuid and Grania* (1951)

Diarmuid and Grania marks Yeats's first direct use of Celtic mythology; though the play was performed in 1901, it remained unpublished for the next fifty years. When the play opens, the banqueting hall at Tara is being prepared by servants of Cormac, the high king of Ireland, for the reception of the warrior Finn MacCool and his followers, the Fianna. Cormac has arranged a marriage between Finn and his daughter with a view to settling an old antagonism between Finn and himself, and more specifically to establishing a military alliance that would protect his kingdom from the foreign invasion he anticipates. Grania, however, wilfully asserts her independence. Her first words to her confidante Laban are "I will not marry Finn." After the Fianna have arrived and begun to feast, Grania persuades Laban, who has magical powers, to bewitch the ale, which she then serves to Finn and his retinue, but not to Diarmuid, "the youngest and comeliest" of the Fianna.

Finn and his companions fall asleep, but not before Conan, the crass messenger of the Fianna and enemy to Diarmuid, tells the story of Diarmuid's predestined death. Diarmuid is to be killed by a boar: "He shall be torn by the tusks, and his face shall be foul, because it will be bloody. I would that the women of Eri could see him when he is foul and bloody." When Conan and the others fall asleep, Grania tells Diarmuid, whom she had never seen before this night, that she has fallen passionately in love with him. They run away together, Diarmuid rather regretfully, for this elopement will mean, he understands, the end of his friendship with Finn and the Fianna.

The second act is set in Diarmuid's house seven years later. The two lovers had been pursued across Ireland by Finn, but at present enjoy an uneasy truce with him. Now Cormac discloses that he has persuaded Finn to seek reconciliation with Diarmuid. Cormac's motivation seems to be based on his urgent need to employ Finn to fight the Lochlanders, who have finally launched an invasion of his kingdom. Grania, it is clear, has grown weary of the pastoral existence she leads with Diarmuid, though she will not admit this to him. Diarmuid is suspicious of her desire to see him make peace with Finn and rejoin the Fianna. He knows that Finn has never forgotten her, and suspects Grania of being attracted to Finn. Grania confesses to Laban that this is, indeed, the case: "how can I forget the greatness of Finn." She prepares a feast to mark the reconciliation of Diarmuid and Finn, significantly putting on her jewels to receive Finn, something she refused to do seven years ago when she reluctantly prepared to welcome him at her father's bidding. The attempt at reconciliation fails when Finn tells Diarmuid that he had pursued Grania and him so relentlessly not out of a desire for revenge on Diarmuid, but out of love for Grania. Conan brings news of the sighting of a gigantic boar in the nearby woods, and Finn challenges Diarmuid to join the hunt. Diarmuid and everyone else know that he is destined to be killed by a boar, yet he nevertheless accepts Finn's challenge.

The wooded slopes of Ben Bulben provide the setting for the third and last act. Grania discovers Diarmuid asleep under a tree, and tries to persuade him not to continue hunting the boar. She proclaims her love for him, though she also tells Diarmuid that she has dreamed he is dead and she is sitting by Finn's side. Diarmuid claims that she is obsessed with Finn, drives her away with his sword, and exits to search for the boar. Grania meets up with Finn and beseeches him to save Diarmuid's life, but Finn replies that Diarmuid's death is fated, and no one can prevent it. A cry from a nearby thicket indicates that the boar has wounded Diarmuid. Finn helps him out of the thicket and reluctantly responds to his plea for water, but Diarmuid, looking at Grania and Finn together, then refuses to drink. He refuses again, when Grania brings him water, and dies. Finn says, "The gods chose you, Grania, to give him love and death." The last words of the play are given to Cormac, who reflects rather complacently that while Diarmuid is dead, "the Fianna are united and the Lochlanders shall be driven into the sea," and to the cynical and cowardly Conan, who foretells that while Grania is plunged into great sorrow for Diarmuid, "her welcome to Finn shall be greater."

Diarmuid and Grania, by Yeats and George Moore, was first performed on October 21, 1901, at the Gaiety Theatre in Dublin. It was produced by an English company, F. R. Benson's Shakespearean Company, at the request of the Irish Literary Theatre, and was followed by Douglas Hyde's *Casadh an*

tSugain (The Twisting of the Rope), which was also
sponsored by the Irish Literary Theatre. Hyde had
used, incidentally, a scenario by Yeats as the basis for
his play.

The audience for the plays seems to have been
made up largely of young members of the Gaelic
League, and their nationalistic fervor embraced a play
written on an Irish subject by Irish playwrights. Their
enthusiasm seems to have permitted the audience to
overlook the fact that *Diarmuid and Grania* was produced by an English company and its music was by
the English composer, Edward Elgar. Yeats recounts,
in *Dramatis Personae,* how enthusiastically the audience responded after the play: "when Maud Gonne
and I got into our cab to go to some supper-party after the performance, the crowd from the gallery
wanted to take the horse out of the cab and drag us
there, but Maud Gonne, weary of public demonstrations, refused." [4]

Diarmuid and Grania was the product of Yeats's
uneasy collaboration with George Moore, a collaboration both men have described amusingly, Yeats in
Dramatis Personae, Moore in *Hail and Farewell.* As
the more experienced dramatist, Moore was supposed
to be chiefly responsible for the play's construction,
and Yeats, as poet, was to concern himself chiefly with
style. There was, predictably, a clash not only of personalities, but of ideas, a clash that marked the end
of the experiment that was the Irish Literary Theatre,
and the end, virtually, of George Moore's association
with the Irish dramatic movement. In his review of
the play for *The United Irishman,* Frank Fay doubted
if "two authors of such opposite literary temperaments
as Mr. W. B. Yeats and Mr. George Moore benefit by
collaboration," and reflected that "much of the disappointment I have heard expressed about the play is
really the result of the execrable—I can use no milder

word—acting it received at the hands of Mr. Benson and his company." [5] *Casadh an tSugain,* though, had been directed by Fay and acted by amateurs. Yeats consequently realized the necessity of using Irish actors and directors if his own plays were to be part of a distinctly Irish drama, and only rarely failed to act on this realization.

The immediate source for Yeats's and Moore's play is a synopsis of the story of Diarmuid and Grania prepared by Lady Gregory. Proinsias MacCana points out that while the tale of Diarmuid and Grania is found only in a late text, "it is already mentioned . . . in a tenth century saga-list, and was undoubtedly a proximate source of the famous romance of Tristan and Iseult." [6] While the intrinsic merit and interest of *Diarmuid and Grania* has usually been underestimated, there are certain obvious shortcomings to the play. Its undue length, for instance, reflects the difficulty the play's authors did not entirely resolve—that of transforming the rambling narrative of the legend into a clear line of dramatic action. Yeats for one was not at his best when attempting plays of a conventional length, and the fact that it is in prose, even if it is Yeats's prose, robs this play of the lyrical utterance that would undoubtedly have graced it if Yeats had composed it as a verse drama. Despite the play's drawbacks, though, and despite its being the fruit of collaboration with Moore, *Diarmuid and Grania* anticipates much that is characteristic in Yeats's later plays.

The chief strength of the play lies in the creation of Grania as a woman whose passion and beauty have destructive personal and public consequences, and in the structuring of the play as a conflict between spontaneity and instinct, on the one hand, and social and political considerations, on the other. In the myth, a supernatural visitor puts a mark on Diarmuid's forehead that makes every woman who sees it fall in love with him. In the play, all reference to the love spot has been omitted, thereby making the character of Grania more strong-willed and passionate, because she acts in accordance with her own desire and will and not some supernatural influence. This conception of a beautiful and passionate heroine obviously anticipates the tragic figure of Deirdre, as indeed the whole play anticipates Yeats's *Deirdre* in the conflict it stages between love and power. Yeats's handling of the Deirdre myth is much more assured than his treatment of Diarmuid and Grania: in *Deirdre* Yeats has omitted what is extraneous to a clearly conceived dramatic action, given it the heightened and more intense language of his verse—has created, in short, a much more unified and affecting play.

Finally, we can see in Grania's attraction to two very different men (Diarmuid seems sensitive and romantic, Finn defined by power and war) the note of advanced thinking about sexual matters a contemporary reviewer insinuated was Moore's contribution. The guess was probably inspired by Moore's reputation as a naturalistic novelist and his admiration for the Ibsenesque drama, in both of which the heroines often assert their sexual identity: Diarmuid and Grania, the reviewer charged, "have become characters which it is easy to fancy in modern garments. So far has the process been carried out that Grania recalls recent heroines of the novel and the stage." [7] At the same time, though, the play's action can be seen as a personal allegory that depicts a familiar yearning of Yeats's and an equally familiar awareness of the impossibility of fulfilling that yearning. The flight of Diarmuid and Grania and the pastoral idyll of their life after they have fled suggests the typical way in which Yeats imagined wooing Maud Gonne away from her commitment to politics to live "naturally," and his understanding that such hope was mere fantasy. Maud Gonne's marriage to Major John McBride did not take place until 1903, but Yeats portrays in Grania's attraction to the warrior Finn (she says to Diarmuid "I shall love you better when you come to me with the reek of battle upon you"), something of Maud Gonne's preference, of which Yeats was painfully aware, for a man of action over a poet and dreamer.

9. *The King's Threshold* (1904)

In Celtic Ireland, the poets were a respected, privileged, and feared caste who produced literature and historical chronicles, possessed magical powers, and shamed enemies with powerful satire. Seanchan belongs to this caste. When the play opens he is lying on the steps of King Guaire's palace at Gort, in County Galway. The King enters and explains to Seanchan's pupils that he has summoned them to save the poet's life by persuading him to eat and drink, for Seanchan is on a hunger strike in protest of his exclusion from the King's council of "Bishops, Soldiers, and Makers of the Law." The right or wrong of the decision to exclude the poet is of no significance, says the King; what is important is that having made such a decision, he cannot go back on it: "I cannot give way, / Because I am King."

The King, however, is afraid Seanchan's hunger strike may turn the people against him, and he authorizes the Oldest Pupil to offer Seanchan a house with land, a pension, jewels and clothes (anything, in short, except the restoration of the ancient right of the poets to be heard in the King's council), if only he will give up his strike. This is the first of the series of vain attempts to make Seanchan see "reason" that

comprises the action of the play. The pupils are succeeded in turn by the mayor of Seanchan's home
town of Kinvara, his servant, the King's Chamberlain,
a monk, a soldier, two young princesses, and finally,
his beloved Fedelm, all of whom attempt to persuade
him to give up his hunger strike. But the absolute
nature of Seanchan's idealism leads him to resist
even the pleadings of the woman he loves. Like the
protagonists of several of the early plays, Seanchan
turns his back on love and life, but for artistic rather
than patriotic or mystical reasons. Seanchan passionately insists on the importance of poetry:

> ". . . cry out that not a man alive
> Would ride among the arrows with high heart,
> Or scatter with an open hand, had not
> Our heady craft commended wasteful virtues."

The King resorts to threats, parades Seanchan's
pupils before him with their necks in halters, and orders them to beg Seanchan to break his fast. But both
the Oldest and Youngest Pupils tell Seanchan to die
and thereby assert the integrity of the poets. Seanchan
dies proclaiming his triumph to the King. The play
ends with the pupils carrying Seanchan's body from
the stage to the accompaniment of solemn music.

The King's Threshold was first performed by the
Irish National Theatre Society in the Molesworth
Hall, Dublin, October 8, 1903. The production was
financed by Annie Horniman, who designed and
made the costumes. With its cast of seventeen, the
play was the most ambitious the Society had put
on. Yeats thought it was the best verse play he had
done to date. In his dedication of the play, he praises
Frank Fay's "beautiful speaking in the character of
Seanchan." It pleased the audience, too, if one may

go by Joseph Holloway's entry in his journal describing the opening night:

> Everybody that is anybody in artistic or literary Ireland was there, and W. B. Yeats's new one-act play in verse, *The King's Threshold,* was proved a thing of exceptional beauty to the eye and ear. The chief role, that of the banished poet, "Seanchan," was marvellously well played by F. J. Fay, whose conception and acting of the difficult part were both well nigh perfect. Truly he lent the beauty of the voice to the poet's words; and his delivery of the final speeches was as musical as the songs of birds, and fascinated the senses quite in the same indescribable manner. . . . The grouping, considering the limited space at command, was remarkably effective, and the stage lighting very successful. No footlights were used, but two lime-lights—one at either side of the stage—and one from the back of the hall, were substituted.[8]

The play is based on Old and Middle Irish romances, but Yeats also acknowledged the influence of *Sancan the Bard,* written ten years earlier than his own play. Yeats had collaborated with its author, Edwin Ellis, on an edition of Blake. In its previous versions, Yeats's play concluded with Seanchan's victorious return to the council table; but Yeats had always been inclined to give it a tragic ending, and he finally did so in 1922. By this time the tactic of hunger strike had been used as political protest by many Irish patriots, including Terence MacSwiney, mayor of Cork, who died in 1920 after a seventy-four-day hunger strike in an English jail. While Yeats had anticipated the use of the hunger strike as a political weapon in modern Ireland (though it had often been used in ancient Ireland, as is pointed out in the play), there can be little doubt that he was moved to give the play a tragic ending by contemporary events. It was also an artistic decision, and a wise one, for the play as it now stands has a greater emotional unity than it did in its previous versions.

The familiar Yeatsian theme of *The King's Threshold* involves the conflict between idealism and the "real" world of money, business, politics, social status, power, and fulfillment in love. But in this play the idealism is neither patriotic as in *Cathleen Ni Houlihan*, nor mystical, as it tends to be in *The Shadowy Waters*. It is the idealism of an art whose value is triumphantly exalted, unlike the self-deprecating and ineffectual art of the poet Aleel when confronted with his beloved's social responsibility in *The Countess Cathleen*. The art of the poet Seanchan involves not a withdrawal from life, but rather an active struggle with the representatives of power and influence in society, and the assertion of the superiority of the "wasteful virtues" inculcated by art over the materialistic corruption of society.

Yeats's own ideas about the role of the artist in society had changed from those of an aesthete who accepted the premise that art has little relation to society, to those of a poet who believed in the high role of art in civilization. Now he further demanded the recognition of art's spiritual significance in "a community of which one half was buried in the practical affairs of life, and the other half in politics and a propagandist patriotism." [9] Inspired by the role of artists in ancient Ireland and in Renaissance societies, Yeats insisted on the need for the poet to be heard in public affairs. Yeats's work in theater management was not the example of a poet who believed in an aesthetic withdrawal from life's problems. And his public life as a senator in the Irish government was, as it were, a vigorous attempt to champion the values of the poet in the King's council.

Yeats's dramatic verse in *The King's Threshold* is, he claimed, the best he had yet written. It is indeed more dramatic than the verse of the earlier plays, which, however beautiful, tends to be lyrical rather than dramatic. One has the sense, in *The King's Threshold,* that the characters actually speak to each other, and do not merely soliloquize. Moreover, the verse registers states of mind with considerable complexity, as when (at the start of the play) the King tries to get the Oldest Pupil to persuade Seanchan to give up his fast. The Oldest Pupil's ambivalence, as he expresses his conflicting loyalties to the King and to Seanchan, is conveyed with an admirable immediacy:

> "My head whirls round;
> I do not know what I am to think or say.
> I owe you all obedience, and yet
> How can I give it, when the man I have loved
> More than all others, thinks that he is wronged
> So bitterly that he will starve and die
> Rather than bear it? Is there any man
> Will throw his life away for a light issue?"

Seanchan is portrayed in more detail than the heroes of Yeats's previous plays. He passionately articulates a philosophy that is intellectually and emotionally convincing (though this aspect of his character gives the play, to some degree, the complexion of an artistic manifesto). Seanchan is, moreover, endowed with a father and mother and pupils, as well as a lover, and his responses to their appeals humanize his character. The other characters are near-allegorical types—King, Mayor, Monk, Soldier—but they are lively, ironically conceived types; Yeats is not heavy-handed here, though there is never any doubt about his identification with Seanchan.

The play's shortcomings lie, indeed, in a too discernible conviction on Yeats's part that Seanchan is wholly in the right; this may be responsible for a certain lack of tension in the plot, and of complexity in the character of the protagonist. So the conclusion reverts somewhat to the typical ending of the morality plays. As Roger McHugh puts it:

> . . . despite a magnificent climax in which Seanchan's pupils, who had vainly tried to persuade their master to abandon his hunger-strike, suddenly, when threatened with death by the King, swing around in support of him, a certain rigidity in the main character betrays the ending; Seanchan will not yield but will pluck victory out of the defeat of death, like Countess Cathleen, like young Michael, like the Wise Man.[10]

10. On Baile's Strand (1904)

The first of his plays to employ the mythological figure of Cuchulain, On Baile's Strand is, of all Yeats's plays, one of the most intense and moving. The setting is an assembly-house on the seashore in ancient Ulster. A Fool and a Blind Man, "their features made grotesque and extravagant by masks," anticipate eating a hen they have just stolen; the Fool is anxious to eat, but the Blind Man insists that the hen is not yet properly cooked. The Blind Man tells us that Conchubar, the High King of Ulster, will today insist that his champion, Cuchulain, take an oath of allegiance "that will stop his rambling and make him as biddable as a house-dog," and that a young man, son of Aoife, the queen of Scotland, who has landed on the shore, has come to kill Cuchulain. The Blind Man knows that the young stranger is Cuchulain's son but will not reveal his secret. Cuchulain's voice is heard outside, raised in anger; he and Conchubar enter the hall, arguing.

Cuchulain is "a dark man, something over forty years of age," while Conchubar is older. Cuchulain complains about the oath Conchubar wants him to take because he has killed men without the king's sanction, and rewarded others according to his own judgment. Conchubar adds another grievance to the list: the stranger from Aoife's country was able to land on the shore of Ulster without being challenged because Cuchulain and his companions were off amusing themselves instead of guarding the shore. Cuchulain insists that he will hunt or dance, quarrel or make love, wherever and whenever he feels like it.

When Conchubar says that he must leave a strong and orderly kingdom to his children, Cuchulain responds "I do not like your children—they have no pith, / No marrow in their bones, and will lie soft / Where you and I lie hard." Cuchulain also despises Conchubar's wife, who constantly dances attendance on her lord and master. He has no child of his own, but a woman he once loved, the beautiful warrior Aoife, was "fitted to give birth to kings." Cuchulain's notion of love is not of a sustaining, nurturing affection, but of "a brief forgiveness between opposites." Aoife now hates him, and because of her hatred is waging war on Ulster.

Conchubar concludes the argument by asserting that he and Cuchulain are mutually dependent: "I need your might of hand and burning heart, / And you in my wisdom." The minor kings who owe allegiance to Conchubar congregate outside the door of

The taking of the oath in *On Baile's Strand*. A University of Vermont production, 1973. Directed by Sidney Poger and Ghita Orth.

The Blind Man tells the Fool that Cuchulain has slain his own son in *On Baile's Strand*. A University of Winnipeg production, 1969. Directed by Reg Skene.

the assembly-house and urge Cuchulain to take the oath. He contemptuously tells them they have been tamed by their wives and children, but agrees to take the oath.

While he is swearing obedience to Conchubar and his children, the women sing a prayer that the fire into which Cuchulain plunges his sword, as part of the ceremony, will drive away the "Shape-Changers" (also known as the Sidhe), the female spirits of the air who are antagonistic to the stability and settled domesticity of "threshold and hearthstone." As soon as Cuchulain has taken the oath, the youth from Aoife's country enters the hall with his sword drawn and challenges Cuchulain to fight.

Cuchulain sees the Young Man's resemblance to Aoife and admires his courage; he offers friendship and exchange of gifts, and when the kings clamor to be allowed to fight the Young Man, Cuchulain addresses him as a comrade: "Boy, I would meet them all in arms / If I'd a son like you." When Conchubar denounces this behavior, Cuchulain seizes him; at this violent treatment of his kingly person, Conchubar alleges that Cuchulain has been maddened by witchcraft, and the other kings take up this cry. Cuchulain seems shocked that he has laid hands on the High King, agrees that he must have been bewitched to be so friendly to the Young Man, and orders him outside to fight.

The Fool drags in the Blind Man, abusing him for having eaten all the hen and left him only the feathers. This is typical of his behavior, the Fool exclaims; the Blind Man always sends him to do the dirty work but keeps any profit for himself. Cuchulain rushes in, takes note of the quarrel between the two and wipes the bloody sword with which he has killed the Young Man on a handful of the hen's feathers. The Fool guilelessly reveals the secret the Blind Man has by now entrusted to him: the Young Man was Aoife's son by her only lover, Cuchulain. The Blind Man feels the bench on which he sits tremble, and thinks it is the Fool trembling with fear that Cuchulain is about to kill him for disclosing such awful news. But the Fool says that it is Cuchulain who is trembling.

Cuchulain first blames witchcraft, then rushes out to slay Conchubar, but—the Fool tells us—only approaches Conchubar, then runs down to the sea, slashing at the waves with his sword as though he were fighting them, until the waves overpower him. This implies that Cuchulain realizes that the responsibility for his son's death rests ultimately with him, and Fate, which works through him, not with Conchubar's demands for allegiance. Since everyone has run down to the shore to watch Cuchulain, the Blind Man calculates that he and the Fool have a good opportunity to steal food from the ovens in the empty houses; they exit with that intention.

On Baile's Strand, Lady Gregory's *Spreading the News,* and revivals of *Cathleen Ni Houlihan* and Synge's *In the Shadow of the Glen,* made up the first program at the Abbey Theatre on December 27, 1904. Maire Nic Shiubhlaigh, who played Cathleen in that production, describes the set for *On Baile's Strand:*

> Amber-coloured hangings draped the interior of a great hall. A huge door, closed, showed intricate Celtic interlacings on panel and lintel. When it was opened, a glimpse was revealed of a luminous blue sky over a bay. Two plain thrones stood in the centre; brilliant handpainted medallions on the walls completed the fittings. A golden arc played across the front, helped the colourful costumes of kings, councillors and the resplendent Cuchulain of Frank Fay to blend into a pale background.[11]

It is a significant indication of Lady Gregory's influence on Yeats that the first version of *On Baile's Strand* was published shortly after her translation of the Ulster saga, *Cuchulain of Muirthemne*. In Lady Gregory's version Cuchulain knows that he left Aoife with child and the Young Man discloses his identity before he dies at Cuchulain's hands. Yeats alters the saga material by adding the dramatically effective subplot involving the Blind Man and the Fool; also, by leaving it to his audience to infer that the Young Man is Cuchulain's son by Aoife, Yeats is able to give the play a powerful sense of tragic irony. By the time of the play's second version, the one included in *Collected Plays*, Yeats had conceived of it as the first of a cycle of plays with Cuchulain for hero. *The Green Helmet* (1910), *At the Hawk's Well* (1917), *The Only Jealousy of Emer* (1919), and *The Death of Cuchulain* (1939), are the later plays which deal with Cuchulain.

Yeats was very pleased with *On Baile's Strand;* before the play was performed, he wrote to Lady Gregory that *On Baile's Strand* was the best play he had written: "It goes magnificently, and the end is particularly impressive." [12] Many shared Yeats's good opinion of the play when it was performed, and he was gratified by the play's reception. Yet he realized after the first production that it suffered from a cloudiness of theme, and he rewrote the entire first part up to the entrance of the Young Man. The result is, in the 1906 version, a highly unified structure, and a play that has been described as one of "the best poetic plays of this century," one Lennox Robinson thought the most perfect of Yeats's verse plays.[13]

Yeats's source for all five Cuchulain plays is the Celtic saga material describing the adventures of the Red Branch knights, the heroes of Ulster. The quarrel between Cuchulain and Conchubar involves a dialectic that is typical of Yeats's poems as well as his plays. Cuchulain is the superhuman, heroic warrior of Ulster who has become an embarrassment to his politic king and compatriots because he is self-ful-filling, interested only in doing what pleases him. In Conchubar's view such inclinations are dangerous, and need to be transformed into the acceptable and so-cially useful behavior of safeguarding the state from within and without. This sort of responsibility is what Cuchulain lacks and despises. Although he is aging (the notes describe him as something over forty, Yeats's age when he wrote the play, whereas in the saga he dies at the age of twenty-seven), he regards the domesticity of Conchubar and his friends with con-tempt. He remembers the wildness of Aoife with plea-sure, so different from the subservience of Conchu-bar's wife, and imagines an heroic son who is the antithesis of Conchubar's soft, privileged children. One's interest in the debate is sustained because of its human implications:

> It is the sheer humanity of Cuchulain and Con-chubar that ultimately touches the heart and engages the mind; Cuchulain's disdain for Con-chubar's life of settled ease is mingled with his longing for a son; Conchubar's arrogant awareness of his power is mingled with his envy of Cuchu-lain's wild abandon.[14]

It is this human element, as opposed to the mys-ticism of *The Shadowy Waters,* or the strangely im-personal quality of the Noh plays, that makes *On Baile's Strand* so affecting. The story of Cuchulain's battle with his son has several prototypes in biblical and classical literature, and its mythic properties clearly touch something deep in human experience. Yeats's own father wrote to him after seeing the play:

I cannot tell you how much I enjoyed your play. As I lay awake most of the night I had plenty of time to think about it. The scene between father and son over the duel was the most thrilling and enthralling experience I ever went through. You touched at the same moment the fountain of joy and tears.[15]

It is interesting to recall that the central action of another of Yeats's best plays, *Purgatory,* involves the murder of a son by his father.

The subplot involving the Blind Man and the Fool parodies and generalizes the conflict between Conchubar and Cuchulain. Though they are, to some extent, low characters who provide comic relief, their function is also, more importantly, that of extending the significance of the quarrel between protagonist and antagonist, a function Yeats emphasizes by giving them masks. Their inclusion marks the first appearance in Yeats's plays of figures on the edge of society whose varying functions usually include the traditional dramatic capacity of possessing knowledge or wisdom unavailable to the other characters. In *On Baile's Strand,* the Blind Man would seem to be emblematic of secret and intellectual knowledge, the Fool of intuitive and natural understanding.

The scene in which the Blind Man cheats the Fool by eating the hen and leaving him only the feathers presents an ironic parallel to the tragic action in which Conchubar orders Cuchulain to kill his own son. Cuchulain exists in the same exploited relationship to Conchubar as the Fool does to the Blind Man. The correlation is made very effectively at that point in the action when Cuchulain enters the hall after killing the Young Man and seizes a bunch of feathers—all that remains of the hen after the Blind Man has finished with it—with which to clean his bloody sword. Figuratively speaking, Cuchulain has the feathers and Conchubar the hen: Cuchulain has killed his son, making Conchubar's kingdom, and that of *his* sons, secure.

In addition to parodying the main plot, the Fool and the Blind Man externalize Cuchulain's inner conflict; significantly, they appear only to Cuchulain and the audience. In their exchanges, they mysteriously seem to affect the outcome of the main plot—their playing at being Cuchulain and Conchubar is "a ritual enactment that somehow determines the main plot." [16]

By taking the oath of allegiance to Conchubar and his children, Cuchulain betrays his very selfhood; this action must have tragic consequences. Those consequences are dramatically foreshadowed when, immediately after Cuchulain has taken the oath, his own son appears onstage. The scene in which the three Women, guardians of home and hearth, administer the oath to Cuchulain, is dramatically effective for another reason, too. The dialectic of the play, the struggle between Cuchulain and Conchubar, and what they stand for, is convincingly extended to the supernatural in this scene: the ritual of the three Women lends a supernatural dimension to Conchubar's way of being in the world, as the evocation of the Sidhe, spirits of anarchic heroism, suggests the opposing life-force embodied in Cuchulain. There can be little doubt that *On Baile's Strand* with its archetypal, intensely human theme, and its complexity artfully accommodated within a clear and tightly unified dramatic structure, is one of Yeats's best plays.

11. *Deirdre* (1907)

Yeats's *Deirdre* is based on the romantic and heroic story of Deirdre and Naoise in the Cuchulain mythological cycle. (Diarmuid and Grania, in the

Fenian cycle, is a variant of the same myth.) It is evening in a primitive wooden house in the woods of Ulster; on one side of the room stands a small table holding a chess game, on the other, a fire burns in the hearth. Through the windows one can see the woods and anyone who approaches the house. Three women with musical instruments have arrived by chance at this "old guest house built for travellers" near King Conchubar's house. The First Musician recalls what happened "some dozen years ago," when Conchubar found Deirdre in these woods being nursed by an old witch. He visited the child every day until she grew up to become a beautiful woman, then determined to marry her. But the old king was disappointed, for a month before the wedding Deirdre ran away with Naoise, a young man "in the laughing scorn of his youth."

The former king of Ulster, Fergus, now an old man, enters with the news that Deirdre and Naoise are expected, for due to his good offices, Conchubar has forgiven them. He asks the women to play welcoming music. Despite the First Musician's reflection that "old men are jealous," Fergus tries to explain why Conchubar has found it politic to pardon the young lovers, who have been wandering the world for the six years since their elopement. Armed men in barbaric dress pass ominously by the window, and will not answer Fergus when he questions them. The First Musician realizes that these are "such men / As kings will gather for a murderous task." The musicians play their instruments and sing of the extreme nature of love as Deirdre and Naoise arrive. The lovers are both uneasy at the atmosphere in the house, though Naoise attempts to persuade Deirdre that all will go well. Deirdre exclaims: "An empty house upon the journey's end! / Is that the way a king that means no mischief / Honours a guest?"

The stage directions here indicate that Naoise and Fergus leave the house; they can be seen through the door or window, where they talk or look expectantly along the road leading to Conchubar's house. Inside, the First Musician suggests to Deirdre that Conchubar means to murder Naoise and marry her; he has sewed magical stones "that have power / To stir even those at enmity to love" into the curtains around the bridal bed. Deirdre threatens to destroy her beauty, then, when Naoise returns, succeeds in persuading him to flee. Fergus, however, convinces them that Conchubar will think they mean to mock him and will easily capture them, so there is no point in flight. A dark-faced messenger comes to the door and announces that Conchubar awaits his guests. Naoise and Fergus are greatly relieved, but Deirdre waits to hear the rest of the message, which bears out her worst fears: "the traitor that bore off the Queen," Naoise, is not wanted, for "It is enough that the King pardon her [Deirdre], / And call her to his table and his bed."

Naoise attempts to send a challenge to Conchubar, but the messenger jeers at him. Fergus at last realizes his mistake in trusting the king, and leaves to gather his friends and oppose Conchubar. Naoise exits and comes back to report that they are hopelessly surrounded, with the woods full of armed men. Naoise and Deirdre determine to play a game of chess while waiting for their murderers to appear.

But Deirdre cannot go on stoically playing chess, knowing that Naoise is doomed to die, and beseeches him to kiss her. For her, their love is the supreme value in life and should be passionately expressed even in the face of death. Naoise notices Conchubar spying on them, and pursues him into the woods. Deirdre takes a knife from the First Musician and conceals it in her clothes. Conchubar and his men enter with Naoise entangled in a net. Conchubar offers to let Naoise go free, if Deirdre will marry him, and indicate to the people that she has done so of her own free will.

Deirdre is at first willing to sacrifice herself, but then, on Naoise's urging, rejects Conchubar's offer. In a vain attempt to exculpate Naoise, she accepts all the responsibility for their elopement. Unseen by Deirdre, Naoise is gagged, and forced behind a curtain. When she misses him, it is too late even to protest, for the executioner emerges from behind the curtain with blood on his sword. Deirdre pretends calmness and willingness to go with Conchubar, if he will but let her lay out the dead body of Naoise as custom demands. Conchubar reluctantly allows her to go behind the curtain. There is shouting outside and Fergus enters, demanding that Naoise and Deirdre be handed over to him; he leads a thousand men armed with scythes and sickles. Conchubar says that he has triumphed and commands the curtain to be opened to show the proof of his victory.

The open curtain reveals the dead bodies of Naoise and of Deirdre, who has killed herself with the knife she earlier concealed in her clothing. As Fergus asks of Conchubar, "What's this but empty cage and tangled wire, / Now the bird's gone?" Although Fergus's men outside shout "Death to Conchubar," Conchubar unrepentantly proclaims that he did right to choose Deirdre, for she was "most fitting to be Queen."

Deirdre was first performed on November 24, 1906, at the Abbey by the National Theatre Society, that is, the Abbey Company. W. G. Fay thought that *Deirdre* was the first verse play that was genuinely appreciated by the audience, but he criticized the effect produced by using a professional English actress, Miss Darragh, in the role of Deirdre. Combining her style with that of the Abbey players was "like putting a Rolls Royce to run a race with a lot of hill ponies." [17] The part

of Deirdre was later played (in 1907 and 1908), at the
Abbey and in London, by another star of the English
stage, Mrs. Patrick Campbell, widely regarded as one
of the great actresses of her time. Yeats's use of professional English actresses was a deviation from the
normal Abbey policy of employing nonprofessional
Irish actors in the interests of maintaining a distinctive Abbey style of acting. Yeats had not yet recognized, Hone tells us, "the lyrical and subtle genius" of
the Abbey actress Maire O'Neill.[18]

The source for Yeats's play is the love story of
Deirdre and Naoise, one of the best-known of Irish
myths. Yeats relied on Lady Gregory's translation in
Cuchulain of Muirthemne. He points out the resemblance of the Irish story to Greek myth: "Deirdre was
the Irish Helen, and Naoise her Paris, and Conchubar her Menelaus." [19]

As was his custom after seeing his plays performed,
Yeats revised *Deirdre,* even though he thought the
original version "most powerful, even sensational." [20]
The effect of the revisions was to make Deirdre even
more emphatically the central figure of the play. Consequently the play depends on its protagonist more
than any of the earlier dramas. Deirdre is like the
strong women characters in plays by the Jacobean
dramatists, Webster and Ford: surrounded by male
deceit and treachery, deeply enamored of a romantic
but rather ineffectual lover, she is finally more intelligent, noble, and heroic than any other character in
the play. Not only that, but her enemy Conchubar is
a far lesser man than the character who opposed
Cuchulain in *On Baile's Strand*. While one has little
sympathy for Conchubar in *On Baile's Strand* and
Guaire, the king who is Seanchan's enemy in *The
King's Threshold,* they are felt to be formidable representatives of all that Cuchulain and Seanchan oppose; but in *Deirdre,* Conchubar, however selfish and

violent, is of inconsequent stature when compared with the play's heroine.

Deirdre is more aware than her lover of what fate holds in store for them. Because it is against her better judgment that she has allowed herself to be persuaded by Naoise to seek a reconciliation with Conchubar, she swiftly comprehends the trap they have fallen into. She sees through Naoise's and Fergus's ill-founded optimism when they attempt to persuade her, and themselves, that all is well. She puzzles out the riddling utterances of the prophetic Musicians and understands that Conchubar intends to kill Naoise and marry her (a worse teachery, for Deirdre, than the murder of them both). She knows that the relief promised by the first lines of the messenger's announcement is false, that Naoise is to be excluded. And she decisively urges Fergus, who foolishly wants to reason with Conchubar even at this juncture, to flee and seek help.

Naoise's stoicism impresses Deirdre enough to agree that they should play chess together while waiting for the inevitable, but she is much more passionate than he. She recalls the first night they spent in the woods together, and, remembering "that old vehement, bewildering kiss," asks him to kiss her for what may be the last time before their death. She prepares for death by seizing a knife from the First Musician, exhibiting her courage and decisiveness. Her calmness after Naoise's death, and ability to persuade Conchubar that she accepts his mastery, demonstrate her heroic will. Her suicide reveals a triumphant nobility of character that impresses even the ignoble and despicably selfish Conchubar.

Yeats described Deirdre's actions as "Red-heat up to Naoise's death, white-heat after he is dead." [21] Certainly, after Naoise's death, Deirdre's control of her passionate nature in order to shape her own destiny (to die with Naoise) gives the impression of over-whelming passion and energy heroically controlled. The play thus attains, chiefly through Deirdre's character, the combination of "overflowing turbulent energy" with "marmorean stillness" which Yeats described in "Poetry and Tradition" as one of the noble qualities of art.[22]

Yeats's increasing mastery of plot is evident in *Deirdre*. To start the play at the climax of the tragic story greatly compresses the play's action and helps sustain its austere, tragic mood. The play is dominated by growing suspense, premonition, and foreshadowing up to the arrival of Conchubar's messenger, the turning point in the action; after that point, by the violent and tragic resolution.

The setting of the isolated house in the sinister woods, the imagery of nets and traps, Naoise's being dragged onstage by Conchubar entangled in a net, all embody the theme of betrayal and entrapment in admirably dramatic fashion. The visual presence of the play's most important stage property, the chess game, suggests both the preordained working out of fate, and the heroic stoicism which accepts that fate. As a contest which is a battle of wits, the chess game is also an apt analogy for the action of the play. The Musicians, much more effectively than in *On Baile's Strand*, perform the function of chorus: they briefly inform us at the beginning of the play what the story is about, they hint at the tragic outcome, they take part in the action as well as comment on it, and they describe in their songs the absolute nature of heroic love.

A series of ironies emphasize the tragic nature of the action; one is that the murder of Naoise occurs while Deirdre is praising him to Conchubar in an attempt to save his life. Another is Deirdre's speech to the Musicians as she goes ostensibly to lay out

Naoise's body, in fact to kill herself with the knife she has taken from the First Musician. (Conchubar, of course, places a different construction on her speech than the audience and the Musicians do.) Deirdre says:

> "Now strike the wire, and sing to it a while,
> Knowing that all is happy, and that you know
> Within what bride-bed I shall lie this night,
> And by what man, and lie close up to him,
> For the bed's narrow, and there outsleep the
>   cockcrow."

Deirdre is an impressive demonstration of Yeats's growing accomplishment as a dramatist. Like *On Baile's Strand,* it has an element of human psychology often missing from later plays that are calculatedly remote and impersonal in effect. *Deirdre* summons up other instances of the situation it dramatizes; not only do Deirdre and Naoise remind us of other Yeatsian lovers, but they also recall those archetypes of tragic and romantic love, Tristan and Iseult, and Paolo and Francesca.

12. Sophocles' *King Oedipus* (1928) and Sophocles' *Oedipus at Colonus* (1934)

Yeats began his translation of Sophocles' *King Oedipus* in 1911; the text in *Collected Plays* is the seventh version of this translation. Very surprisingly, in view of his own theory and practice, Yeats turned this play and *Oedipus at Colonus* into prose, with the exception of the choruses' lines. Not only did Yeats put "readers and scholars" out of his mind in doing these translations aimed at the average theatergoer, but he also "cut down on the meta-

phoric, ambiguous, and ironic language of Sophocles." [23] What Yeats was interested in, to the near exclusion of the complexities of Sophocles' dramatic
verse, was the clear structure and the action of the
play. Yeats's translation of *King Oedipus* in particular has been proved to be a very popular and stage-
worthy version on many occasions.

The first production of Sophocles' *King Oedipus*,
on December 7, 1926, was extremely successful, as an
article in the *New York Times* attests:

> One does not expect to see an audience drawn
> from all ranks of life, crowding a theater beyond
> its capacity and becoming awed into spellbound,
> breathless attention by a tragedy of Sophocles. Yet
> that is exactly what happened at the Abbey Thea-
> tre on the evening of Dec 7 when the W. B. Yeats
> translation of *Oedipus the King* was presented for
> the first time by the Abbey Players. It was com-
> pletely a night of unlooked-for-revelations which
> embraced the play, translator, players and audi-
> ence alike.
>
> It was an event hitherto unequaled in the his-
> tory of the Abbey and when the chorus, standing
> before the closed curtain, spoke the concluding
> line: "Call no man happy while he lives," there
> followed a scene of enthusiasm surpassing all
> similar scenes with which the career of the theatre
> is dotted. . . . Yeats's *Oedipus the King* is not only
> great, it is magnificent. . . . he has brought Greek
> classic drama within the reach and understanding
> of audiences to whom it has heretofore represented
> the highest standard of intellectuality.[24]

Yeats's translation was also used in later, memorable productions of *King Oedipus:* Laurence Olivier
played the title role at an Old Vic production at the
Century Theatre in New York in 1946, as did James
Mason at a Stratford Ontario Festival production di-

rected by Tyrone Guthrie in July 1954. In July 1973, a production at the Abbey was staged by a Greek director, Michael Cacoyannis. Alec Reid pays tribute to Yeats's contribution to the success of this Abbey production:

> It is astonishing . . . that this inevitability should have been caught in a translation, yet as we watched Doom stalk, almost tangible, on the Abbey stage, it needed a conscious effort to remember that the words were the words of an Irishman, not of a Greek, of Yeats not of Sophocles. . . . The English version is as hard, as cold, as unyieldingly magnificent as marble.[25]

Sophocles' *Oedipus at Colonus* was performed for the first time at the Abbey, on September 12, 1927. The fact that Yeats worked on these translations of Sophocles over a period of many years, and the manner in which he translated them, helps account for the compression of structure and intensity of emotional effect which Yeats was able to attain in his own plays. Significantly, he subtitled each of the translations "a version for the modern stage."

VI. NOH PLAYS

Yeats was discouraged that his verse plays had not attracted the popular audience he had dreamed of, and dispirited at the difficulties of staging them, even though he could count on a relatively sophisticated audience at the Abbey: "I have begun to shrink from sending my muses where they are but half-welcomed; and even in Dublin, where the pit has an ear for verse, I have no longer the appetite to carry me through the daily rehearsals." [1] Despite experimentation with Gordon Craig's screens, costumes, and masks in Abbey productions of *The Hour-Glass* and *The Countess Cathleen* as early as 1911, Yeats continued to find himself frustrated and inhibited by conventions of the contemporary commercial theater. He could not as yet see an acceptable way of eliminating the limitations of painted scenery, artificial lighting, and an undue emphasis on the personalities of the actors.

Moreover, though Yeats had worked diligently for a decade or more at finding ways of keeping the Abbey financially solvent, he must have experienced the guilty suspicion that the unpopularity of his own plays had done nothing to avert the financial crisis in which the theater found itself by 1914. There are, then, elements of understandable defensiveness, bitterness, and exaggeration in the artistic manifestoes Yeats issued at this time, and these elements show up clearly in his rationale for adopting the Japanese Noh play as a model for his drama. Yeats wants to make it clear that he has rejected the conventional theater more than it has rejected him, and his excitement at discovering a new and congenial dramatic form is often accompanied by an elitist glee that the form is an aristocratic one.

Yeats had first encountered the Noh plays in 1913, when he shared a cottage in Sussex with Ezra Pound, who was finishing Ernest Fenollosa's translations of Noh plays. Yeats contributed an introduction to the translations, published in 1916 as *Certain Noble Plays of Japan,* in which he claimed "with the help of these plays" to have "invented a form of drama, distinguished, indirect and symbolic, and having no need of mob or press to pay its way—an aristocratic form. . . . In the studio and in the drawing-room we can found a true theatre of beauty." [2] Yeats rejoiced at being able to substitute a beautiful, sculptured mask "for the face of some commonplace player, or for that face repainted to suit his own vulgar fancy." [3] The tone of these and similar remarks should not distract us from appreciating that Yeats had encountered the dramatic form that seemed to embody all he had, however uncertainly, striven for in the past. And there would be compensations for neglecting the traditions of realistic drama: "whatever we lose in mass and in power we should recover in elegance and in subtlety." [4]

What Yeats admired in these Japanese plays that flourished during the fourteenth and fifteenth centuries, and what he imitated in his own plays, was a nonmimetic dramatic form, symbolic and ritualistic in mode and highly stylized in convention. He admired, too, the impressive continuity of cultural tradition which preserved those plays: as Fenollosa pointed out, "the same plays are today enacted in the same manner as then; even the leading actors of today are blood descendants of the very men who created this drama 450 years ago." [5] Indeed, not only did the actors belong to certain families which trained new generations in the conventions of the plays, but the families actually preserved the texts and choreography for the plays.

The Noh plays originated, like English and Greek drama, in religious ritual. Shinto and Buddhist religious festivals gave rise to the form, which is characterized by dance, music, and a mixture of verse and prose. Though music was an integral part of the play, it was not written down; the musicians were expected to accompany the verse by playing the appropriate traditional music. "The actors intoned their speeches, the chorus chanted theirs"; the dance was characterized by "slow steps and solemn gestures." [6] The masks were sculptured, the costumes rich and fine. There was no drop curtain on the small square stage. The plays were short and often performed in a sequence of as many as five or six. The three or four characters in each play have formal titles—hero, priest, a country gentleman, a fisherman, and so on. Direct action does not take place on stage; instead, action "is lived through again in dance and narrative by the ghost of one of the participants in it." [7]

Fenollosa sums up the concentration of the Noh: "All elements—costume, motion, verse, and music—unite to produce a single clarified impression." That "impression" takes the place of direct action:

> Each drama embodies some primary human relation or emotion. . . . The emotion is always fixed upon idea, not upon personality. The solo parts express great types of human character, derived from Japanese history. Now it is brotherly love,

now love to a parent, now loyalty to a master, love
of husband and wife, of mother for a dead child,
or of jealousy or anger, of self-mastery in battle,
of the battle passion itself, of the clinging of a
ghost to the scene of its sin, of the infinite com-
passion of a Buddha, of the sorrow of unrequited
love. Some one of these intense emotions is chosen
for a piece, and, in it, elevated to the plane of
universality by the intensity and purity of treatment. Thus the drama became a storehouse of
history, and a great moral force for the whole
social order of the Samurai.[8]

The influence of the Noh is apparent in almost all
of Yeats's plays written after 1916, but it is particularly obvious in the plays discussed in this chapter.
The publication of *At the Hawk's Well, The Only
Jealousy of Emer, The Dreaming of the Bones* and
Calvary in the collection entitled *Four Plays for
Dancers* (1921) suggests a Noh sequence; Yeats had intended *The Cat and the Moon* "to be what the Japanese call a *Kiogen,* and to come as a relaxation of attention between, let us say *At the Hawk's Well* and
The Dreaming of the Bones."[9] The emphasis on
aesthetic considerations in the staging of these plays,
the use of masks, music and chorus, the absence of a
drop curtain (though Yeats introduces a cloth to be
folded and unfolded that is its symbolic equivalent),
the themes of heroism and passion and encounters
with the supernatural—all these, as well as Yeats's
own explicit acknowledgment, demonstrate the impact
on his work after 1916 of the Noh drama.

Yet it is easy to exaggerate this influence, for Yeats
had been working toward the same kind of drama as
the Noh on his own, as his earlier plays, his theorizing
and experimentation reveal. Yeats's subject matter
remained Irish, as in the Cuchulain plays and *The*

Dreaming of the Bones; as far as the themes of all the plays in this group are concerned, Yeats was demonstrably interested in heroism, romantic passion and the supernatural long before he encountered the Noh. To make that point, he included *The Land of Heart's Desire* and *The Countess Cathleen* with the four dance plays in *Plays and Controversies* (1923). Yeats had also employed verse and occasional music and songs in his earliest plays. Gordon Craig had given him (in 1911) the opportunity to experiment with a symbolic set, costumes, and masks, had encouraged him to suppress any expression of mere personality on the parts of the actors, and generally supported the idea of a theater of beauty that was the antithesis of the realistic theater of the day. "I don't want to imitate man or Nature or anything else on the boards of a theatre," Craig proclaimed, "I want to create a new world there—not to copy the real world imperfectly." [10] Yeats would have agreed with these sentiments, undoubtedly, but it took the Noh plays to trigger in him a full sense of awareness of the kind of theater and plays he had been working toward; he was, naturally, encouraged to move in this direction, to sever his residual, emotional ties with the realistic theater by the relative failure of his work in that context.

Yeats, of course, did not first encounter the use of masks and choruses in the Noh drama, since these are an obvious feature of classical Greek drama. Although there can be little doubt that the Noh exerted the more profound influence on Yeats's development as a dramatist, it is sometimes difficult to separate these two influences on Yeats's plays, for they are often parallel. Then again, the function of setting in the Noh was similar to its function in Irish myth and folklore, as Yeats pointed out in his introduction to *Certain Noble Plays of Japan:*

These Japanese poets too feel for tomb and wood the emotion, the sense of awe that our Gaelic-speaking country people will sometimes show when you speak to them of Castle Hackett or of some Holy Well; and that is why perhaps it pleases them to begin so many plays by a Traveller asking his way with many questions. . . . The men who created this convention were more like ourselves than were the Greeks and Romans, more like us even than are Shakespeare and Corneille.[11]

What the Noh play, as distinct from other parallel influences, did for Yeats, was to crystallize his sense of the kind of drama he wanted to write, to unify a number of disparate interests evident in his earlier work. It also gave him a prestigious model and authority for his work that was not available to him in western culture. Yeats's Noh plays are not, then, a willful imitation of an esoteric tradition. Essentially they are the culmination of his own art, and like the work of any great artist, ultimately they assimilate influences only to transcend them. Perhaps the most impressive demonstration of this assimilation of influence lies in the fact that *At the Hawk's Well* was not only translated into Japanese and performed in Japan several times, but was also "adapted into a complete Noh form" in which "the original version had of course undergone considerable transformation." [12]

Yeats's Noh plays are, of all his dramatic works, most attractive to our contemporary experimental theater; the "total theater" approach exploits their purely theatrical possibilities—especially their emphasis on music, dance, mask, and song—to impressive effect, as recent productions in New York by La Mama and the Open Eye Theater have demonstrated. And a British drama critic reports the interest of influential British directors and dramatists in Yeats's plays for dancers: "Peter Brook . . . uses dance plays

for the exercizes his company practise in his theatre
workshop in Paris; Harold Pinter would like to produce a dance play. . . ." [13]

13. *At the Hawk's Well* (1917)

The time is the Irish heroic age. The Musicians' song accompanies the unfolding and folding
of a black cloth with "a gold pattern suggesting a
hawk." Their song evokes the setting of a bare
mountain place at nightfall; a well and a stripped
tree whose leaves "choke the dry bed of the well" are
the only features of this barren landscape. Throughout the play the Three Musicians "accompany the
movements of the players with gong or drum or
zither." The Guardian of the Well crouches on the
ground, "entirely covered by a black cloak." An Old
Man, doubled over with age, enters and makes a fire,
"complaining of the Guardian's silence and the "broken rocks, / And ragged thorns."

A Young Man then appears, whom the Old Man
judges by his golden dress not to be one of those (like
himself) "who hate the living world"; the Young
Man announces that he is Cuchulain, come from afar
in quest of the miraculous water from this well that
confers immortality. Fearful that Cuchulain will
drink all the water, the Old Man wants him to leave.
The Old Man feels that he has a prior claim on the
magical waters, having waited these fifty years for the
well to fill up. On three occasions during that time,
the Old Man recounts, he was beguiled into sleep
only to find, upon awakening, the tantalizing evidence
of wet stones around the empty well that it had
filled with water while he slept. Cuchulain magnani-
mously promises the Old Man a share of the water
when the well fills. Cuchulain will not be tricked

The Old Man in *At the Hawk's Well*. A Centaur Theatre production, Montreal, 1971. Directed by James W. Flannery. Mask design by Felix Mirbt.

JAMES W. FLANNERY

The Musicians in *At the Hawk's Well*. A University of Winnipeg production, 1969. Directed by Reg Skene.

REG SKENE; DAVID HEWLETT

into sleeping; if needs be, he blithely resolves, he will
pierce his foot to stay awake. The Guardian of the
Well cries out like a hawk, apparently possessed by
Fand, the Woman of the Sidhe. The Old Man
warns Cuchulain that to gaze directly into her eyes
lays one open to a terrible curse.

The Guardian of the Well throws off her cloak,
revealing a dress that suggests a hawk, and begins to
dance, "moving like a hawk." The Old Man covers
his head to avoid her eyes and falls asleep. Cuchulain
looks fearlessly into her eyes. Water splashes into the
well, and although Cuchulain hears it, he follows the
Guardian offstage as though in a dream. The Old
Man awakens to find the stones wet, but the water
gone, and curses bitterly. Cuchulain returns, describing how the Guardian eluded him to hide on the
rocky hillside.

There are cries and the noise of swords striking
shields, which the Old Man interprets for Cuchulain:
the Guardian

> ". . . has roused up the fierce women of the hills,
> Aoife, and all her troop, to take your life,
> And never till you are lying in the earth
> Can you know rest."

Cuchulain is excited by the clash of arms, and the
prospect of an encounter with Aoife. He shoulders
his spear "no longer as if in a dream," and exits asserting his identity as "Cuchulain, son of Sualtim."
The Old Man then exits, and the Musicians sing a
song disparaging those who seek immortality and
praising an easy, unambitious life.

In his eagerness to be done with "the stupidity of
an ordinary audience," Yeats seems to have confused intelligence with social status.[14] *At the Hawk's
Well* was first staged in the drawing-room of Lady

Cunard in London on April 2, 1916, with a small, invited audience, then a few days later at Lady Islington's, where "Queen Alexandra's presence attracted three hundred fashionable people." [15] The Queen had admired Yeats's poetry, but when he gave a talk on the Noh drama before his own play, she quickly became bored, and "sent a message by her lady-in-waiting to ask for it to be cut short." [16]

Yeats was delighted to have found for this, his first play in the Noh tradition, a Japanese actor and dancer who had seen Noh plays performed in Japan. Michio Itoh played the part of the Guardian of the Well, and accompanied by Yeats, attracted a good deal of puzzled attention at the London Zoo, where he was seen imitating the movements of the caged hawks in preparation for his role in Yeats's play. Itoh produced *At the Hawk's Well* in Japan in 1939, and again in 1958; after his death, the play was performed in the Tokyo Culture Hall as a memorial tribute (July 13, 1962), and has been staged in Japan at least twice since then.[17]

The stage directions are unusually elaborate for Yeats, and indicate how far he had moved away from the conventions of the realistic stage. The players are masked, or, in the case of the three Musicians, their faces are made up to resemble masks. The movements of the Old Man, "like those of the other persons of the play, suggest a marionette." These directions show, no doubt, the influence of Gordon Craig, as well as of the Noh drama, but they derive, too, from Yeats's belief, expressed in his essay "The Tragic Theatre" (1910), that highly individualized character has a function only in comedy, and not in tragedy.

Both the blank verse spoken by Cuchulain and the Old Man, and the lyric verse sung by the Musicians show the beneficial influence of Ezra Pound, whose help Yeats sought in trying to purge his poetry of abstraction and vagueness; the verse of *At the Hawk's Well* employs "a terse, vivid diction," it is "more spare, the images are exactly delimited by the words, every shadow is removed." [18] The simple music for the play was composed by Edmund Dulac, who also played the part of the First Musician. Yeats and Dulac had difficulty persuading the other musicians that their music and singing should occupy a background role in the play, distinctly subordinate to the actors' speech.

The stage is "any bare space before a wall against which stands a patterned screen." Again, Craig's influence coincides here with the influence of the Noh and with Yeats's own distaste for conventional "scenery;" he relies mainly on the poetry to create setting. "The most effective lighting," he tells us in the stage directions "is the lighting we are accustomed to in our rooms." Yeats thus hoped to discard the conventions of theater lighting and scenery which he found merely distracted the audience from the play.

At the Hawk's Well portrays the initiation of the Irish mythological hero, Cuchulain. He is called the Young Man in the play as though to emphasize not only his naïveté but also his courage and strength in this crucial encounter whereby the future tragic implications of his heroic career become apparent. There is no source for the play's action in Irish saga, and Yeats was probably inspired by the Noh plays, in which "the adventure itself is often the meeting with ghost, god, or goddess at some holy place." [19]

The play's setting, a haunting spiritual wasteland, is an apt testing-ground for heroic courage and resolution. Cuchulain's inevitable failure to complete his quest for immortality by drinking the magical well-water serves to direct our attention to the distinctive nature of his heroic identity. Unlike the Old

Man, Cuchulain will achieve immortality, but it is by living his life so intensely and by meeting his death with such courage that he gains renown forever, not by drinking from the well. Indeed, Cuchulain is much less interested in the magic water than is the Old Man, and unlike him, wastes no time regretting being diverted from it by the Guardian, as if he realizes that it is impossible to gain immortality by such means, anyway. He instinctively realizes his immortality will be achieved through conflict.

The Old Man wears an heroic mask, but the remorseful withdrawal from life into which his pursuit of an ideal has led him is a form of sterility; he can hardly be distinguished from the barren landscape around him, as Cuchulain remarks: "You seem as dried up as the leaves and sticks / As though you had no part in life." He counsels Cuchulain against his stoical resolution to stay awake if need be by wounding himself, and fearfully warns him that he will be cursed if he looks into the eyes of the hawk woman:

> "That curse may be
> Never to win a woman's love and keep it;
> Or always to mix hatred in the love;
> Or it may be that she will kill your children,
> That you will find them, their throats torn
>   and bloody,
> Or you will be so maddened that you kill them
> With your own hand."

Cuchulain refuses to concern himself with the bitterness in store for him because of his daring to face the hawk woman, but an audience familiar with Yeats's other Cuchulain plays cannot but think of the consequences of this heroic defiance of the supernatural. Cuchulain's pursuit of Aoife with which this play ends, we know, leads to an amorous as well as a martial encounter; the fruit of this love-hate relationship is the son whom Cuchulain unwittingly kills in *On Baile's Strand*. We know, too, from *The Only Jealousy of Emer* that his love for Emer is blighted in a tragic way, and from *The Death of Cuchulain* that Cuchulain is, despite his heroism, to meet his death at the hands of a cowardly blind man.

The Musicians play the role of chorus, doing the work of exposition and commentary; they seem as imperceptive as "average" people about the attraction of the ideal, and reject the idea of life as heroic conflict, as their closing song indicates: "I choose a pleasant life / Among indolent meadows; / Wisdom must live a bitter life." The Musicians disparage the Old Man's idealism for the wrong reason. The play certainly condemns the self-absorbed idealism of the Old Man that is essentially a withdrawal from life; we know that he will die before tasting the water of immortality, and that he will be wracked with remorse until then by the knowledge that he has failed to live. But he has at least attempted something more than those the Musicians praise who have settled for a comfortable home with "children and dogs on the floor." The Musicians cannot understand, either, the choice of strife that characterizes Cuchulain's life. The curse laid on Cuchulain really is "only" his fate. His instinctive engagement with life, his determination to live his life and be himself, leads ineluctably to that tragic fate, which is far from being simply the effect of a curse. The contrast between Cuchulain and the Old Man anticipates some of the finest poetry of Yeats's later career, like "A Dialogue of Self and Soul," in which the poet rejects withdrawal, asceticism and remorse for the affirmation of life itself, however bitter and ignominious it has proved to be in the past and will continue to be in the future.

The opening of the Lyric Theatre in Belfast, in

October 1968, was marked by a production of four of the Cuchulain plays—*At the Hawk's Well, On Baile's Strand, The Only Jealousy of Emer,* and *The Death of Cuchulain:*

> It was in the first play of the four—*At the Hawk's Well* that the company were at their best. The disposition of the chorus, consisting of three men which, in itself was an admirable innovation, gave it an authority that was the main factor in ensuring success. By turns it melted into and emerged from the slabs like spirits of the rock intermittently made visible.
>
> Germaine Donnelly, as the Guardian of the Well, had the same quality, helped in her case by a very impressive headdress. Between them they conjured the quality of the doom of Cuchulain; it scarcely needed the actual appearance of the young hero in the arrogant strut of Geremy Jones or the babblings of Frank McQuoid as the Old Man to underline the point. . . .
>
> This [production] was a little model of how the verse of Yeats should be taken—robustly and simply without any prolongation of vowels or accentuation of rhythm.[20]

14. *The Only Jealousy of Emer* (1919)

Yeats's stage directions draw our attention to this play's resemblance to the first of the dance plays: the Musicians are costumed and made up as in *At the Hawk's Well,* they play the same musical instruments, the stage "as before" can be against the wall of any room, a song accompanies the unfolding and folding of a black cloth by the Musicians. The play is about the heroic love of Cuchulain's wife, Emer.

The First Musician sings of woman's beauty that is "like a white / Frail bird . . . thrown / Between dark

Bricriu stands over Cuchulain with Emer in the background in *The Only Jealousy of Emer*. A University of Michigan production, 1978. Directed by Irene Connors.

IRENE CONNORS

Fand, the Woman of the Sidhe, with Bricriu, the Figure of Cuchulain, in *The Only Jealousy of Emer*. A La Mama Experimental Theatre Club production, New York, 1970.

LA MAMA

Fand and the Ghost of Cuchulain embrace behind the anguished Emer in *The Only Jealousy of Emer*. A La Mama Experimental Theatre Club production, New York, 1970.

furrows upon the ploughed land," or a pale shell deposited on the shore by the stormy sea, and wonders what labor or violence went into the creation of this loveliness. Then he evokes the setting for the play, a fisherman's cottage, in which "a fisher's net hangs from a beam, / A long oar lies against the wall."

The cloth is folded, revealing on one side of the stage Cuchulain's apparently lifeless body lying on a bed, wearing burial-clothes and an heroic mask. Cuchulain's wife Emer sits by the bed and reasons that Cuchulain cannot really be dead, for his death would have been accompanied by supernatural portents, "like the world's end." Unknown to Emer, this Figure of Cuchulain is possessed by Bricriu of the Sidhe, the supernatural instigator of discord among men and gods. Near the front of the stage, unseen by Emer, crouches the Ghost of Cuchulain, identical in appearance to the figure on the bed. Cuchulain's mistress, Eithne Inguba, enters hesitantly. Emer encourages her to sit beside the bed, telling her not to be ashamed. She herself sent for Eithne, for they too, Emer says, loved "that amorous, violent man" best in the whole world. Emer explains to Eithne how Cuchulain arrived at his present state after killing his own son and fighting the sea (the events portrayed in *On Baile's Strand*): "the waves washed his senseless image up / And laid it at this door."

It may have happened, concludes Emer, that supernatural forces have possessed him and put this image in his place; accordingly she stirs up the fire to try to dispel enchantment, and persuades Eithne to kiss Cuchulain in order to awaken him. Eithne kisses him, but recoils from something she feels to be evil and inhuman, noticing with horror the figure's withered arm. Emer challenges the figure, who reveals that he is Bricriu of the Sidhe. Eithne flees in terror at the sight of his distorted face and withered arm. Bricriu proceeds to tell the fearless Emer that Cuchulain will be restored to life only if she will renounce any claim to his love; she must not be under any illusion about what this means:

> "He'll never sit beside you at the hearth
> Or make old bones, but die of wounds and toil
> On some far shore or mountain, a strange woman
> Beside his mattress."

Bricriu touches Emer's eyes, and now she sees the Ghost of Cuchulain. She sees, too, Fand, the Woman of the Sidhe, whose mask and clothes "suggest gold or bronze or brass or silver, so that she seems more an idol than a human being." Fand dances around the Ghost, seductively draping her hair over his head. The Ghost awakens during the dance, and recognizes Fand as the hawk-woman he had encountered at the hawk's well. She claims to be "all woman now" and promises Cuchulain, if he will but kiss her, an eternity of love, beauty, and relief from the "intricacies of blind remorse" that characterized his earthly existence. But just as he is about to kiss Fand, the Ghost of Cuchulain remembers Emer and turns away. Fand scornfully reminds him of his unfaithfulness to Emer, and exits; he follows her.

The Figure of Cuchulain (Bricriu) tells Emer she has only seconds to prevent Fand's enticing Cuchulain away to the other world, and finally she cries out in anguish, "I renounce Cuchulain's love forever." The Figure of Cuchulain now lies back on the bed, partly drawing the curtain. Eithne reenters, sees him stir and naively believes that she was responsible for bringing Cuchulain back to life. Cuchulain is now himself, neither the image possessed by Bricriu nor the Ghost tempted by Fand. He addresses words of love to Eithne, and confides to her his fearful sense of having been "in some strange place."

The Musicians unfold the cloth, wondering at the bitter fate of an unnamed woman who is "a statue of solitude." The woman is Fand, whose superhuman nature desperately craved the love of the human Cuchulain to complete its existence: "When your mouth and my mouth meet / All my round shall be complete." But it is also Emer, whose heroic self-denial has turned her into something more (and less) than human. There is, indeed, a kinship and similarity between Emer and Fand; Emer's only jealousy is of Fand, the sole woman capable of taking Cuchulain from her, and Fand's "seduction" of Cuchulain is halted at a crucial stage by his memory of Emer. The irony is that neither gets Cuchulain, and an ordinary passing fancy like Eithne thinks she has saved Cuchulain's life. Either Emer or Fand, then, is perfectly described as "a statue of solitude" with a beating heart. When the cloth is folded again, the Musicians' song is finished and the stage is bare.

The Only Jealousy of Emer was first produced in a Dutch translation in Amsterdam in 1922, by a Dutch actor called Albert Van Dalsum; the sculptor Hildo Krop designed the masks for this performance. Yeats rewrote the play in prose, which he tried to make "very simple," and allowed considerable freedom of interpretation to dancers, singers, and musicians.[21] This prose version was entitled *Fighting the Waves,* and was staged very successfully in August, 1929, in the small experimental theater, the Peacock, which had been attached to the Abbey two years previously. An American composer, George Antheil, wrote what Yeats described as "exciting dramatic music." [22] Ninette de Valois, an original member of Diaghilev's ballet and founder of the Abbey School of Ballet, danced the part of Fand and was responsible for the choreography, and Krop's superb masks were used again (Krop was in the audience). Yeats seemed strangely content to have thus turned his play into what he described as "a mere occasion for sculptor and dancer." [23] To have allowed a play modelled on the Noh drama such an elaborate production runs counter to Yeats's rationale in adopting this model in the first place. Yeats's complaisance may have derived from the fact that he supervised the direction of the original version of *The Only Jealousy of Emer* in a not very successful production at the Abbey, on May 9, 1926.

Like the other plays collected under the title *Four Plays for Dancers, The Only Jealousy of Emer* shows the strong influence of the Japanese Noh plays Yeats admired so much; its action involves an encounter between human and supernatural characters, and utilizes dance, verse, and song. The only prop employed, besides the black cloth folded and unfolded by the Musicians, is the curtained bed on which the Figure of Cuchulain rests.

Yeats's source for the play is a story in Lady Gregory's *Cuchulain of Muirthemne,* but there are many analogues which employ this romantic motif of a love so pure that it transcends its object. The play's primary concern is to dramatize Emer's tragically heroic renunciation of self, as she saves Cuchulain by giving up her future with him. A quarrel between Bricriu and Fand precipitates the human conflict of the play; as in Greek myth, the gods interfere with human destinies. The human interest of the play lies in the action involving renunciation of the person one loves most, precisely because one loves that person so passionately. In her renunciation of Cuchulain, Emer achieves her husband's bitter ideal of heroism.

Emer's struggle is presented in sharp, symbolic form

on stage; as she sits with the Figure of Cuchulain, Fand entices the Ghost of Cuchulain. As Peter Ure points out, more than Cuchulain's choice in *At the Hawk's Well* or that of any of the earlier tragic protagonists in Yeats's drama, Emer's choice of her destiny is a moral one, for she understands what the consequences of her action must be.[24] The tragically ironic consequences of Emer's act are forcefully presented on stage when Cuchulain awakens and calls for Eithne. We are conscious, too, that Cuchulain's return to his remorseful if heroic existence is an ambiguous good. Emer is ennobled by her action, but in an ambivalent way, as the metaphor of sculpture suggests: she partakes of the nobility and heroic quality of a piece of sculpture, but at the cost of lessening her humanity by what Yeats calls, in "Easter 1916," "too great a sacrifice." The sculptured masks employed in the first performance and in *Fighting the Waves* must have externalized this sense of stoniness very finely.

Emer's superhuman rival, Fand, is a seductive figure who represents an ideal, unworldly state of existence outside the cycle of birth, death, and rebirth. (It is important in this context to remember that Yeats believed in reincarnation.) In Yeats's esoteric system, Fand belongs to the fifteenth phase of the moon, a condition of absolute beauty and of spiritual enlightenment that exists outside of the normal, sublunary conditions of life, death, and successive incarnations. The state of existence Fand represents may be thought of as a more astringent and philosophical version of the other world of the early plays, the Tir na nOg of Celtic myth and folklore. Fand offers Cuchulain the immortality she had cheated him of in *At the Hawk's Well;* but now it is clear that the cost of achieving that immortality is the loss of human life and the obliteration of earthly existence and memories. Cuchulain is rather weary of life, complicated as it is for him by remorse and bitterness. But his love for Emer, even though he has been unfaithful to her so often, makes him hesitate long enough for Emer to make her decision. That decision brings Cuchulain back into the time-bound cycle of earthly existence. The conclusion of the play's action thus interestingly reverses the final movements of the early folk and morality plays in which the protagonist leaves his world behind, and anticipates the outcome of such famous debate poems as "A Dialogue of Self and Soul," "Vacillation," and arguably, "Sailing to Byzantium."

The verse of *The Only Jealousy of Emer* ranges from an admirably flexible blank verse which is spoken by Emer, Eithne and Bricriu, to the varied lyric meters of the Musicians' speeches and songs, to the octosyllabic couplets of the supernatural exchange between Fand and the Ghost of Cuchulain. The recurrent imagery of the sea suggests the bitterness of death; it was the sea, after all, which "mastered" Cuchulain at the end of *On Baile's Strand,* and leaves him hovering between life and death at the beginning of *The Only Jealousy of Emer.* The associated imagery of seashell and seabird suggests mortal beauty's tenuousness and susceptibility to change.

The dance of Fand is well integrated into the dramatic action of the play; since it represents an alluring temptation for Cuchulain to be done with this world, it is a functional and not at all a decorative sequence. Yeats's revisions of this play lessen Fand's prominence, and install Emer at the center of the play's significance. Perhaps as a consequence *The Only Jealousy of Emer* seems more human and less remote in its concerns than *At the Hawk's Well,* and inherently more effective because of the poignancy of the dramatic action.

The emotional intensity that characterizes the play may derive from the circumstances of Yeats's marriage in 1917 to Georgie Hyde-Lees:

> In the year preceding his marriage Yeats had once again proposed to and been turned down by Maud Gonne. Then he fell in love with and was rejected by Maud's beautiful seventeen-year-old daughter, Iseult. In a state of severe emotional depression he turned to Georgie Hyde-Lees and was accepted by her. It is little wonder that shortly after his marriage Yeats wondered if he had not "betrayed three people." It is not difficult to find these three people—Georgie, Maud, and Iseult—portrayed, respectively, as Emer, Eithne, and Fand.[25]

In 1970 the Experimental Theater Club of La Mama in New York mounted an extremely successful production of *The Only Jealousy of Emer*. Clive Barnes, writing in the *New York Times*, described the play as having "great qualities of pure theatrical imagination" that were excitingly realized in the "total theater" treatment by La Mama. He praised "the operatically styled score by Barbara Benary and a ritualistic performance of great authority by a cast that included William Finley as the lost Cuchulain, Murrell Gehman as the faithful, tortured Emer, and a sensuous dancer, Susan Topping, as the vision of the Woman of the Sidhe."[26]

In a later review of the same production, Walter Kerr remarked that Yeats was concerned, in such plays as *The Only Jealousy of Emer*, "to do consciously what Aeschylus had done instinctively, to make a gesture big enough to summon up myth." Kerr had high praise for the "imperious, serene staging," especially at two of the play's high spots:

From Cuchulain's bier at least two figures rise, uncoiling themselves as from a nest of snakes. And while the power of renewal, at whatever cost, is asserting itself, the carved figures of waiting women wheel in great clockwork circles, evading one another, embracing one another, as though they were moved by the rotating of the earth.

There is an astonishing moment in which Margaret Benczek, as the mistress whose kiss may have set blood coursing through Cuchulain again, flies to a doorway in fright. But she doesn't approach the door directly. Instead she dramatizes, with Oriental precision and restraint, the frozen half-steps, the feeling of being unable to make headway against pressing space, that sometimes over-takes those who are running in panic. By the time she ends with her fingers splayed against the doorway, huddled and hidden, she has given us a sense of flight that is all the greater for having taken so long and for having conjured up such invisible resistance.

The Only Jealousy of Emer, Kerr concluded, permitted us "to look at drama as it is, or was, not long after stepping from the womb." [27]

15. *The Dreaming of the Bones* (1919)

The time is 1916, immediately after the Easter Rising. The stage can be "any bare place in a room" against a wall, on which is hung a screen or curtain suggesting mountain and sky. The three Musicians enter and unfold a cloth, as in the other plays for dancers, singing of the way dreams emanate from "the dry bones of the dead" and fill the valley to overflowing, like wine that fills a jade or agate cup. The First Musician reveals that it is the dark hour before dawn in a lonely mountain place in County Clare, on the western coast of Ireland.

A Young Man stumbles wearily in the darkness, praying in Irish. Then a Stranger and a Young Girl enter, dressed "in the costume of a past time," and wearing heroic masks. The Young Man raises his lantern to see who they are, but the Young Girl blows it out; in response to the Stranger's question, the Young Man explains that he has fled from Dublin, where he fought in the Post Office, the headquarters of the rebels in the Easter Rising. He is to be met at daybreak by a coracle from the Aran Islands. The Stranger says that he knows all the hiding places of the hills, though they used to be even better for hiding in. The Young Man understands his reference—in the sixteenth and seventeenth centuries, the woods had been destroyed by the English in order to deprive Irish rebels of cover:

> "You'd say they had better before English
> robbers
> Cut down the trees or set them upon fire
> For fear their owners might find shelter there."

The Young Man is alarmed by a noise; he fears it may be the Irish police whom he and his comrades hate more than English soldiers because they are fellow Irishmen who betray the nationalist cause. The Stranger promises to lead him to a hiding place where only ghosts, and no living man, could discover him. The Young Man has had an explanation of ghosts from his grandmother—they do penance by living their lives through again; the Stranger adds that the spirits "dream" their lives again. Then he and the Young Girl lead the Young Man past a ruined abbey to the stone ridge of the mountains. This action is symbolically expressed as the characters go around the stage three times, pausing after each circle while the

Musicians describe their progress. The Musicians sing of the lonely, "bitter sweetness" of the night, and urge the cock to crow and announce the morning. As the travelers pause near the summit, the Stranger recalls days when the bells would be rousing the monks in the abbey at this hour. The Young Man again reflects on the ancient wrongs suffered by Ireland, this time on the English destruction of Irish monasteries:

> "Is there no house
> Famous for sanctity or architectural beauty
> In Clare or Kerry, or in all wide Connacht,
> The enemy has not unroofed?"

The Stranger reveals that one Donough O'Brien is buried in the abbey, an Irishman who rebelled against an Irish king; the Young Man condemns him as one of those "who made Ireland weak," and asks if those ghosts the Stranger has referred to who "work out a penance / Upon the mountain-top where I am to hide" come from the same abbey graveyard. (Up to this point in the play the conversation has been between the Young Man and the Stranger; from here on the dialogue involves only the Young Man and the Young Girl.) The Young Girl answers no, that the two ghosts in question have a more lonely fate than those, like O'Brien, who "mix in a brief dream-battle above their bones."

For a space of seven hundred years, she says, no other ghost or man has spoken to these lonely ghosts. The ghosts are those of young lovers whose "lips can never meet," for the recollection of their crime keeps them apart. When the Young Girl explains the crime,

> "Her king and lover
> Was overthrown in battle by her husband,
> And for her sake and for his own, being blind

And bitter and bitterly in love, he brought
A foreign army from across the sea"

the Young Man realizes that she is describing Diarmuid and Dervorgilla, "who brought the Norman
in," and thus began the seven hundred years of English rule in Ireland. The Young Girl says that the two
ghosts would not be "wholly miserable and accursed /
If somebody of their own race at last would say, / I
have forgiven them." The Young Man adamantly
refuses: "O, never, never / Shall Diarmuid and Dervorgilla be forgiven."

The dawn begins to break, and the characters go
around the stage once more, to reach the mountain's
summit, where the Young Man can see "the Aran Islands, Connemara Hill, / And Galway in the breaking
light." The Young Man reflects on what the towns
of Ireland would have been like "if that crime were
uncommitted." These towns would not have been pil-
laged by the English and would still have had the
mark of a distinctive Irish culture, but,

"The enemy has toppled roof and gable,
And torn the panelling from ancient rooms;
What generations of old men had known
Like their own hands, and children wondered at,
Has boiled a trooper's porridge. That town had
    lain,
But for the pair you would have me pardon,
Amid its gables and its battlements
Like any old admired Italian town."

At these unforgiving sentiments, the Stranger and
Young Girl dance, gazing passionately into one another's eyes, and drift from rock to rock into the dis-
tance. The Young Man realizes they are Diarmuid
and Dervorgilla, and is deeply moved, especially when

he sees the two cover their eyes "as though their hearts / Had suddenly been broken." He is tempted to forgive them: "I had almost yielded and forgiven it all— / Terrible the temptation and the place!" The Musicians fold and unfold the cloth, and sing of the night bird's song and the alluring "music of a lost kingdom" they have heard in the night; now, however, the night is gone and the cocks crow to greet the morning.

Yeats found the idea on which the play's action is based, that the dead relive moments of intense and passionate experience, in a number of sources, as he explains:

> Spiritism, whether of folk-lore or of the séance-room, the visions of Swedenborg, and the speculation of the Platonists and Japanese plays, will have it that we may see at certain roads and in certain houses old murders acted over again, and in certain fields dead huntsmen riding with horse and hound, or ancient armies fighting above bones or ashes. . . . all passionate moments recur again and again, for passion desires its own recurrence more than any event. . . .[28]

The action of *The Dreaming of the Bones* possesses marked similarities to that of the Japanese Noh play *Nishikigi* which Pound and Fenollosa had translated. As Yeats pointed out in his introduction to *Certain Noble Plays of Japan,* there was also a common emphasis in the Irish and Japanese traditions on supernatural encounters and the numinousness of places associated with such encounters. The mixture of Irish historical and political subject matter with the romantic action of *Nishikigi* gave Yeats's play "as strong an appeal for an Irish audience as *Cathleen Ni Houlihan.*" [29]

The Dreaming of the Bones was first performed at

the Abbey on December 6, 1931. Yeats recorded in a letter that it was "enthusiastically received," and there is also reported to have been an excellent production of the play in the drawing room of Yeats's house in Dublin.[30] Unfortunately, *The Dreaming of the Bones* has rarely been staged since, though the Lyric Players Theatre of Belfast mounted successful productions in 1961 at the Dublin Theatre Festival and the Yeats International Summer School at Sligo.

There is no incongruity whatever in this play's being, of all Yeats's plays, the one closest to the artistic model of the Noh, and at the same time a play whose subject matter is distinctly Irish. *The Dreaming of the Bones* possesses a lucid and satisfying dramatic and aesthetic structure. And the play's dramatizing of the opposing claims of romantic love and patriotism gives it, potentially, at least, a wide appeal.

The Young Man is portrayed sympathetically, though with a slight edge of criticism. His disguise as an Aran fisherman emphasizes his identity as a native Irishman, in touch with a primitive sense of race. He speaks of ancient historical wrongs suffered by Ireland as though they had just happened. This obdurate determination not to forget is mitigated by his strong sense of the beauty that would have distinguished the Irish countryside and towns if they had not been ravaged by the English. Though the Young Man sees the world in political and historical terms and has something of the character of the puritanical revolutionary, yet he is moved by the lovers' appeal almost to the point of forgiveness.

The pivot of the action, the lovers' seeking forgiveness from *this* young man, is of course the irony around which the play is structured. The lovers' crime has caused untold hardship and misery for generation upon generation of the Irish people. They must ask forgiveness, then, from a man who realizes the extent of their crime. But that same man is one who, precisely because he is aware of the grievousness of the lovers' sin, cannot forgive Diarmuid and Dervorgilla. The latest in a long line of rebels, his heroic purpose is to change the course of Irish history by taking arms against the English. He must not be weakened by sympathy for the human motivations of those who would frustrate that aim. In a sense, Ireland is the disembodied protagonist of *The Dreaming of the Bones* (in *Cathleen Ni Houlihan,* she was actually embodied in the figure of the old woman who is turned into a beautiful young girl by the approach of the 1798 rebellion), and Ireland's history, in which the past chronically obtrudes upon the present, is the play's theme.

The lovers' purgatorial existence is portrayed with bittersweet poignancy. They committed the original sin of Irish history, because their passion blinded them to the consideration of anyone or anything except each other. They saw the world only in terms of personal fulfillment, with little or no sense of the enormous social, political, and historical consequences of their deed. Now they suffer the appropriate punishment—that of lovers who cannot be united despite their tremendous yearning for each other. The passionate side of their nature is sympathetically presented, and their desperate need for forgiveness is also touchingly portrayed. Like all the other lovers of romance whose love is so strong that it survives into the supernatural world, Diarmuid and Dervorgilla compel our admiration. But as with Dante's guilty lovers, Paola and Francesca, our pity is compounded by our sense of the justice of their fate: "the dance in which Diarmuid and Dervorgilla act their love and torment takes place before the backdrop of the Irish land, Irish history, a framework which places and diminishes the lovers' torment, reveals it as only a part of the whole picture." [31]

The division of the lovers' roles gives the play its simple, dramatically satisfying division into two parts. The Stranger's task in the first half of the play, in which he alone speaks to the Young Man, is ostensibly to guide him to a hiding place, in reality to a holy place in the landscape where past and present, natural and supernatural, can meet. Once there, the Young Girl begins to speak to the Young Man, and she alone speaks to him for the duration of the play. Her role is to sway the Young Man, to persuade him to forgive; it seems likely that if anyone could win forgiveness for a crime of passion, it might be a young girl who could win it from a young man.

The play's setting is the landscape familiar from many of Yeats's poems—"cold Clare rock and Galway rock and thorn," as he describes it in "In Memory of Major Robert Gregory." This mountainous area along the western coast of Ireland, a primitive landscape remote from the cities in which an alien, English culture has taken root, affords a quintessentially Irish setting in which the peasant is an organic part of the natural world. Yeats evokes the beauty and mysterious animism of this landscape much more effectively in the verse of the play than any "scenery" could. The music of Irish names, such as Corcomroe, Aughanish, Bailevelehan, and Aughtmana, and the evocation of

> "the shallow well and the flat stone
> Fouled by the drinking cattle, the narrow lane
> Where mourners for five centuries have carried
> Noble or peasant to his burial"

help to create the sense of a place untouched by the English from whom the Young Man is fleeing, and of an idealized rural community made up of peasant and noble from which the unheroic life of the urban middle classes has been excluded.

The imagery of the play, found in particularly concentrated form in the Musicians' songs, involves a contrast between night and day. The mysterious, enchanted darkness is associated with the ghostly lovers; the plaintive cry of the nocturnal curlew and the mysterious "wandering airy music" of the night air suggest their homeless fate. The imagery of day and light is associated with the Young Man's purposiveness, the music of cockcrow with his assertive commitment to action. Yet both image clusters are emotionally complicated. The nocturnal dreaming of the lovers' bones, that is, the reliving of their lives, darkens the sun and withers the wheat; in other words, the sterility of the past obtrudes upon the present both in national and personal terms, and remorse for the past blights life in the present. Similarly, the images of daylight and the cock of March have connotations of rawness, insensitivity, and unloveliness—their music and vitality represent a vigor that is somewhat crude.

This complication of the associations of the play's imagery is an index to the ambivalence of our response to the lovers and the Young Man. Our pity for the lovers is qualified by our sense of the terrible strife they introduced into Ireland, just as our admiration for the Young Man's purposefulness is qualified by the hardness of heart he must cultivate to be politically effectual. The dawn may well signal the birth of the "terrible beauty" Yeats portrays in the poem "Easter 1916." The beauty brought into being by the heroic self-sacrifice of the revolutionaries of Easter week cannot be separated from the hardness of heart they required to realize their goals.

The Musicians in *The Dreaming of the Bones* fill the same role of exposition and commentary on the

The Dreaming of the Bones. An Abbey Theatre production.
THE ABBEY THEATRE
The dance of the Roman Soldiers in *Calvary*. A Trinity College, Dublin, production at the Dublin Theatre Festival of 1965. Directed by James W. Flannery.
JAMES W. FLANNERY

action as those in the other three *Plays for Dancers;* most notably, through their songs, they draw the audience's attention to the ambivalence of emotional response the characters and events in this play demand.

16. *Calvary* (1920)

Calvary is one of two plays (the other is *The Resurrection*) in which Yeats assimilates the Christian myth to his own system of thought. The stage directions for *Calvary* describe the setting only as "a bare place," with no mention even of the screen used in earlier plays as a symbolic indication of place. The audience is seated around three sides of the stage. As in the other *Plays for Dancers,* three Musicians unfold and fold a cloth while singing. The line "God has not died for the white heron" is repeated three times. The First Musician sets the scene on the road to Calvary on Good Friday, "the day whereon Christ dreams His passion through," apparently in the same sort of recurrence as that portrayed in *The Dreaming of the Bones.* (Yeats's theory, that "all passionate moments recur again and again, for passion desires its own occurrence more than any event," helps to explain the action of both plays.) [32] The Musicians seat themselves at the back of the stage with their instruments—drum, flute, and zither. Christ enters and leans upon his cross, surrounded by a hostile crowd who call on him to work a miracle and save himself.

Lazarus comes on stage and Christ appeals to him: "Seeing that you died, / Lay in the tomb four days and were raised up, / You will not mock at me." But Lazarus rejoins bitterly that he had wanted to die in order to escape Christ's love, and thought he had accomplished this until Christ restored him to life:

"I saw you stand
In the opening of the tomb; 'Come out!' you
called;
You dragged me to the light as boys drag out
A rabbit when they have dug its hole away."

The crowd shrinks from Lazarus's "death-stricken and death-hungry" face, and he leaves determined to seek his death in the desert. Now Martha and the three Marys and those other disciples who "live but in His love," gather around Christ, kissing his hand and washing his bloody feet with their hair.

But the street suddenly empties, "as though all fled in terror," when Judas appears. He explains to Christ why he betrayed him: he had sought (and won) the freedom to be beyond Christ's redemption and to defeat God's power. The Three Roman Soldiers enter and order Judas to hold up the cross on which Christ is to be crucified. According to the stage directions, "Christ stands with His arms stretched out upon it." The Soldiers tell Christ they will keep the crowd away and let him die in peace. Christ asks them who they are that they ask their God for nothing. One of them responds that they are the gamblers who will throw dice for his garment when he is dead. Another tells him, "Whatever happens is the best, we say, / So that it's unexpected." Then they dance "the dance of the dice-throwers" around the cross, in which they quarrel for a while, then settle the quarrel by throwing dice. Christ calls out "My father, why hast Thou forsaken me?" The Musicians sing while folding and unfolding the cloth; the line "God has not appeared to the birds" is repeated three times.

While the remarkably intense effect of *Calvary* does not depend on an understanding of Yeats's ideas about history and human personality (Yeats always labored to transform his ideas into autonomous theatrical ex-

periences), more than most of Yeats's plays it demands an acquaintance with those ideas. The director of a notable production of the play records, on the
basis of discussion after the play, that the audience
found "the symbolism of *Calvary* . . . difficult to grasp
on a first hearing."[33]

In the esoteric philosophical system that he began to
develop after his marriage in 1917, though he did not
publish *A Vision*, which sets forth this system, until
1925, Yeats posited the belief that history occurred in
cycles of two thousand years. Yeats thought of each
historical cycle as being either subjective or objective
in attributes; similarly, he theorized that human personality types could also be categorized as subjective
or objective. (These terms may be compared to Jung's
classifications of introvert and extrovert.) Moreover,
each historical age and personality generally characterized as subjective or objective is assigned varying
degrees of subjectivity and objectivity according to the
twenty-eight phases of the moon.

Yeats characterizes Christianity as an objective (or
primary) era because it is oriented to belief in redemption through the external acts of Christ's birth and
crucifixion; Yeats categorizes as subjective (or antithetical) those eras that are to be defined spiritually
in terms of the immanence, as opposed to the transcendence, of self, including the one that is to begin in
Yeats's lifetime with the end of the Christian dispensation. Yeats's notes to *Calvary*, in *Four Plays for
Dancers*, explain that Lazarus and Judas, because of
their subjectivity, have moved beyond the reach of
Christ's redemptive love, as have the Roman soldiers
because of their extreme objectivity.

The action of the play is similar to that of *The
Dreaming of the Bones*, though in reliving his passion
at Calvary, Christ is of course not looking for forgiveness, as Diarmuid and Dervorgilla are; rather he is

fated to confront those beyond the power of his love. It is toward the revelation of this bitter knowledge whereby Christ realizes the limit to his love, rather than its triumphant ability to redeem all mankind, that the play moves. The dance of the Roman Soldiers around the cross, in which Christ and Judas are included, conclusively and dramatically embodies the proposition that Christ and all he represents are only part of the vast, cyclical movement of history that includes ways of being in the world that cannot be encompassed by the Christian scheme of things.

Yeats considered the birds referred to in the play—heron, eagle, and swan—as the "natural symbols of subjectivity," and so the refrains—"God has not died for the white heron" and "God has not appeared to the birds"—emphasize how much the inner-directed soul which they symbolize is beyond the care of Christ. Judas's betrayal and Lazarus's seeking after death are the human equivalents of the birds' subjectivity. Their completely gratuitous acts are assertions of self that put them beyond the reach of a Christian God. Both Christ and the Roman soldiers are objective personalities because they have relinquished self to authority, Christ to His Father, and the soldiers to the Roman Empire they serve. What makes the soldiers' objectivity different from Christ's, however, and what puts them beyond the power of his redemption, is that they believe in chance, in the throw of the dice. In contrast, Christ has *chosen* to act the role of redeemer.

Calvary is the only one of Yeats's plays not to have been performed at the Abbey. A striking presentation of the play directed by James Flannery, at the Dublin Theatre Festival of 1965, won high praise from the critics. The London *Times* called it "an outstanding production," and the German *Theater Heute* was sufficiently impressed to venture that Yeats "would be considered one of the world's major dramatists if he were given productions which employed the full theatricality his plays seem to call for." [34]

17. *The Cat and the Moon* (1926)

The Cat and the Moon is one of the most popular and frequently staged of Yeats's Noh plays. As with the *Four Plays for Dancers,* the setting is suggested symbolically. A patterned screen or curtain is meant to suggest Saint Colman's holy well. Three Musicians sit against the wall on which the screen is hung. After the First Musician's song about Minnaloushe (the cat) and the moon, two beggars enter wearing grotesque masks, the Lame Beggar on the Blind Beggar's back. They have long been wandering the roads on their way to the holy well of Saint Colman, but their mutual dependence all this time does not prevent the blind man from suspecting that his lame partner takes advantage of him.

Throughout the play the First Musician speaks the lines of the saint, who never materializes on stage. The saint offers the beggars the choice of physical wholeness or blessedness. The blind man wants to see, but the lame man is content to remain lame if he will be blessed. The saint grants their wishes. The blind man sees the holy well and everything else around him, but, unlike the lame man, he cannot see the saint. Then he notices that the lame man is wearing the skin of a sheep that was stolen from him, and he beats his companion. "The beating takes the form of a dance," the stage directions tell us. Then the Blind Beggar leaves.

The saint climbs on the back of the Lame Beggar, to whose great relief he proves no heavier than a grasshopper. Then the saint tells the rather incredulous

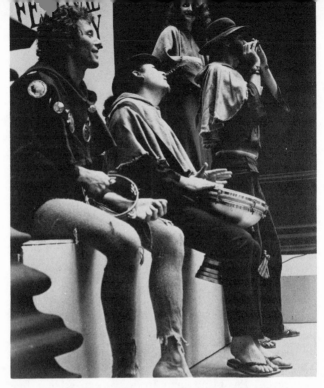

Above, The Musicians, *below,* the Lame Beggar and the Blind Beggar in *The Cat and the Moon.* A Theatre of the Open Eye production at McGill University, Montreal, 1973. Directed by Jean Erdman.

beggar to dance. The Lame Beggar begins clumsily, leaning on his stick, but then throws the stick away and dances faster and faster. He exits dancing. The play is concluded by the First Musician's song describing the change in the phases of the moon that has taken place, a change reflected in the eyes of Minnaloushe the cat.

Yeats tells us in a note to this play that he originally intended to include it in *Four Plays for Dancers*. The inclusion of *The Cat and the Moon* in this volume of plays modelled on the Noh would have provided a most appropriate context for the play, for as Yeats goes on to explain: "I intended my play to be what the Japanese call a *Kiogen,* and to come as a relaxation of attention between, let us say *The Hawk's Well* and *The Dreaming of the Bones,* and as the Musicians would be already in their places, I have not written any verses to be sung at the unfolding and the folding of a cloth." [35] The *Kiogen* was a brief farcical interlude traditionally interposed between the serious plays of a Noh sequence. "The principal characters are usually the *daimyo* or nobleman and the comic servant who hoodwinks him, the *daimyo* generally triumphing and beating the servant violently." [36] Yeats retains this element of the *Kiogen* in the beating of the Lame Beggar by the Blind Beggar.

Like most of the other Noh plays, however, *The Cat and the Moon* is Irish in its inspiration. The holy well of Saint Colman, at which the two beggars have almost arrived as the play opens, was near to Yeats's home in Galway. The mention of "Kiltartan river" emphasizes the locality in which the play is set, as does the dialect Yeats uses for the light-hearted dialogue. When the Lame Beggar asks his companion—"Do you think now will the saint put an ear on him at all, and we without an Ave or a Pater-noster to put before the prayer or after the prayer?"—it is hard not to hear the influence of Lady Gregory. And though Yeats recalls "some story, which I have half forgotten, of a lame man and a blind man's arrival at it [Saint Colman's well], though not of their quarrel there," it is hard, too, not to see the influence of Synge's *The Well of the Saints* on the plot of Yeats's play.[37]

In the restoration of the Blind Beggar's sight (recalling Christ's miracles in the New Testament), Yeats shows up, as did Synge in his play, the limitations of the orthodox Christian conception of blessedness. The divorce of body from soul in the Christian tradition is revealed and criticized in the unhappiness the gift of sight causes in both plays. Bodily wholeness, effected by Christian miracle, does not solve what Yeats conceives of as one of man's greatest afflictions, the disjunction between body and soul. Yeats's blind man can only see that he has been robbed. That he cannot see the saint indicates that he remains blind to spiritual reality.

Yeats's play is, however, much lighter in tone and more optimistic than Synge's. In Synge's play, what Martin Doul first sees when his blindness is cured are the bleeding feet of the ascetic, barefoot Saint. The implication is that, for the Christian, spiritual joy can only be achieved by the denial of the body. But Yeats is concerned in *The Cat and the Moon* only to touch on the limitations of Christian dualism. Though he often registers, in such poems as "A Dialogue of Self and Soul," that aspect of Christian belief whereby the soul is exalted only at the expense of the body, Yeats does not fashion *The Cat and the Moon* out of the negative tension between body and soul.

Yeats's play emphasizes a conception of blessedness that unites body and soul, a positive dialectic between opposites. Thus there is nothing censorious or repressive about Yeats's saint, as there always is in Synge's

representatives of Christianity. The Lame Beggar does
worry briefly if the Saint will require devout prayers
(perhaps even in Latin) from two sinners before he
will consider their wishes. But the Blind Beggar asserts a dialectical principle that is axiomatic in Yeats:
saints are much more interested in sinners than in people as pious and holy as themselves. The Blind Beggar
cites as evidence for his point of view "the holy man
in the big house at Laban" who goes "knocking about
the roads with an old lecher from the county of
Mayo"; Yeats's sly reference here to his friends Edward Martyn and George Moore is not simply gratuitous—he saw their friendship as being based on a si-
multaneous attraction and repulsion.

The lame man on the blind man's back does suggest soul and body, as Yeats acknowledged in his notes
to the play; their relationship emphasizes, however, the
separation of body and soul. The Lame Beggar's elevated position, his identity as the guide in this oblig-
atory relationship with the Blind Beggar that has
worked for forty years or so, his "flighty" nature which
disregards the mundane, comically yet effectively symbolizes the duality of soul and body. The Lame Beggar's acceptance of the burden of the saint, on the
other hand, is a symbol of Yeatsian "unity of being."
That the Lame Beggar is made not merely to walk,
but to dance in spiritual ecstasy, is a characteristically
Yeatsian image of a joyful union of body and soul.
The spectacle of the Lame Beggar dancing with the
invisible saint on his back recalls that other, brilliant
and moving image in "Sailing to Byzantium" of the
soul singing all the louder "for every tatter in its mortal dress" (that is, its scarecrow-like body).

Though the setting and characters of this play are
identifiably Christian, perhaps the image of sanctity
with which the play ends suggests more the ecstasy of

eastern religion. Maybe this is why Yeats thought that the play was possessed of "an odour, a breath, that suggests to me Indian or Japanese poems or legends." [38]

A good number of esoteric interpretations of this little play have been put forward by critics since Yeats first suggested, rather hesitantly, in his notes to the play in 1924 that

> Minnaloushe and the Moon were perhaps . . . an exposition of man's relation to . . . the Antithetical Tincture [a subjective, emotional and aesthetic condition of existence], and when the Saint mounts upon the back of the Lame Beggar he personifies a certain great spiritual event which may take place when Primary Tincture [objective, reasonable and moral] . . . supersedes Antithetical. . . .[39]

But this sense of the large historical cycles which determine the condition of man's existence is only present in the play, and then in a rather general way, in the opening and closing songs. The first of these describes the dance of Minnaloushe the cat, "close kindred" of the moon, whose eyes reflect its changing shape. The song that ends the play describes how "the sacred moon overhead / Has taken a new phase," indicating that the change in the lives of the two beggars has been accomplished. The function of these songs in the play is doubtless to give the audience a generalized sense of large historical forces, by means of poetic images. However aesthetically pleasing these images are, though, it is very doubtful that they can carry the heavy freight of the detailed symbolic significance Yeats and many critics who follow his lead attribute to the play.

An aspect of Yeats's thought that *is* integrated into the play, however, and complements the generalized suggestion of determinative historical forces, is the idea that a significant element of choice allows man to make his own destiny despite those forces. The Lame Beggar, epitomizing the body, with all of its inherent limitations, attains unity of being when he chooses to unite himself with his opposite, the saint, who symbolizes the soul and its ecstatic possibilities. In the language of Yeats's system, the Lame Beggar achieves unity of being by joining with his anti-self.

This play was published in 1924 (though Yeats dated it 1926 in the *Collected Plays*). It was first performed on May 9, 1926, at the Abbey, and has been produced many times since. It was produced very successfully in 1976 at the Project Arts Centre in Dublin by James Flannery. The drama critic of the *Irish Independent* wrote: *"The Cat and the Moon* is a great delight, with magnificent masks and costumes by Nicola Kozakie-wicz, and a marvellous musical accompaniment by Thomas O'Brien on the fiddle and Eoin Ruari O Brolchain on the bodhran [small drum]." [40]

Jean Erdman's Open Eye theater group put on a superb production at McGill University in 1973, and then again in New York in 1975 and 1976. The magnificent dancing and music that perfectly embodied the play's theme made these productions extremely satisfying and appealing. One critic wrote, "The remoteness and esoteric quality of [Yeats's] plays which one may sense when reading them were all but forgotten: Yeats's words, spoken and sung, accompanied by lively movements and dancing . . . were rendered with great insight and a touch of inner grace." [41]

18. *The King of the Great Clock Tower* (1935)

It is apparent from this play that by the time of its composition the influence of the Noh on Yeats's

drama had abated somewhat, and that his radical intentions to found an anti-theater had moderated considerably. Yeats's note to the play explains why, in
very practical terms, he dropped or modified the conventions of his earlier plays that imitated the Noh
drama:

> When The Abbey School of Ballet was founded
> I tried these [Noh] plays upon the stage where
> they seemed out of place. Why should musician or
> actor fold and unfold a cloth when the prosce-
> nium curtain was there, why carry on to the stage
> drums, gong, and flute when the orchestra was
> there. *Fighting the Waves* and the present play so
> far imitate the Japanese model that they climax
> in a dance, substitute suggestion for representa-
> tion, but like the Japanese plays themselves they
> are stage plays.[42]

While the stage directions for the play do indicate that
it is intended for performance in a more or less conventional theater, as opposed to a drawing room,
Yeats exaggerates (in his note to the play) the extent
to which he has here modified the Noh characteristics
of his earlier plays. If Yeats has dropped the folding
and unfolding of the symbolic cloth he used in the
earlier dance plays to take the place of a drop curtain,
and his stage directions refer to a drop curtain and
a proscenium, he has retained something comparable
to that cloth in an inner curtain with "a stencilled
pattern of dancers." The musical instruments, drum
and gong, are still present on the stage, and not in the
orchestra. The Queen and the Stroller both wear
masks to indicate their personalities: the Queen's is
beautiful and impassive, the Stroller's "wild" and
"half-savage." Finally, the role of the Attendants,
though the first speaks the part of Captain of the
Guard, is essentially the same as that of the Musicians
in the earlier dance plays.

As the play begins, the parted inner curtain reveals King and Queen on their thrones, which are represented by two cubes. The King recalls how he made this mysterious woman his Queen "a year ago tonight" when she walked into his house. No one knew then, or knows now, her origin; the King, therefore, asks her again, "before the assembled court," her "country, name and family." The Queen remains silent and utterly impassive. The Stroller enters. He is a reckless and extravagant poet who extols the beauty of the mysterious Queen in his songs, and has become so obsessed with the image of her beauty he has created that he longs to see her face to face. Ironically, he does not realize that he is in her presence. When his attention is directed to the Queen, the Stroller notes that she is "neither so red, nor white, nor full in the breast" as he had thought, but says he will, nonetheless, proclaim her beauty everywhere. Not content with this audacity, he declares that the icy Queen will dance and sing for him, and kiss his lips on the stroke of midnight "when the old year dies."

The outraged King orders him to be beheaded. The Stroller insists that even if he is executed, what he has insisted on will come to pass. The First Attendant, as Captain of the Guard, takes him off-stage, and shortly after, the King lays the head of the Stroller on one of the thrones. The Queen dances before it, then faces the audience with the severed head on her shoulder. The head sings of an erotic afterworld where "crossed fingers" can exceed the pleasure of "the nuptial bed of man," and "A nuptial bed exceed all that / Boys at puberty have thought." The Queen dances again and kisses the head on the last stroke of the clock which tolls midnight.

The action of *The King of the Great Clock Tower* blends several narrative traditions that involve a sexually charged encounter between a prophet or poet and a woman, and the consequent decapitation of the prophet or poet. The bible story of John the Baptist and Salome is one obvious source for Yeats's play, though Oscar Wilde's play *Salomé* (1892) is, Yeats acknowledges in notes to his own play, a more immediate source. From the classical tradition, *The King of the Great Clock Tower* recalls the myth of Orpheus, in which the severed head of the poet continues to sing after he has been dismembered by the Thracian women. There is also an ancient Celtic cult of the severed head: Yeats cites as a source an "old Gaelic legend" in which "a certain man swears to sing the praise of a certain woman, his head is cut off and the head sings." [43] Yeats had written a prose version of this legend of Aodh and Dectira as far back as 1895. There may be an autobiographical element here, too, of Maud Gonne's sexual coldness toward Yeats, and of his sense of having sacrificed so much to that "barren passion," as he describes it in the dedicatory poem to the volume *Responsibilities*.

There is, at any rate, a mixture of the mannered and the mythic in this play. The note of sexual sadism and perversity that one finds in Wilde's *Salomé* and in the drawings of Aubrey Beardsley is particularly strong in the Queen's erotic dance with the severed head. This dance takes place, it should be noted, not before the decapitation, as in Wilde's play, but afterwards. It seems to be intended (to go by the climax of the revised version, *A Full Moon in March*) not only as an expression of sexual yearning and satisfaction, but also of a Yeatsian unity of being that is achieved in the blending of opposites. The dance is, for Yeats, a perfect image of unity of being, and it takes place here, as it does in *The Cat and the Moon*, against the background of a significant turning point in time.

Though one may see in the play a parable of the

The King of the Great Clock Tower. A University of Ottawa Drama Guild production, 1972. Directed by James W. Flannery. Costumes and mask design by Jacques Lemothe.
JAMES W. FLANNERY

Poet's relation to a destructive Muse, Yeats's reflection that the play is "spiritually incoherent" accurately registers the fact that the Queen and the Stroller are not sufficiently symbolical of an opposition of principles. Their union in the dance is, therefore, not a thoroughly convincing representation of unity of being. Yeats very effectively remedies this shortcoming in *A Full Moon in March*.

The King of the Great Clock Tower was produced in a prose version at the Abbey on July 30, 1934. Yeats wrote in a letter "It has proved most effective

—it was magnificently acted and danced." [44] Ninette de Valois played the part of the Queen. However, the play has not been staged often since then because most producers prefer *A Full Moon in March.*

19. *A Full Moon in March* (1935)

Most critics have properly followed Yeats's lead in treating this play as a more intense, compressed, and artistically coherent version of *The King of the Great Clock Tower.* Both the elimination of the King from the later play (both works are, confusingly, given the same date in *Collected Plays*), and the change of title may be seen as indicative of the dramatic compression and unity Yeats achieves in *A Full Moon in March,* and of this play's more satisfactorily symbolic nature. Among other elements, the realistic motive of the King's outrage is discarded. Yeats must have realized that the King's jealousy lent the earlier play a plausible element of cause and effect that was at odds with its symbolic nature, and his mere presence would call into question the Queen's icy chastity. The title of the play not only reflects the King's absence, but refers, in Yeats's symbolism, to the fifteenth phase of the moon, a phase of complete beauty in which unity of being is accomplished. This unity is represented, much more successfully than in *The King of the Great Clock Tower,* in the dance which ends the play.

With the exclusion of the King, the plot of *A Full Moon in March* attains a more arbitrary quality, like that in certain rather chilling fairy tales. Thus the Queen offers herself to whoever can sing best of his love for her, but decapitates whoever displeases her. The Queen's fascinated horror at all the Swineherd represents is made much more explicit in this play, and so it is easy to see her character as a symbolic embodiment of aloof spirituality that loathes and also craves its opposite. That opposite is the Swineherd, no longer merely an earthy poet like the Stroller, but a symbolic figure who stands for the gross and purely instinctual, physical world.

The action of this play, much more so than that of *The King of the Great Clock Tower,* is meaningfully symbolical. The interaction of fair and foul is comparable to the dialectic of Yeats's "Crazy Jane" poems, which culminate in such conclusions as "Love has pitched his mansion / In the place of excrement." The language of the Swineherd's song is strongly reminiscent of these poems: he offers to the indignant Queen "A song—the night of love, / An ignorant forest and the dung of swine." The union of physical and spiritual at the end of the play is manifested in the Queen's unambiguously sexual and orgasmic dance with the Swineherd's head. Denis Donoghue describes this dance as "the fitting climax to Yeats's best play. The feeling at this point is so intense that speech is too crude, too circumscribed, to express it. . . . the dance, with its climactic kiss, is the most eloquent event. Speech alone, for once, is insufficient. It is the dance which vibrates as symbolic enactment of the complete, the 'perfect' life." [45]

Though *A Full Moon in March* was not performed in Yeats's lifetime, it has been produced with great success on a number of occasions in the recent past. Writing of a University of Ottawa Dramatic Guild production of the play in 1971, a *Toronto Telegram* reviewer applauded James Flannery's staging as "an outstanding theatrical event," and continued:

> This play is astonishingly modern. In its ritualism, mythical roots and sexual tension, it is far more like some of the most interesting experi-

Above, Queen, Swineherd, and Attendants in *A Full Moon in March. Below,* The Queen dances before the head of the Swineherd. A Theatre of the Open Eye production, New York, 1976. Directed by Jean Erdman.

JEAN ERDMAN; SCOTT JOHNSON

Above, Queen and Swineherd in *A Full Moon in March.* *Below,* Climactic dance in *A Full Moon in March.* A University of Ottawa Drama Guild production, 1970. Directed by James W. Flannery.

JAMES W. FLANNERY

mental drama of today than like the plays of its own period.

This amazingly anachronistic quality may well account for its lack of acceptance when it was originally done in Ireland—and it certainly is responsible for the recognition with which Toronto audiences are greeting it.

The settings and costumes are dramatic and colorful, with oriental overtones which are strangely appropriate to the simplicity of the story and the austerity of physical movement.[46]

Jean Erdman's production in 1976 at the Open Eye theater in New York was also glowingly reviewed:

Deftly presented, the Queen and Swineherd speak straight to our souls of man's most basic drives and needs. Unlike "logical" theatre, Yeats uses the combined force of music and dance as an integral part of the performance. The drama makes our blood race as we are pulled into a world of emotional intensity and sinister beauty. Our involvement is total, not momentary as in a suspenseful scene. The driving music and poetic imagery grabs and demands complete concentration.[47]

20. *The Death of Cuchulain* (1939)

This is Yeats's last play, written in anticipation of his own death. Though he discards some of the features of his earlier plays in the same mode, it is essentially as a Noh play that Yeats conceives of *The Death of Cuchulain*. The stage directions indicate only that the scene is "a bare stage." The producer, an old man "looking like something out of mythology" enters and addresses the audience. In his irascible and extravagant speech, he explains the "principles" which have guided his production: there is to be dance, music, and if not a severed head, then a symbol for one. He hopes the audience numbers no more than fifty or one hundred; if there are more, the old man warns, they must not "shuffle their feet or talk." They must realize that this is the last in Yeats's series of plays about Cuchulain, and they should be familiar with those earlier plays and with the mythology" on which they are based. He snobbishly hopes that the audience is made up of such well-informed people, and not of opinionated individuals bent on self-improvement "who are educating themselves out of Book Societies and the like." The play and its dance must be understood to be symbolic, and utterly unlike modern, realistic art. The stage darkens and the curtain falls.

After the curtain has risen again, Eithne, Cuchulain's mistress, enters and calls out the hero's name. When Cuchulain enters, Eithne tells him she has a message from his wife Emer: Queen Maeve and her Connacht army have invaded Ulster, and "No matter what's the odds, no matter though / Your death may come of it, ride out and fight." Cuchulain replies that he has anticipated the message, for he is armed and eager to do battle. Then he notices a letter in Eithne's hand which she seems unaware of. The letter is from Emer, but it urges him *not* to fight until the following morning when his ally, Conall, will join him with a great army.

The Morrigu, the crow-headed Celtic goddess of war, appears to Eithne and touches her. Eithne now understands that she has been bewitched to lead Cuchulain to his death, but Cuchulain scoffs at her explanation. She only wants to be rid of him, he says, because she desires another, younger lover. Nonetheless, he is determined to fight. Eithne passionately

Left, Eithne Inguba and Cuchulain in *The Death of Cuchulain.* A University of Vermont production, 1973. Directed by Sidney Poger and Ghita Orth.

SIDNEY POGER

Below, The Blind Man kills Cuchulain in *The Death of Cuchulain.* A production of the Yeats Ensemble of the University of Michigan at The New Theatre Festival, Baltimore, 1976. Directed by Irene Connors.

IRENE CONNORS

Opposite, The Morrigu, Goddess of War, in *The Death of Cuchulain.* A University of Winnipeg production, 1969. Directed by Reg Skene.

REG SKENE; DAVID HEWLETT

Opposite below, The Street-Singer at the end of *The Death of Cuchulain.* An Abbey West Theatre Group production, Santa Fe, 1974. Directed by Dan Gotch.

DAN GOTCH

resents his blithe dismissal of what he takes to be her infidelity, and swears she will join Cuchulain in death to prove that she is no traitor to him. Cuchulain orders his servants to protect Eithne's life.

The stage darkens, there is music of pipe and drum, then the lights come up, revealing an empty stage. Cuchulain enters, wounded, and attempts to tie himself upright to a stone. Then Aoife, the mistress of his youth and mother of the son whom Cuchulain unwittingly killed, comes on stage. She tells Cuchulain that she has come to kill him. As she helps to tie him erect, Cuchulain acknowledges to Aoife that she has the right to kill him. She exits, however, at the approach of the Blind Man. The Blind Man discloses that Queen Maeve has promised him a reward of twelve pennies for the head of Cuchulain. He ominously lays his bag on the ground (we can guess its function), and feels Cuchulain's body until he reaches his neck. Cuchulain sees the first incarnation his soul is to take after he dies. It is "a soft feathery shape," apparently a bird, which he asserts is about to sing. The stage darkens and the curtain falls. When the curtain rises again, the Morrigu is on stage holding a black parallelogram meant to represent Cuchulain's head. The stage directions tell us that "there are six other parallelograms near the backcloth," representing the men who gave Cuchulain his mortal wounds.

Emer enters and dances. Her dance expresses anger and rage at the six who wounded Cuchulain and "adoration and triumph" before the head of Cuchulain. She stops when she hears "a few faint bird notes." The stage darkens, and there is music "of some Irish fair of our day." Then the stage brightens to reveal three ragged musicians. Two of them play pipe and drum while the third sings a song of the harlot and the beggar man.

Yeats was still working on this play two days before

his death, and while he would have, according to his constant practice, continued to revise and improve it had he lived longer, there is no compelling reason not to think of the play as complete. Yeats's source for *The Death of Cuchulain* is Lady Gregory's *Cuchulain of Muirthemne,* though he would seem to have invented the circumstance of Cuchulain's death at the hands of the Blind Man. Also, the Cuchulain of the original saga dies while still a young man. Yeats's conception of him in this play as an aging man reflects the way in which Yeats remade the traditional hero in his own image.

While *The Death of Cuchulain* is no doubt a Yeatsian adaption of the Noh drama, Yeats has seen fit, in this play, to modify considerably, or discard, what had become the stage conventions of his earlier plays in the same mode. There is no indication that the characters wear masks, and the severed heads (represented by masks in *A Full Moon in March* and *The King of the Great Clock Tower*) are represented abstractly by the black parallelograms. Instead of the ritualistic folding and unfolding of a cloth at the beginning and end of the play, there are stage directions for the lights to darken four times and the curtain to fall twice within the course of the play, suggesting that Yeats had in mind, probably, a small experimental theater like the Peacock, rather than a drawing room. The brief dance of Emer does not fulfill the organic and climactic role of the dances in the earlier plays based on the Noh. The musicians scarcely fill the role of chorus as they do in the dance plays, though their song and music ends the play. Their music is heard mainly in the breaks in the action, when the stage lights darken. In insisting on the Irishness of these musicians—the Old Man has picked them up on the streets, and their instruments are probably the traditional Irish varieties of pipe and drum—Yeats seems to want to stress the significance of his play for an Irish audience.

Cuchulain meets his fate in circumstances dominated by female figures emblematic of love, hate, and death. Emer and Eithne adore Cuchulain with a selfless passion. Eithne is a more resolute and courageous figure in this play than she was in *The Only Jealousy of Emer;* indeed, she is given the most passionate lines in the play when she reacts to Cuchulain's assertion that she no longer loves him:

> "When you are gone
> I shall denounce myself to all your cooks,
> Scullions, armourers, bed-makers and messengers,
> Until they hammer me with a ladle, cut me with
> a knife,
> Impale me upon a spit, put me to death
> By what foul way best please their fancy,
> So that my shade can stand among the shades
> And greet your shade and prove it is no traitor."

Maeve and Aoife have been Cuchulain's mistresses, but now they hate him and seek his death. The balefulness of the hawk-headed goddess, the Morrigu, who "arranges" Cuchulain's death, is reflected in Maeve's monstrous transformation: she has an eye in the middle of her forehead. Despite her determination to kill Cuchulain, Aoife, on the other hand, retains some of the tenderness of her love for him. Finally, it is the Harlot of the song that closes the play who pays ambivalent testimony to the resurgence of Cuchulain's heroic spirit in modern Ireland.

Cuchulain's male enemies do not even appear in the play; though they know he is mortally wounded, they dare not pursue him. And though the Blind Man, rather than Aoife, administers the *coup de grâce* to Cuchulain, he does so because of Maeve's promise. The Blind Man symbolizes the malevolent, mean-spirited cowardice and avarice of the modern world. He understands nothing of what is good or noble in man, only the economic "good sense" of bringing Cuchulain's head to Maeve for the pathetic bounty of twelve pence. The betrayal is all the more base for being rewarded not by gold or silver, but by copper pennies.

More than any of Yeats's other plays on the theme of heroism, *The Death of Cuchulain* is marked by an astringent sense of irony. The most exalted heroism, it seems, must confront and accept to the bitter end the prevalence of dishonor and humiliation. This theme can be seen in many of Yeats's last poems, and involves an heroic assertion of the value and meaning of life despite its ignominies, particularly those of old age. The Old Man who gives the play's prologue, his rage inspired by a general sense of the depravity of modern times, is no doubt a somewhat extravagant self-portrait of Yeats.

What Yeats does in this play is to present to himself and the modern world an image of heroism that is all the more heroic and noble for being beset on all sides by hatred, cowardice, and cupidity. Cuchulain's stoic acceptance of his fate, his composure and aloofness, his aristocratic magnanimity toward those who would undo him, are the heroic attributes Yeats holds up to a degenerate modern world for its edification. Heroism must be created in scorn of the ignoble reality of life, the play asserts.

Some of the bitterness of *The Death of Cuchulain* stems from Yeats's disillusionment, shared by many Irishmen, with post-revolutionary Ireland. In Yeats's eyes, the heroes of 1916 were the sole reincarnations of the heroic spirit of ancient Ireland symbolized by Cuchulain. They were the grand exceptions to the prevailing atmosphere of "shivering prudence" which characterized modern Ireland. The insurgents of Easter Week also invoked Cuchulain, of course, and the

Irish government commemorated them by erecting in the Post Office a statue of Cuchulain in his tragic triumph, tied upright to a stump, sword in hand. The Morrigu, in the shape of a crow, sits on his shoulder.

There are, in fact, a number of interesting and significant parallels between this symbolic play and the historical circumstances of the Easter Rising. Cuchulain epitomizes the magnanimity of its leaders, and the spiritual exaltation of Padraic Pearse in particular. The opening of the play recalls the confusion and misunderstanding among the leaders of the rebellion about whether or not to stage the revolt, and the determination of those who decided to fight against overwhelming odds.[48]

The resolution of Yeatsian tragedy, and of this play in particular, poses a problem analogous to that raised by tragic plays which demand a Christian interpretation. If one is made to feel that a hero's death is followed by an eternity of bliss, then the play which culminates in his death will not arouse feelings of pity and terror (at least, not to the same extent as a play whose universe is amoral). Yeats's world is not Christian, of course, but our sense of doom, disaster, and defeat is alleviated somewhat because Cuchulain's death, the play makes clear, is succeeded by his transformation into an image of spiritual perfection. And his spirit survives, even if fleetingly, in modern Ireland. Yeats's tragedy, consequently, results not in the Aristotelian effect of catharsis, but in what Yeats calls "tragic ecstasy," a state of being the hero or heroine shares, at the play's climactic moments, with the audience: "in theatrical terms, the supremely intense experience of tragic ecstasy was intended by Yeats to provide the audience with an experiential perception of his own mystical 'faith.' "[49]

The Death of Cuchulain was first performed at the Abbey on December 2, 1949 by the Lyric Theatre

Company, founded by the Irish poet and verse dramatist, Austin Clarke. It was performed twice in 1960 by Mary O'Malley's Lyric Players, first at the Dublin Theatre Festival and then at the Yeats International Summer School in Sligo, as part of a sequence which included *At the Hawk's Well, On Baile's Strand, The Only Jealousy of Emer, Purgatory,* and *The King's Threshold.* The five Cuchulain plays were also successfully staged by the Dublin University Players in 1965, and by Reg Skene, director of theater at the University of Winnipeg, in 1969. The last two productions treated the five brief Cuchulain plays almost as five acts of one longer play. Skene argues convincingly that Yeats structured the Cuchulain plays in terms not only of his private system, but also of solar mythology. Thus the plays are "seasonal rituals marking certain crisis points in the solar year. . . . *The Death of Cuchulain* [marks] the summer solstice." [50] Skene's account of the ritualistic significance of the series of plays further reinforces the positive sense that Cuchulain's spirit will renew itself, despite the awful bitterness of his death:

> As the Blind Man's hands reach Cuchulain's neck and he moves to cut off Cuchulain's head, the stage is plunged into darkness. When the lights come on, Cuchulain's head is represented by a black parallelogram. The ritual pattern here seems derived from events associated with solar eclipse—surely one of the most frightening and mysterious events in the life of the sun as seen by primitive man.[51]

VII. TRAGI-COMEDIES

Yeats said that he had intended *The Player Queen* to be a tragedy, but could not finish it until he decided to turn it into a "farce." [1] There are elements of traditional farce, most notably those of broad, physical comedy, in *The Green Helmet* and *The Herne's Egg* as well as in *The Player Queen*. But it seems more useful to use the term tragi-comedy to describe the distinctive mixture of tragic and comic which Yeats achieved in these plays. It seems particularly appropriate to employ this term since these three plays, characteristically Yeatsian as they are, are reminiscent thematically (and occasionally stylistically) of Elizabethan and Jacobean tragi-comedy, in which the tragic possibilities of doom and death are ultimately defeated, and life and creativity affirmed.

In *The Player Queen* disaster is narrowly averted in a plot which involves love, intrigue, and disguised characters who belong to high and low estates. The play's "savage undertones of tragedy" are resolved happily, though not unambiguously, since several major characters are excluded from the happiness of the play's conclusion.[2] Moreover, destruction on a cataclysmic as well as a human scale is prevented in the play: Yeats parodies his own ideas about history, and the apocalyptic violence one expects to attend the change from one historical dispensation to another simply does not take place.

In *The Green Helmet,* the threatened disaster of Cuchulain's death at the hands of the Red Man is averted when the god recognizes the greatness of Cuchulain's heroism in his willingness to sacrifice himself for the common good. Cuchulain is heroic because he is in touch with life's elemental energies and the natural cycles of death and rebirth, which are epitomized in the Red Man. In a less obvious way, Shakespeare's tragi-comedies achieve the universality of life-affirming myth by evoking the archetypal pattern of death and rebirth associated with the changing seasons.

The Herne's Egg is the most modern in tone of Yeats's tragi-comedies, and arguably anticipates the theater of the absurd. It is at once savagely ironic and grotesquely comic. The disaster which threatens the protagonist of this play is not prevented (he dies at the hands of a fool, that is, himself), but is mitigated by virtue of the sardonic perspective through which Yeats insists we view the play's characters and events. The fact that Congal is reincarnated as a donkey allows for little in the way of tragic exaltation at the play's close, though he does momentarily attain the proportions of a tragic hero as he anticipates his death on the mountain top. The bitterly ironic treatment not only of heroism, but also of the supernatural, is unparalleled in Yeats's work, and helps give to this play, above all his others, a strong sense of the absurdity of the human condition.

21. *The Green Helmet* (1910)

The farcical rambunctiousness of *The Green Helmet* seems particularly uncharacteristic of Yeats, given his treatment of the Cuchulain material in his other plays. The time is the heroic age of Ireland, the place is the interior of a house; through its windows can be seen the moon-lit sea, through its door, rocks of the shoreline and the sea beyond. The stage directions go into considerable detail to describe the setting at the Abbey Theatre's original production of the play:

> . . . the house is orange-red and the chairs and tables and flagons black, with a slight purple tinge which is not clearly distinguishable from the black. The rocks are black with a few green touches. The sea is green and luminous, and all the characters except the Red Man and the Black Men are dressed in various shades of green, one or two with touches of purple which look nearly black. The Black Men all wear dark purple and have eared caps, and at the end their eyes should look green from the reflected light of the sea. The Red Man is altogether in red. He is very tall, and his height increased by horns on the Green Helmet. The effect is intentionally violent and startling.

The play opens with Conall and Laegaire, champions of Ulster, apprehensively watching for the approach of someone from the sea. They hear a distant shout, but reckon with some relief that it came from the land. A young stranger, presumably the man who gave the shout, nears the door, but the two determine not to let him in, for they want no one to know the shameful reason for their fear. However, the young man effortlessly forces his way in. Conall and Laegaire recognize him as Cuchulain, and reluctantly tell him their story.

Two years ago to the hour, the Red Man, a huge man with a foxy appearance and "a great laughing mouth," came into their gathering and joined in the singing and dancing and drinking. This Red Man wanted to play a game he called "whip off my head." Laughing all the time, he explained to Conall and Laegaire that one of them would cut off his head, and then he would cut off one of theirs. Cuchulain objects: "How could he whip off a head when his own had been whipped away?" Conall says that of course they asked him the same question, but his response was only to laugh all the more, until Conall in exasperation whipped off his head. The man picked up his head (still laughing) and "splashed himself into the sea."

Cuchulain says it is a good story, but they must have imagined it while drunk. No, they say, for exactly twelve months later, the Red Man "ran up out of the sea with his head on his shoulders again" to claim his debt of a head from Conall or Laegaire. The warriors are afraid they will be shamed in everyone's eyes because they will not take part in this bizarre game. After all, Conall whipped off the Red Man's head; now he or Laegaire should let the Red Man whip off one of theirs. There is "a splash and a rumble" from the shore, and the Red Man appears, leaning on a large two-handed sword, laughing "like the sea." Cuchulain addresses this boisterous giant fearlessly. But the Red Man claims that the game of whipping off heads was only "a drinking joke and a gibe and a juggler's feat," and that he has come to bring a gift, his green helmet. It is to be worn by the bravest of the three champions of Ulster, he says as he leaves.

Conall and Laegaire immediately start arguing about who is to wear the helmet, but Cuchulain takes it, fills it with ale, and says they will all drink from it. There is a great noise of shouting and horns outside, and the warriors' chariot-drivers, stable-boys and scullions come running in. They are disputing the relative rights of their masters to wear the green helmet, for the Red Man has let them know about the troublesome gift he had left. Cuchulain proclaims the helmet a "cup of peace," but Laegaire objects that Cuchulain and Conall have drunk from it before him.

Then the wives of the three heroes come to the door and argue about who will enter first. Cuchulain solves the problem by ordering the wall to be broken down so that the three wives can enter at the same time, and he then throws the green helmet into the sea to avoid any more argument. But Conall and Laegaire consider themselves robbed by Cuchulain. Emer, Cuchulain's wife, flourishing a dagger, provokes their wives with a song praising her husband. The wives of Conall and Laegaire order their servants to drown Emer's song by blowing their horns, clapping, and shouting. This results in "a deafening noise and a confused fight." Three black hands are seen to come through the windows and put out the torches.

The moonlight gradually reveals the Red Man standing in the room, with black, cat-headed men who "crouch and stand about the door." One of them carries the helmet, another the Red Man's sword. The Red Man demands that the rules of the game be observed. Someone must kneel down and have his head cut off "or all shall go to wrack." Cuchulain volunteers, to Emer's great sorrow and despair. When she offers to kill herself instead, he upbraids her and commands her to "Bear children and sweep the house." The Red Man now reveals himself the guardian of Ireland who tests its heroes, and benevolently places the green helmet on the head of the kneeling Cuchulain, marking him as a true hero, whose heroism is joyful and selfless.

The Green Helmet is a verse play based on an earlier prose drama *The Golden Helmet,* but very much superior to it, by all accounts: "In characterization, structure, and satiric intensity, *The Green Helmet* is an immense improvement over its banal predecessor in prose." [3] The sources of Yeats's play are two stories

Cuchulain offers his head to the Red Man in *The Green Helmet*. A University of Winnipeg production, 1969. Directed by Reg Skene.

REG SKENE; DAVID HEWLETT

from Lady Gregory's *Cuchulain of Muirthemne*, "The Feast of Bricriu" and "The Championship of Ulster." "The Feast of Bricriu" has numerous analogues in English, French, and German literature of the Middle Ages in which a beheading game figures prominently. The most famous of these is the English poem "Sir Gawain and the Green Knight"; the Green Knight is obviously a vegetation god whose life is bound up with the natural cycle of death and rebirth. Yeats's play not only uses the beheading game and vegetation symbolism, but employs a comparably humorous, even rollicking, tone. Yeats described *The Green Helmet* as an "heroic farce," an unusual term that gives some indication of the play's unique combination of broad physical comedy, pungent satiric elements, and playful yet startling mythic content; there is, in addition, a serious attempt to define the qualities of character Yeats felt were so desperately lacking in modern Ireland.

Yeats links the two stories from *Cuchulain of Muirthemne*, making the Red Man not only Bricriu, the instigator of discord, but also CuRoi, the tester of the champions of Ulster. Thus the play shows how reconciliation and self-sacrifice for the common good are the key to a true heroism like Cuchulain's, and how braggartly self-esteem and vainglorious competitiveness, leading to divisiveness and strife, are the marks of false heroism like that of Conall and Laegaire. Cuchulain's self-sacrifice is offered, not in agonized pursuit of martyrdom, but thoughtlessly, in a spontaneous gesture that comes from an innate nobility and generosity of character, and that laughs at spite and betrayal. The Red Man acknowledges this in acclaiming Cuchulain's heroism:

"I choose the laughing lip
That shall not turn from laughing, whatever rise
    or fall;
The heart that grows no bitterer although
    betrayed by all;
The hand that loves to scatter; the life like a
    gambler's throw."

These are the virtues that are particularly lacking in modern Ireland, Yeats insinuates: mere physical courage, which might have brought distinction to an ancient hero, is not enough to deal with the chronic divisiveness that makes the quality of life in Ireland so bitterly unpleasant. As Conall complains,

"Here neighbour wars on neighbour,
  and why there is no man knows,
And if a man is lucky all wish his luck away,
And take his good name from him between
  a day and a day."

Conall and Laegaire, perpetually on the alert for any undervaluing of their worth, are like the strutting roosters of the barnyard, whereas Cuchulain is compared to "the great barnacle-goose" in his noble transcendence of mean, calculating worldliness. There is grave need in modern Ireland for Cuchulain's qualities. The mean-spiritedness of latter-day embodiments of Conall and Laegaire will lead to the ruin of the country; such men will sacrifice all to their personal self-esteem. The darkness and confusion which descends on all, and which can only be dispersed by Cuchulain's gesture, is a metaphor for the ruinous state of affairs caused by those in Irish public life who possess a psychology similar to that of Conall and Laegaire.

The farcical disputations that climax in the great noise and fighting between the advocates of the three champions are a general satiric indictment of self-destructive, partisan tendencies in Yeats's homeland. But the blowing of horns by the champions' servants to drown each other out specifically mocks those men in the audiences of *The Playboy of the Western World* who made it impossible for anyone to hear Synge's play. Yeats wrote *The Green Helmet* in the months following the first production of *The Playboy of the Western World,* and he chose to have it produced, at its first performance, as a curtain raiser for Synge's play.

It is not far-fetched to see in the Cuchulain of *The Green Helmet* an idealized version of Yeats, who showed great moral courage in his support for Synge and *The Playboy of the Western World* during the disturbances that attended the first week of its performance in Ireland. Like Cuchulain, Yeats also came home from Scotland (where he was lecturing) to confront a crisis in Irish public life. His defense of the play in which he attempted to pacify an inflamed public by appealing to reason and light, no doubt provided the experience for Yeats's conception of Cuchulain's character and function in *The Green Helmet*.

One Yeatsian critic has suggested that Cuchulain is a sun god; yet in the case of *The Green Helmet*, it might be more accurate to say that Cuchulain is a hero who is intimately *associated* with the solar source of energy and life, embodied in the Red Man.[4] The Red Man's color and boundless energy, the fact that he controls the light of the moon, apparently rises out of the sea, and returns to Conall and Laegaire in precisely twelve-month spans of time, strongly suggest the Red Man's solar nature. His exemplary powers of recuperation and his joyful demonstration of them in his ability to rejoin his severed head to his body suggest the way in which the death of life in the winter, when the sun goes away, is followed by regeneration in the spring, when it returns. His gift of the *green* helmet reminds us also of the dependence of the natural world on the sun to foster life. This mythic element would seem to be employed in the play in order to link Cuchulain's heroism with the exuberance and self-assuredness of natural and cosmic forces. Cuchulain's heroism in *The Green Helmet* is not shown to be in conflict with society, as it is in *On Baile's Strand*, but rather in harmony with a higher order—the creative energy of the life force. Conall and Laegaire, in contrast, futilely try to defeat that order by refusing to play the Red Man's game and by fighting with his followers.

The ballad meter of this play's verse differs sharply from the iambic blank verse of the plays that precede it, and gives *The Green Helmet* a more native Irish feel than the earlier plays, which have a faintly Elizabethan flavor. Yeats himself realized this: "When I wrote in blank verse I was dissatisfied; my vaguely medieval *Countess Cathleen* fitted the measure, but our Heroic Age went better, or so I fancied, in the ballad metre of *The Green Helmet*." [5] The ballad meter is, indeed, the perfect vehicle for embodying the energy and vitality of this play.

The Green Helmet was staged as a curtain raiser for a revival of *The Playboy of the Western World* at the Abbey on April 10, 1910. It has not often been performed since then. A director who staged the five Cuchulain plays in 1965 found that *The Green Helmet* was "well-nigh unstageable in any acceptable dramatic idiom," and tended to clash with the mood and content of the other Cuchulain plays. [6]

22. *The Player Queen* (1922)

The Player Queen is set in some unspecified country, at some uncertain time in the past; its characters, uniquely in Yeats's plays, have no nationality. The first scene of this unusually lengthy play takes place in "an open space at the meeting of three streets." Two Old Men who wear "grotesque masks" remark on the crowd of men which passed by an hour ago, and mention the Queen's castle, which sits outside town on a great hill. The audience is thus indirectly alerted to the mob's revolutionary intentions.

Septimus, "a handsome man of thirty-five," staggers drunkenly on to the stage, knocking on doors, looking for somewhere to sleep and complaining about the town's lack of charity to a dramatist and poet of his eminence. He complains, too, about his bad wife, who "has hid herself, has run away, or has drowned herself." Then he exchanges insults with two "bad, popular poets" who leave him by the roadside, where he lies down to sleep. Septimus is self-pityingly conscious of his own resemblance to the victim in the story of the Good Samaritan: "Robbed, so to speak; naked, so to speak—bleeding, so to speak—and they pass by, on the other side of the street."

The crowd of citizens and countrymen which had earlier made the Old Men so uneasy, fills up the stage, looking forward to "a bloody day's business." They have never seen the Queen, and are predisposed to believe the worst about her. So they eagerly seize on the Tapster's story that the Queen is a witch who couples with "a great white unicorn." Unable to sleep because of the noisy crowd, Septimus drunkenly defends the chastity, not of the Queen, but of the unicorn, and insults a big countryman, who knocks him down. The crowd goes purposefully up one of the streets towards the castle, but returns "in confusion and fear," having met the Old Beggar. This "horrible old man," the citizens recall, marks the changeover from the rule of one monarch to that of another. He will lie down in straw and bray like a donkey at the exact moment when the crown changes hands. The First Countryman explains that the donkey that possesses the Old Beggar at such times "is the donkey that carried Christ into Jerusalem, and that is why it knows its rightful sovereign." Septimus and the Old Beggar leave the stage together.

The second scene takes place in the throne room of the Queen's castle. The Prime Minister is trying to arrange for a play about Noah and the Flood to be put on by some travelling players, but Decima, the leading lady and wife of Septimus, cannot be found. The pretty and vain Decima is, in fact, lying hidden under the throne, determined not to play the role of an old woman (Noah's wife). The Queen comes in, dressed in "a badly fitting state dress." She is young, "with an ascetic timid face," and says rather dubiously that she is prepared for martyrdom at the hands of the crowd, though the Prime Minister has only urged her, in a politic but tardy anticipation of the sort of trouble we have seen brewing in the first scene, to show herself to her angry subjects.

Nona, another of the players, entices Decima out of hiding with a lobster and a bottle of wine, and tries to get her to dress for the part of Noah's wife. But Decima responds, "the only part in the world I can play is a great queen's part." Then the two actresses argue about Septimus, and Nona reveals that he is her lover. She decides, moreover, that she will play Decima's part in the play. Decima contemptuously pretends happiness at this outcome, "I threw away a part and I threw away a man—she has picked both up." As she dances with the players, who are dressed as animals for the Ark, Septimus comes in announcing "the end of the Christian Era, the coming of a New Dispensation, that of the New Adam, that of the Unicorn." The prosaic and unimpressive harbinger of this great change is reflected in the fact that the mob we encountered in the first scene is now preparing to attack the castle.

All the players flee except Septimus, Decima, and Nona. Nona gathers a bundle of properties and ties them on Septimus's back. But Decima has locked the gate against their departure, and says she will unlock it only if Septimus promises to drive Nona from the company. Nona eventually manages to snatch the key and leave with Septimus. Decima feels herself betrayed by Septimus and is about to stab herself with Nona's scissors when the Queen comes in and stops

Septimus and Nona in *The Player Queen*. A Peacock Theatre production, Dublin, 1971. Directed by Edward Golden. Set by Bronwen Casson.

THE ABBEY THEATRE; DERMOT BARRY

her. But Decima is determined to die and thinks if she could only wear the Queen's gold brocade and gold slippers she would die happily. The Queen has seen the angry mob and no longer wants to be a martyr, so she hands over her clothes and leaves for a convent: "I have long wanted to go there to lose my name and disappear."

A Bishop enters, addressing Decima as Queen and telling her that the people are henceforth to be loyal and obedient because the Prime Minister has told them he and the Queen are to be married. The crowd has, apparently, accepted this as evidence of her normality. The Prime Minister is taken aback when he enters and sees that Decima has taken the place of the Queen, but he can only go along with the pretense, for her regal manner and good looks please the crowd. Septimus now reappears, and insists that the Queen is his bad wife. The Prime Minister orders him banished. The bray of a donkey is heard and the Old Beggar is hauled on stage. He is denounced as an impostor who has attempted to foment conspiracy, for all except the Prime Minister and Septimus believe that Decima is the true Queen, and that the crown has not changed hands. The new Queen covers her face with the mask of Noah's sister, so as not to be recognized by the players, who return to perform a dance. She gives them money but forbids them ever to come back into her kingdom.

Yeats had great difficulty completing *The Player Queen* as a verse tragedy that seriously employed his esoteric system; he was able to finish it rapidly, however, once he had decided it should be a prose farce. Though he started work on it in 1908, Yeats was to revise the play constantly for the next ten years or so.

The Player Queen has been described as "the type of play which actors and producers invariably enjoy but which leaves an audience bewildered if amused." [7] The audience is likely to be puzzled if it is unaware of Yeats's ideas about history and his theory of the Mask, both of which are parodied in the play. For many critics, *The Player Queen* is of particular importance in tracing the evolution of Yeats's ideas: "the ten years during which he wrestled with the play are the crucible in which he remade his ideas and prepared the way for . . . *A Vision* and the major poems and plays." [8] Yeats conceived of history as unfolding itself in cycles of two thousand years, each of which reversed the characteristics of the previous age. At the point where one period changes to the next there is a

miraculous incarnation, the fruit of intercourse between a woman and an animal or bird (a god in disguise), and subsequent apocalyptic violence. All of this
is given serious and brilliant expression in Yeats's poetry, but in *The Player Queen,* he treats this myth of
destruction and renewal sardonically, and seems to be
mocking his own ideas.

Yeats's theory of the Mask, basically the notion that
an individual achieves fulfillment by the assumption
of his anti-self, of all that he is not, seems of real significance in *The Player Queen* only for the character
of Decima. Yeats explains his theory of the Mask thus:

> I think all happiness depends on the energy to
> assume the mask of some other life, on a re-birth
> as something not oneself, something created in a
> moment and perpetually renewed; in playing a
> game like that of a child where one loses the in-
> finite pain of self-realisation, in a grotesque or
> solemn painted face put on that one may hide
> from the terror of judgement. . . .
>
> If we cannot imagine ourselves as different
> from what we are, and try to assume that second
> self, we cannot impose a discipline upon ourselves
> though we may accept one from others. Active
> virtue, as distinguished from the passive accep-
> tance of a code, is therefore theatrical, consciously
> dramatic, the wearing of a mask. . . .[9]

Even if one is unfamiliar with Yeats's ideas, however, one can still respond to the extremely lively and
varied theatrical experience the play provides. The
complexity and irony of the relationship between
Septimus and Decima, for example, is masterfully
handled, as is Septimus's drunken pleading of the
cause of true poetry.

One's expectations, if one is familiar with Yeats's

ideas, about the outcome of the action are constantly defeated in *The Player Queen* in an ironic and playful way. The threatened violence (the necessary instrument of historical change, one would think, according to Yeats's usual account), is averted. The hints at the likelihood of Decima becoming the sexual mate of the unicorn, and thereby engendering a new race of men, also come to nothing. Instead, she marries the Prime Minister. Then again, the Old Beggar suggests that, contrary to expectation, the afterlife is no place for heroes and lovers, for he has known only an old jackass to come from there, and "Maybe there is nothing else." Decima should, moreover, according to Yeats's theory of the Mask, have attained happiness in becoming the queenly opposite to her actress-self. But she partly regrets her rejection of Septimus. Her emotional ambivalence is dramatized effectively and movingly by Septimus's wearing the hat of Noah as he leaves, while she wears the mask of Noah's sister, who was left behind and perished in the flood.

The dramatic symbol of the unicorn is not the more or less straightforward indication of the fruitful destruction that precedes a new order, as it is in *The Unicorn from the Stars*. In *The Player Queen* the unicorn's symbolic associations are complicated by the subjective interpretations of the various characters. An excitable boy tells the crowd that he shot and wounded the unicorn on one occasion, and on another saw it copulating with the Queen. The ascetic young Queen conceives of the unicorn as the embodiment of chastity and spirituality. Septimus thinks of the unicorn as the image of a new order. Yet he understands that the time for that new order has not yet come, for the unicorn is reluctant to "trample mankind to death" and too chaste to "beget a new race."

All of the premonitions of earth-shattering change

—the unicorn, the prophetic Old Beggar, the violence of the mob, the references to Noah's flood—are, with deliberate irony, revealed to be misleading.

Change has been accomplished by the end of the play, and one might be tempted to interpret it as radical change. Certainly the death-oriented Christianity of the Queen has been banished in favor of the vital energy of Decima. But Decima is to marry a politician, who will make sure that (unlike the real Queen) her clothes fit her properly, and that she shows herself to the populace, and that she conceives an heir to the throne. The Prime Minister is skilled in political survival and expediency, as his orders to banish Septimus and hang the Old Beggar demonstrate, and he will give the people what they want in order to ensure his self-preservation.

It is interesting that Yeats was not able to complete this play until early in 1917. Perhaps a skeptical but well-founded intuition that mediocrity would persist, in Ireland as elsewhere, despite intimations of radical change afforded by the Easter Rising of 1916, helped define the sardonic mood of anticlimax that so distinguishes *The Player Queen*.

The Player Queen was first performed by the Stage Society on May 25, 1919 at the King's Hall, Covent Garden, London. It was played at the Abbey on December 9, 1919, when Barry Fitzgerald played the First Old Man and his brother, Arthur Shields, played Septimus. This was evidently a successful production, and the play was revived twice at the Abbey in the next two years.

Joseph Holloway thought that the audience was particularly pleased by the setting, for which Yeats used the canvas screens Gordon Craig had invented for his *Hamlet,* produced at the Moscow Art Theater. Craig also designed the costumes and masks for *The Player Queen.* Yeats said that the characters in his play had no nationality just as these screens, "where every line must suggest some mathematical proportion, where all is phantastic, incredible, and luminous, have no nationality." [10] The value of these anti-realistic sets was that, used in conjunction with experimental lighting, they freed the stage from what Yeats considered the constrictive conventions of painted scenery.

Vivian Mercier gives an interesting account of a later production at the Abbey by Austin Clarke's Lyric Theatre Company:

> The style of the entire production was homogeneous, being essentially that appropriate to Elizabethan comedy. The world of the stage was a fairytale or folklore one that yet remained continuous with the everyday world of Bottom or the troop of players in *Hamlet*. Once she appeared in the second act—the first is little more than a prologue reminiscent of the crowd scenes in *Julius Caesar*—Decima, the player queen, dominated the action. Cyril Cusack's wife, Maureen, played her as a sly, earthy, scheming little road-company *femme fatale,* who suddenly put on regal beauty and dignity with the crown and robes. One could not miss the dramatic contrast between the "real" queen, who had nothing queenly about her, not even the courage for martyrdom, and the player queen who, though born in a ditch, was a queen to the tip of her greedy tongue. Art triumphed over nature: the point was not the conflict between appearance and reality but that in order to *be* a real queen one must also *act* the part; the mask, worn long enough, becomes the face itself.[11]

23. *The Herne's Egg* (1938)

The preoccupations of *The Herne's Egg* are typically Yeatsian, but there are also aspects of this

sprawling play that demonstrably anticipate the Theater of the Absurd. The set for the play's first two
scenes is a symbolic representation of mist, rocks, and
a great herne (heron). A stylized, dance-like battle
takes place between the armies of King Congal of
Connacht and King Aedh of Tara. The two Kings
pause to reckon their losses: both are equal in this,
their fiftieth battle. To celebrate the truce at which
they arrive, Aedh gives a banquet at Tara. Congal decides to gather the herne's eggs as a delicacy for the
feast, and calls the priestess Attracta mad when she
warns him that the eggs are sacred to the Great Herne,
and can only be eaten or handled by women priestesses
like herself, who are betrothed to the god. When
Congal's men gather the eggs anyway, Attracta in-
vokes an ancient curse on the King: he will meet his
death at the hands of a fool. Congal rationalizes this
prophecy into the probability that, as a soldier, he will
die on the battlefield at the hands of some fool or
other.

The next three scenes are set at Aedh's castle, at
Tara. In the banqueting hall Congal, drunk, calls his
men to arms. He is insulted because he has been served
"a common hen's egg" at the feast, while everyone else
had a herne's egg. Aedh is also drunk, and resents
this behavior on the part of his guest, whom he calls
a "beastly drunken liar." The two fight with table legs
—they have left their swords outside the city, presumably to avoid having an argument turn into a pitched
battle—and their followers join in, armed with table
legs and candlesticks. As in the opening scene, the
fighting is stylized, and weapons do not touch. So it
comes as a surprise when Congal kills Aedh offstage.
Congal is dismayed at this termination of his ritualistic feud with Aedh, and blames the Great Herne.

Attracta is seen carrying a herne's egg, and Congal
understands that she had substituted a hen's egg for

it on his plate and thereby "brought bloodshed on us all." Congal and his men determine to cure what they perceive as her mad belief that she is betrothed to the Great Herne by raping her:

> "we seven in the name of the law
> Must handle, penetrate, and possess her,
> And do her a great good by that action,
> Melting out the virgin snow . . ."

They argue about who is to go first and settle the argument by casting lots to determine the order in which they will rape her.

The following morning, Attracta refuses to acknowledge that she has been raped by Congal and his men. She says, however, the Great Herne came to her in the night, and made love to her. When Congal's men persist in their assertion, she prophesies that as punishment for their lying they will be reincarnated as "cat or rat or bat, . . . dog or wolf or goose." Congal, she repeats, must die on the holy mountain at the hands of a fool. As Attracta pronounces the doom of Congal and his followers, the Great Herne lends credence to what she says by creating thunder, terrifying the soldiers.

The last scene is set on a mountain top at night. Congal is conversing with the Fool, who is armed with a cauldron lid for shield, a pot for helmet, and a kitchen spit for sword. "Somebody" has told him to kill Congal, and promised him pennies if he does. He wounds Congal with the spit, and then drops it, fascinated by the wound. Congal stands the spit upright among some stones and throws himself on it. Thus he attempts to defeat the prophecy that he will die at the hands of a fool, though he is conscious of the cruel irony that he may only be fulfilling that prophecy. Attracta enters with Corney, her servant, and Congal appeals to her with his dying breath, to help him avoid reincarnation as "a brute beast." For some unaccountable reason Attracta seems willing to help and commands Corney to lie down with her and thereby give a human form to Congal's reincarnation. But the off-stage braying of Corney's donkey signals that it has coupled with another donkey and that Congal must be re-born as a donkey. The play ends with Corney laughing at this conclusion: "All that trouble and nothing to show for it, / Nothing but just another donkey."

The Herne's Egg is the antithesis of the concentration and intensity Yeats sought to achieve in his emulation of the Noh drama. Six scenes long, with a comparatively large cast, it is alternately comic and serious, farcical and savage in tone. Like *The Player Queen,* it seems to have been conceived of in terms of theatrical effect, and is also somewhat lacking in unity. *"The Herne's Egg* is crowded and stagy . . . not a play for the drawing room, but more on the scale of the old Abbey plays and *The Player Queen,* with its different locations, its fourteen speaking parts, and an abundance of properties and stage-effects." [12]

In the play, much is made of the fact that Attracta is betrothed to the Great Herne and becomes his bride. For the reader or playgoer familiar with Yeats's thought and with such poems as "Leda and the Swan," *The Herne's Egg* would seem, then, to be about another miraculous impregnation of a mortal woman by a god in the shape of a bird. Such impregnations, of Leda by Zeus in the form of a swan, or of Mary by the Holy Spirit in the form of a dove, signal for Yeats the end of one historical era and the beginning of another that is to be dominated by the progeny of these miraculous conceptions. But the issue of Attracta's impregnation is not raised, and so her relationship with the god is deprived of precisely what

Corney and Attracta in *The Herne's Egg*. A University of Vermont production, 1973. Directed by Sidney Poger and Ghita Orth.

SIDNEY POGER

makes such relationships, in Yeats's mythology, interesting and significant. Our expectations about the outcome of this relationship between woman and god are utterly defeated: Yeats raises the issue only to drop it. This was true also in *The Player Queen,* where his hints that Decima will be impregnated by the Unicorn, and thereby beget a new race of men, remain merely hints. One can scarcely even claim, in this respect, that Yeats is parodying an aspect of his own thought, for this idea about miraculous conceptions would have to be more substantially embodied in the plays before it could effectively be parodied.

Despite this lack of cohesiveness in the play, however, its main concern is still apparent: it is to present, in the form of a savage farce, the encounter of the hero with the supernatural which Yeats treated more sympathetically and tragically in *At the Hawk's Well*. The character of Congal is central to an understanding of the play's theme, and is the best indication of its ironic ambiguity. He is king, warrior, and hero who takes on the supernatural in the form of the Great Herne, but he is also a fool, and a rather villainous fool, at that. Congal's struggle with the supernatural is unwittingly occasioned by his rash decision to take the herne's eggs to the feast at Tara, then consciously pursued in his rape of Attracta (after he has killed Aedh and seeks revenge on the god). In all of his behavior until he goes to meet his death in the last scene of the play, there is little an audience can sympathize with: Congal commits sacrilege and rape with a total lack of moral sensibility. The utterly futile and self-defeating consequences of both acts, though, help make Congal more of a fool than a villain. Moreover, his pompous expatiations on the terse suggestions of his second-in-command, Mike, are foolish and comic.

What redeems Congal in a minimal way is his sheer physical courage and his growing determination to defeat the god. But the first quality is self-evidently limited, and the second undercut because, even if Congal thinks he has triumphed over the god by his suicide, he is the only one to think so. The dignity of Congal's desperate suicide is diminished by the highly undignified consequence of his fated reincarnation as a donkey.

Congal, then is not Cuchulain, but he has his moments. His encounter with death on the mountain does foreshadow the heroic death of Cuchulain in Yeats's last play, and carries distant echoes of Macbeth at bay. Congal's anticipation of his death, and his encounter with the Fool, are the finest things in *The Herne's Egg*. In his weary sense of futility and certain defeat by the god he conjures up a despairing, macabre dance of death:

"Here I must sit through the full moon,
And he will send up Fools against me,
Meandering, roaring, yelling,
Whispering Fools, then chattering Fools,
And after that morose, melancholy,
Sluggish, fat, silent Fools;
And I, moon-crazed, moon-blind,
Fighting and wounded, wounded and fighting.
I never thought of such an end."

The Fool's sly but somehow naive wounding of Congal with the unheroic kitchen spit, and his fascination with the wound—"I must see it, I never saw a wound"—are disturbing intimations of the insanity of soldiering and heroism. The Fool extends our sense of the stupidity and brutality of war which colors this play's treatment of heroism. This last scene, then, achieves an admirable intensity of emotion that is largely missing from the previous parts of the play.

There are strong elements of the absurd in *The Herne's Egg*. The vague sense that the play is an oriental parable in an Irish setting helps make the Great Herne an incongruous and rather absurd figure (Yeats said in a letter that the play was the philosophy of his Indian friend Shri Purohit Swam "in a fable"). The Great Herne's stern demonstration of power by causing thunder suggests a ludicrous, self-important magician more than a wise god. The props of the eggs and Corney's life-size toy donkey, "on wheels, like a child's toy," are gratuitous exploitations of the comic as well as symbols, respectively, of fertility and the particular, ignominious reincarnation awaiting Congal (Corney's donkey used to be a Clare highwayman). The exchanges between Mike and Congal, or rather Mike's laconic prompting of Congal, are exercises in the absurd, anticipating similar exchanges in Pinter's plays. Then again, the indignation with which the drunken Congal describes Aedh's death, and his earnest refutation of the dying Aedh's equally straight-faced accusation that Congal secretly practised fighting with a table leg, are preposterously and outrageously funny:

> "Tara knew that he was overmatched;
> Knew from the start he had no chance;
> Died of a broken head; died drunk;
> Accused me with his dying breath
> Of secretly practising with a table-leg,
> Practising at midnight until I
> Became a perfect master with the weapon.
> But that is all lies."

The Herne's Egg is, then, a somewhat chaotic tragi-comedy, decidedly anti-heroic in tone; but it is also, like *The Player Queen,* rich in theatrical possibilities.

In a preface to *The Herne's Egg,* Yeats described the conditions under which it was written, and noted that the plot was one he remembered from his youth: *"The Herne's Egg* was written in the happier moments of a long illness that had so separated me from life that I felt irresponsible; the plot echoes that of Samuel Ferguson's 'Congal,' and in one form or another had been in my head since my early twenties." [13]

The Abbey production scheduled in 1938 was can-celled because the management considered the play too ribald and irreverent to risk staging. The play was first performed at the Abbey by the Lyric Theatre Company on October 29, 1950. A reviewer for *The Irish Times* commented on the contrast between *The Herne's Egg* and Austin Clarke's verse play, *Sister Eucharia,* which was presented on the same program:

> Mr. Austin Clarke has chosen two curiously contrasting vehicles for the autumn production of his Lyric Theatre Company at the Abbey Theatre. His own play *Sister Eucharia,* is set

around the unworldliness, the mystical ecstasies
and the asceticism of a community of nuns, while
The Herne's Egg, Yeats's second-last play abounds
in the crude earthiness of pre-historic Ireland, and
plays the mystic devotion of Attracta, priestess of
the Great Herne, contrapuntally against the cynical carnality of King Congal and his warriors.[14]

The reviewer went on to praise "the brilliant work" of
Jack MacGowran in the role of Mike, and the beauty
of Anne Yeats's setting and costumes.

While *The Herne's Egg* is not often performed, the
judgment of one critic, that the play has proved "impossible to produce," is obviously wrong.[15] A very
effective production at the University of Vermont in
1973, directed by Sidney Poger and Ghita Orth, leaves
no doubt in my mind about the play's eminently
theatrical qualities. The problem resides, rather, in
the incoherence of those elements of the play which
have some enigmatic and unsatisfying relation to
Yeats's system.

VIII. SUPERNATURAL PLAYS

Generalized affinities with the Noh plays, in particular the revelation of a supernatural world through the manifestation of ghosts, are evident in the three late plays discussed here. But the differences are more significant than the similarities. Yeats's treatment of the supernatural in *The Resurrection, The Words upon the Window-Pane,* and *Purgatory* emphasizes the irrational, but does so in a realistic style; the human significance of that irrationality is presented with a compelling immediacy. The passionate moments that the ghosts relive in *The Words upon the Window-Pane* and *Purgatory* are dramatized with greater psychological realism than in the Noh plays which deal with ghosts, and *The Resurrection* demonstrates the importance of the irrational and supernatural for modern Western culture. That Yeats imaginatively accepts Christ's being both god and man in *The Resurrection,* and the purgatorial existence of the dead in *Purgatory* and *The Words upon the Window-Pane,* also helps make these plays more accessible and realistic to the average audience.

In all three plays, though admittedly with some exceptions in *The Resurrection,* Yeats has jettisoned the conventions of the Noh. Chorus, mask, musicians, dance, and the total theatrical effect of a stylized, impersonal, indirect form of drama have been virtually abandoned. Only *Purgatory* is in verse, and that verse is exceptionally close to the rhythms of actual speech.

From Yeats's notes to *The Resurrection,* it would appear that the play's resemblance to the Noh was the result of an afterthought. In a note at the beginning of *The Resurrection,* Yeats writes that he had begun the play "with an ordinary stage scene in the mind's eye," but because of its controversial subject matter that "might make it unsuited for the public stage," he changed the stage directions so that "it might be played in a studio or drawing-room like my dance plays." The songs at the beginning and ending of the play were also added, Yeats tells us, merely to accompany the folding of the cloth, the symbolic replacement for the opening and closing of the curtain on the conventional stage. The role of the musicians is slight: they have no part in the action, as they do in the Noh plays, and the noise of drum and rattle does not really require their presence on stage. The only mention of a mask occurs in the stage directions when Christ appears, and it is interestingly "a recognisable but stylistic" mask that he is described as wearing; the mask is clearly meant to be more realistic than the masks employed in the dance plays. Again, the climax of the play is the Greek's scream when he feels the beating heart of the risen Christ, and not the ecstatic dance employed in the Noh plays.

James Flannery considered the possibility of directing *The Resurrection* (at the Dublin Theatre Festival, 1965) as though it were a Noh play, but then rightly decided to give it a fairly realistic treatment, stressing the play's human dimension:

> Instead of working for the effect of remoteness that masks and stylized gestures and movement would have given, we endeavoured to engage our audience's attention by stressing the essential humanity of each of the characters. . . .[1]

The Words upon the Window-Pane sets a manifestation of the supernatural (Swift's impassioned dialogue with the two women he loved, enacted uncon-
sciously by a Dublin medium), in the naturalistically
portrayed context of middle-class characters and preoccupations. Yet *The Words upon the Window-Pane*
is no more a naturalistic play than is *The Resurrection*. Indeed, it shares with *The Resurrection* the important characteristic of actually subverting all of the
implications of a social problem play by emphasizing
the irrational and supernatural. "As in *The Resurrection,* Yeats has turned the tables upon the naturalistic
drama by exploding it from inside; from its shattered
ruins there arises the terrible image of an utterly
different kind of life." [2]

Yeats's treatment of the subject matter of *Purgatory,*
earlier in his career, would doubtless have resulted in
a dance play like *The Dreaming of the Bones.* But
while *Purgatory* has all of the intensity and compression of structure of Yeats's Noh plays, its content is,
despite its supernaturalism, intensely human, and is
presented to the audience in a very direct and un-
mediated fashion. We are made to feel that the ghosts
are important not because they are intrinsically interesting psychic phenomena, but because they are psychologically compelling embodiments of a human
relationship that had disastrous consequences. The
supernatural and the human are interrelated in a
thoroughly convincing way, and the presence of the
supernatural in this play does not therefore invite the
stylized production demanded by the Noh plays. A
realistic production of *Purgatory* has been described by
Vivian Mercier as "one of the most shattering experiences that the modern theater has to offer." He
saw the play at the Abbey in 1938, and remembers that
". . . there was no underplaying or stylization. Michael
J. Dolan and Joe Linane, two actors trained exclu-

sively in Abbey realism, were playing two meaty parts for all that was in them." [3]

24. *The Resurrection* (1931)

The Resurrection is a dramatic essay in comparative religion in which Yeats seeks to establish the primitive aspects of Christianity by emphasizing the parallels between Christ's death and resurrection and those of the pagan deity Dionysus. The setting is Jerusalem on the third day after Christ's crucifixion. A Hebrew and a Greek, both disciples of Christ, are guarding the room in a house where the eleven apostles are gathered. There is an anti-Christian mob at large in the city. There is also a band of Dionysian worshippers whose riotous progress through the town is indicated by the noise of their drums and rattles. The Hebrew and the Greek debate the identity of Christ now that he is dead and buried. The Hebrew can no longer believe that Christ is the Messiah, since he has suffered death. The Hebrew is, in fact, somewhat relieved that Christ was nothing more than a good man: it means that he can now settle for the ordinary satisfactions of life, like marriage and children. The Greek, on the other hand, believes that Christ is pure spirit ("I am certain that Jesus never had a human body"), and that it was merely a phantom that seemed to be crucified and buried.

The Dionysian worshippers stop on the street outside the house. The Greek describes, with considerable distaste, their appearance and actions: some men are dressed as women, others dance, slashing themselves with knives, a man and a woman fornicate in the middle of the street, and they all sing a hymn describing the death of Dionysus.

A third follower of Christ, the Syrian, now enters

the house to report breathlessly that the Galilean women have told him how they found Christ's tomb empty, and then encountered the risen Christ. He wants to tell the apostles, but is prevented by the Hebrew and the Greek: the Hebrew feels that these irrational "dreams of women" will upset the apostles unnecessarily, the Greek that the women have merely met the phantom that Christ always was, and that he will soon appear and speak to the apostles. The Syrian believes that Christ is both man and god, both a fully human and a fully divine person.

The followers of Dionysus pass outside the house again. Having hidden an image of their dead god, they now proclaim his resurrection. The Hebrew remarks that "their god arises every year, whereas our god is dead forever." The Dionysian worshippers, however, suddenly and unaccountably, stop outside the house and watch it intently.

The figure of Christ passes through a wall into the room. The Hebrew is terrified, the Greek at first unafraid. Convinced that Christ is mere phantom, the latter touches the figure, but is terror-stricken when he feels the heart of Christ beating. When Christ has passed into the inner room, again through a wall, the Syrian describes how he is received by the apostles and how doubting Thomas puts his hand into the wound in Christ's side. The Greek now realizes the cataclysmic significance of the coming of Christianity for the old Mediterranean civilization, "O Athens, Alexandria, Rome, something has come to destroy you," a realization echoed in the song that closes the play.

Yeats's linking of Christ with Dionysus was no doubt inspired in part by such anthropological works as Sir James Frazer's *The Golden Bough* (1890), and Jessie L. Weston's *From Ritual to Romance* (1920), both of which T. S. Eliot used to such effect in *The Waste*

Land. Implicit in such studies is the idea that Christ is one of many gods worshiped in eastern mystery religions, and that his death and resurrection are not unique, as most Christians believe, but typical of all the gods of these mystery religions. As with Dionysus, Attis, Adonis, and Osiris, Christ's death and resurrection is a spiritual equivalent to the fertility myth that describes the great cycle of palingenesis, that is, the death of the natural world in winter and its resurrection in the spring.

There are, of course, important differences between Christ and these other vegetation gods, most notably in the body of ethical doctrine preached by Christ. Christ's kinship with these gods had been obscured from the beginning by the emphasis on his ethical teachings. By Victorian times his divinity was, in effect, largely disregarded, and Christianity was reduced to a useful, puritanical, social ethic. Yeats's play revolts against the blandness of modern Christianity, powerfully asserting the violent, savage, and primitive aspects of Christ's life and death, and, above all, his supernatural identity.

Yeats was also familiar with Nietzsche's juxtaposition of Christ and Dionysus, though Nietzsche had insisted on the fundamental difference between the two gods:

> Dionysus against the 'Crucified,' there you have the contrast. There is no difference in respect to their martyrdom—it is a difference in the meaning of it. Life itself, its eternal fertility and recurrence, causes pain, destruction, the will to destroy. In the other case, suffering—the 'Crucified as the innocent one'—counts as an argument against this life, as a formula for its condemnation.[4]

In *The Resurrection,* Yeats attempts to reinterpret the meaning of Christ's death, restoring to it the

Dionysian characteristics that Christianity, according to Nietzsche, had always excluded. Yeats's ideas about the Dionysian element in Christianity, and about Christianity's role as the apocalyptic termination of Greek and Roman culture and power, are embodied in this play at first in an oblique way, then with increasing clarity and directness.

The lyric at the very beginning of the play suggests, in its evocation of *sparagmos,* that the death and rebirth of Christ is like that of pagan gods, in particular, Dionysus. Then by having the drums and rattles of the Dionysian worshipers intrude into the conversation of the Greek and the Hebrew at critical moments, and the Greek react so pronouncedly to the barbaric ritual of the Dionysians, Yeats suggests to an alert audience that Christianity may retain some of the barbarism so obviously excluded from it by the humanist and rational conceptions of the play's two main characters. When the Syrian attempts to tell the apostles of Christ's resurrection, the Hebrew will not let him pass, will not allow the apostles to be disturbed by the "irrational dreams of women," as though the Galilean women who claimed to have encountered the resurrected Christ were no different from the followers of Dionysus. The Syrian's argument stresses the irrational element in Christianity (that element which denies the validity of the Greek's Apollonian ideas): "What matter if it contradicts all human knowledge? . . . What if there is always something that lies outside knowledge, outside order? What if at the moment when knowledge and order seem complete that something appears?"

The final appearance of the worshipers of Dionysus brings the parallel between Christ and Dionysus to a climax. Their cry, that "God has arisen," intended to celebrate the rebirth of Dionysus, coincides with the unseen, but mysteriously experienced arrival of

Christ in the house where the apostles are guarded. Their silence as they approach the house, and their staring at it, forcefully bring home the point of all the earlier parallels. The Greek now understands that Christianity is not a product of Greek and Roman culture, but is a radically new and different phenomenon, a new dispensation. The song for the conclusion of the play stresses the element of Dionysian frenzy and unreason that characterizes Christianity and makes it the antithesis, in Yeats's mind, of Greek rationality:

> "Odour of blood when Christ was slain
> Made all Platonic tolerance vain
> And vain all Doric discipline."

The structure of the play is simple and clear-cut. The Hebrew and the Greek debate their respective beliefs in Christ's total humanity and his total divinity. The Syrian's synthesis resolves the dialectic, and Christ's appearance affirms the resolution: Christ is both man and god. The mathematical neatness of the play's structure, however, does not mean that this *drame à these* is undramatic. If the "first sketch" of this play was, as Yeats tells us, "more dialogue than play," this fifth version is thoroughly dramatic.

The debate between the Greek and the Hebrew is neither esoteric nor abstract. We rightly anticipate that the argument is to be resolved by the events of the play. The situation of the two men momentarily expecting the arrival of a mob against whom they are committed to defend the apostles is filled with suspense. The anticipation of the Syrian's return and his news about the Galilean women's experience are similarly dramatic. The appearance of the mob of Dionysian worshipers is effective dramatically because it elicits from the Hebrew and the Greek first

relief that it is not the anti-Christian mob, then con-
tempt and disgust at the worshipers' abandoned behavior. Moreover, the audience is made acutely conscious of dramatic irony, as they see an essential
similarity between Christ and Dionysus and between
their groups of followers; they do not see the complete
antithesis the Hebrew and the Greek, two civilized
men, assume exists. The eventual appearance of
Christ, who passes silently across the stage, is highly
dramatic, but the dramatic tension is raised to a sin-
gularly intense climax when the Greek touches
Christ, and understands that he is not a phantom, but
a resurrected man-god with a beating heart. The audience is made to share the Greek's "terror of the supernatural," "the sense of spiritual reality [that] comes
whether to the individual or to crowds from some
violent shock." [5] The scream uttered by the Greek
when he feels the heartbeat of Christ has been described as "one of the great *coups de théâtre* of the
twentieth century." [6]

Yeats began writing this play in 1925, but it went
through four separate manuscript versions and a
printed version (in *The Adelphi,* 1927), before it
reached its final form. It was first performed at the
Abbey on July 30, 1934. Yeats's misgivings about the
play's suitability for the public stage were not put to
the test, though, for as Yeats remarked with obvious
satisfaction and relief, there was a strike that "prevented the publication of the religious as well as of
the political newspapers and reviews." [7] When the play
was presented by the Abbey players a few months
later in New York, at the Golden Theater, the potentially controversial ideas about Christianity Yeats
was sure would be attacked by the Irish reviewers
were not even mentioned by an American reviewer,
who thought the play piously orthodox.

Although *The Resurrection* is not one of [Yeats's] most tremendous works, it is on the high plane of devout and meditative poetry, and it is worthy of his Olympian genius. Taking a Hebrew, a Greek and a Syrian on the day of Our Lord's resurrection, Mr. Yeats shows how the vanity and security of the common man's thinking is destroyed by that supernatural event. *The Resurrection* is an unpretentious dramatic item and perhaps too literal in some of its ideas, but it is vividly imagined and lucidly phrased, and the lines are beautifully spoken, especially by F. J. McCormick and Michael J. Dolan.[8]

In a very successful production of *The Resurrection* at the Dublin Theatre Festival in 1965, James Flannery deviated from a strict adherence to the play's stage directions. For example, as the play progressed, "A Dionysian heart-image wreathed in ivy . . . was changed to an image which closely resembled the familiar Christian symbol of the two myths." [9] And the Dionysian worshipers were actually present on stage, strengthening the total action of the play, "particularly when, in their final ecstatic dance of joy for their newly risen god, they raised the theatrical temperature for the climax of the play as the Greek touched Christ's heart." [10]

25. *The Words upon the Window-Pane* (1934)

At first sight a naturalistic play in prose, *The Words upon the Window-Pane* would appear to be very atypical of Yeats's plays. It is set in the Dublin of Yeats's day. The action takes place in a lodging house that had, in days of former grandeur, belonged

to acquaintances of Jonathan Swift, the great eighteenth-century Anglo-Irish satirist. The "Dublin Spiritualists Association" is holding a séance, to which its
president, Dr. Trench, has brought the skeptical young
intellectual John Corbet. Corbet appears more interested in the few lines of a poem he finds engraved on a
window than the séance that is to take place. He is a
student of literature and recognizes the poem as one
written by Stella (one of the two women Swift loved)
on the occasion of Swift's fifty-fourth birthday. The
other characters who attend the séance are faintly
comic, earnest persons who want trivial information
from dead relatives: Mrs. Mallett, for example, wants
to reach her dead husband for advice about whether
or not to open a tea-shop. She and the others, including the medium, Mrs. Henderson, are worried about
an evil influence that has been preventing such com-
munication at previous séances.

As the séance gets under way, it becomes clear to
the audience that this evil influence is a manifestation, enacted by the unwitting medium, of two encounters between Swift and the women he loved,
Vanessa and Stella. In the first of these encounters
Swift and Vanessa talk passionately of their relationship. She pleads for physical love and places his hands
on her breasts; he, however, torturedly rejects sexual
love, fearful that a child would inherit the madness
he suspects lies in wait for him, and prays to leave only
his intellect to posterity. In the encounter with Stella,
only Swift speaks, this time more calmly. He praises
her resolutely platonic love for him, though it means
she has no children, lover, or husband, and recites the
poem she wrote to him. The poem includes the lines
that are written upon the window-pane:

"You taught how I might youth prolong
By knowing what is right and wrong,

How from my heart to bring supplies
Of lustre to my fading eyes."

The séance is considered a failure by all except Dr.
Trench and Corbet. Dr. Trench has understood from
the beginning the significance of such a manifestation.
Even before the séance began, he attempted to explain
to the uncomprehending Abraham Johnson how some
spirits

> "think they are still living and go over and over
> some action of their past lives, just as we go over
> and over some painful thought, except that where
> they are thought is reality. . . . Sometimes a spirit
> relives not the pain of death but some passionate
> or tragic moment of life . . . the murderer repeats
> his murder, the robber his robbery, the lover his
> serenade, the soldier hears the trumpet once again.
> If I were a Catholic I would say that such spirits
> were in Purgatory."

The only response to such phenomena, Trench concludes, is a sympathetic patience that will help the
afflicted spirits to pass out of their passion and remorse. Corbet, on the other hand, is impressed by the
séance, but concludes that Mrs. Henderson is an "accomplished actress and scholar" because of what she
has revealed of Swift's character and life. She claims
not even to know who Swift was. After everyone has
left she starts to make tea, but is possessed again by the
spirit of Swift. The play ends with his tragic echo of
Job, "Perish the day on which I was born."

The setting for *The Words upon the Window-Pane*
is sharply atypical. Instead of the bare place of the
dance plays, we encounter the realistic setting for a
séance—"a lodging-house room," chairs around a table, "a kettle on the hob and some tea-things on a
dresser." In startling contrast to the heroic personages

of the dance plays we have the professional middle-class characters of the elderly Dr. Trench and of John Corbet, a Cambridge graduate student at work on a thesis on Swift, and the comic characters of the Evangelical preacher, Abraham Johnson, the lady who is unsure about opening a tea-shop, Mrs. Mallett, and the devotee of the dog-tracks, Corny Patterson. The medium, Mrs. Henderson, is a completely unremarkable woman, as is the secretary of the association, Miss Mackenna.

These characters, writes Yeats in his introduction to the play, were "all people I had met or might have met in just such a séance." [11] Yeats's interest in the occult had led him to partake in many such spiritualist gatherings, and he captures perfectly the atmosphere of earnest Christians and pathetic and comic eccentrics attempting to get in touch with their departed brethren. The situation at the emotional core of the play, that is, the reenactment in two brief but intense scenes of Swift's relationship with Vanessa and Stella, is incomprehensible to the conventional spiritualists.

Yeats acknowledges that the occurrence of this kind of manifestation at a séance is very unlikely—"I have not heard of spirits in a European séance-room reenacting their past lives. . . ." [12] What Yeats has done, and to great dramatic effect, is to enclose, in the naturalistic framework and ambience of this play, the extraordinary kind of supernatural, purgatorial recurrence that is the main focus of such plays as *The Dreaming of the Bones* and *Purgatory*. The dramatic qualities of this play depend largely on its structure, whereby the revelation of the supernatural is unexpectedly accomplished in the apparently spurious surroundings and ritual of the séance. The surface realism is only the setting, then, for a quintessentially Yeatsian intensity. Swift's anguished repression of sexual love for Vanessa, his moving avowal of platonic love for Stella, and his incipient, tragic madness (all in such evident contrast to the mundane surroundings and the realistic mode of the play) are what seize the audience's imagination: "Yeats picks the occasion —a séance—where . . . circumstantial realism will testify against its own completeness or sufficiency as truth. Swift, the most 'real' presence in the play, never appears on the stage." [13]

As his disillusion with modern post-revolutionary Ireland grew, so did Yeats's sense of himself as Anglo-Irish and his idealization of the eighteenth century as "that one Irish century that escaped from darkness and confusion." [14] But the order and reason that Yeats and his character Corbet admire in this most "civilized" period of Irish history (it was civilized, of course, only for that small segment of Ireland's population that was originally English, and not at all for the native Irish) is scarcely found in Swift, at least not as he is presented in this play. It is, rather, Yeats's sympathetic interest in the passion and remorse of Swift's personal life which really provides the inspiration for his appearance in the play, and not Swift's embodiment of all that was noble and great in eighteenth-century Ireland. Also, Yeats felt keenly the possibility of encountering the ghost of Swift in Dublin's streets of eighteenth-century houses, especially in the area of the cathedral where he was dean ("Swift haunts me," Yeats said, "he is always just around the next corner").[15] Yeats's sense of discovery of his own roots in eighteenth-century Ireland and of its civic and intellectual virtues are not dramatically assimilated into this play, then, but his imaginative sympathy with the tormented figure of Swift is.

Though Yeats wrote this play in 1930 and it was produced in the same year, it was not published until 1934. A review in the *New York Times* of the play's first performance at the Abbey (on November 17,

1930) noted only that the audience was enthusiastic, and that the play "makes heavy demands on the power of the actress who must represent the spirits of Swift and Vanessa in turn." [16] In a later review, J. J. Hayes thought the play lacking in point, and not sufficiently dramatic until its conclusion: "The last five minutes of this playlet are strongly dramatic and offer an opportunity to May Craig to round off her brilliant acting, as the medium, with a fine climax. But a few minutes of tenseness at the end of the play is not sufficient justification for the piece itself." [17] One would think that dramatic interest ought to be sustained throughout the play by Yeats's evident craftsmanship, but there have not been memorable revivals that would positively demonstrate the efficacy of this play on the stage.

26. *Purgatory* (1939)

Purgatory is, at one and the same time, an intense psychological drama and an elitist political allegory. The setting for this play is outside the burned-out ruins of a grand house. A bare tree stands in the background. The Old Man and his son have evidently just arrived on the scene. The Boy complains resentfully to his father of having had to shoulder their peddler's pack through the countryside and listen to his interminable talk. When the Old Man claims that souls in Purgatory come back to the scene of their sins to live through their transgressions again and again, and alleges that there is someone in the house, the Boy exasperatedly tells him to be quiet. The Old Man goes on, however, talking as much to himself as to the Boy, to reveal that he was born in the ruined house, and that his mother was a high-born lady who married a groom. She died giving birth to him, and when he

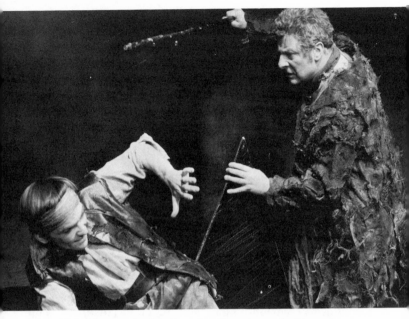

The Old Man and the Boy in *Purgatory*. A Peacock
Theatre production, Dublin, 1970. Directed by Hugh Hunt.
THE ABBEY THEATRE; DERMOT BARRY

was sixteen, his dissolute father burned the house
down. The Old Man confesses that he stabbed his father to death and left his body in the fire, then ran
away and became a peddler. The Boy is moved by the
story only to identify with his blackguard grandfather
because he succeeded in getting the girl and the
money, and to envy the opportunities his father had in
the big house.

The Old Man reveals that this is the anniversary of
his mother's wedding night. The events of that night
are suddenly reenacted in the present: the Old Man
hears the hoofbeats of his father's horse as he returns
from the public-house to his waiting bride, with a whiskey bottle under his arm. A lit-up window shows the
young girl waiting for her husband, who climbs with
her to the bedroom where he begets a child, now the

Old Man. The Boy doesn't hear the hoofbeats or see his grandmother, and takes advantage of what he thinks is the Old Man's madness by attempting to run away with his money. The two fight and scatter the money, the boy threatening to kill his father. The window in the house lights up again, and a man can be seen pouring whiskey into a glass. This time the boy also sees the apparition and exclaims in fright at this appearance of "a dead, living, murdered man!"

The Old Man suddenly stabs the Boy again and again with the same knife he used to kill his father. He hopes thereby to have redeemed his mother's soul from its purgatorial state of having to live through the sin of her misalliance with his father. Killing the Boy will, he hopes, put an end to the consequence of his mother's act, for the Boy would, in marrying and begetting, "have passed pollution on." But the hoofbeats recur once more, and the Old Man understands that the scene he has witnessed between his father and mother is destined to happen again and again. The play ends with his desperate prayer to God to release his mother's soul, and to "appease / The misery of the living and the remorse of the dead."

Purgatory is a very brief but intense and successful treatment, as its title suggests, of the remorseful re-enactment of passion by the dead that is at the heart of *The Dreaming of the Bones* and *The Words upon the Window-Pane*. What Dr. Trench says in the latter play describes the situation of the Old Man's mother in *Purgatory:* "some spirits are earth-bound—they think they are still living and go over and over some action of their past lives, just as we go over and over some painful thought, except that where they are, thought is reality." The mother's transgression was the misalliance into which she entered with a common groom, a betrayal of her self and her station occasioned by sexual passion—she "looked at him and married him." The recurrence of her marriage night in the burnt-out shell of her house, as she couples with her drunken husband to give birth to his murderer, provokes her son to murder again, this time to kill his own son.

The relationship between the characters, especially between the living and the dead, is much more intense than in the other two ghost plays, because it is plausibly human and oedipal in character. The Old Man's resentment of his father (he calls him a beast more than once), and his ambiguous solicitude for his mother (he wonders whether there is pleasure for her in this recurrent sexual union, and vainly beseeches her, "Do not let him touch you!"), make the psychological motivation a unified part of the obsessional subject matter of the play. When the Boy identifies with his grandfather's values, and threatens to repeat the Old Man's sin, "What if I killed you? You killed my grand-dad, / Because you were young and he was old. / Now I am young and you are old," the possibility of a gradual and progressive working-out of the consequences of the misalliance is suggested. But this possibility is only briefly, if suspensefully presented before the Old Man suddenly and savagely murders his son.

The characters' lines, even when expository, are always dramatic, revealing their personalities, experience, and attitudes to one another in a very immediate way. Thus the first words of the play, spoken by the Boy,

> "Half-door, hall door,
> Hither and thither day and night,
> Hill or hollow, shouldering this pack,
> Hearing you talk"

convey his exasperation and weariness at wandering across the countryside, trying to sell his peddler's wares at the half-doors of the peasantry and the hall doors of the gentry, his resentment at the Old Man's garrulousness, and the absence of anything like love in his feeling for his father. The play's verse, mainly in iambic tetrameter lines, is a brilliant dramatic vehicle for the play's meaning. The rhythms and idiom are close to common speech, but at the same time, tautly controlled. T. S. Eliot praised the functional beauty of Yeats's verse in *Purgatory:* "you can hardly say whether the lines give grandeur to the drama, or whether it is the drama which turns the words into poetry." [18] Imagery is dramatically functional, too: the Old Man's memory of the tree in front of the house before a thunderbolt had struck it—"Green leaves, ripe leaves, leaves thick as butter, / Fat greasy life"—reveals the disturbing movement of mind from admiration of life to a fascinated repulsion by it, a movement which recognizes man's inherent potential for self-damnation.

The compression of time also lends a singular intensity to the play. The Old Man murders his son, and the mother reenacts her wedding night in the present time of the play. This foreshortening of time deepens our sense of the tragic, unpitying consequences of the mother's misalliance as she dreams through her wedding night and conceives the child who is to murder his father and his own son.

At one level, the play demands to be interpreted as an angry political allegory of the wanton destruction, in modern Ireland, of a cultured and privileged class (the Anglo-Irish), by a violent and ignorant people irresponsibly intent on tasting power (the native Irish). It is quite clear in this play that the Anglo-Irish big house, and its family of "great people," are the positive images of an admirable culture, typifying what was best in Ireland. In such earlier poems as "Upon a

House Shaken by the Land Agitation" (the house was Lady Gregory's), Yeats would acknowledge, if rather grudgingly, that the Anglo-Irish aristocratic culture flourished largely at the expense of the native Irish; but there is no such admission in *Purgatory*. When the Old Man eulogizes the shell of the mansion and the ghosts of its inhabitants, there is no qualifying irony at work:

> "Great people lived and died in this house;
> Magistrates, colonels, members of Parliament,
> Captains and Governors, and long ago
> Men that had fought at Aughrim and the Boyne.
> Some that had gone on Government work
> To London or to India came home to die,
> Or came from London every spring
> To look at the may-blossom in the park."

The misalliance which is the source of evil in *Purgatory* is wrong, for Yeats, not so much because of the groom's nature, as because of the fact that he belongs to a different race, religion, and class than the woman he marries. The marriage is tragically wasteful and destructive because it violates Yeats's increasingly strong sense of caste.

There is a passage in *On the Boiler* (in which *Purgatory* was published) that provides an interesting parallel for the destruction of the eighteenth-century house in the play, and gives us an indication of Yeats's frame of mind at this time. He exhorts the Lord Mayor of Dublin to restore the Mansion House to "its eighteenth-century state," to make of it a "dignified ancestral building" by rebuilding the facade. What is wrong with it as it presently exists is that "all Catholic Ireland . . . swells out in that pretentious front." [19] *On the Boiler,* is, in fact, a rather cantankerous series of intemperate observations on the degeneracy of mod-

ern Ireland (and indeed, of Europe), including speculations on eugenics that it is charitable to regard as
silly rather than pernicious.

The mood of bitter disillusion that distinguishes
Purgatory and *On the Boiler* is partly due to Yeats's
angry dismay at the nature of the new Free State in
which he found himself senator and citizen. The hopes
Yeats had long nourished for an heroic, modern Irish
society, had been particularly disappointed by the anti-
heroic quality of life in Ireland after the achievement
of political independence. Yeats's admiration for eighteenth-century Anglo-Irish culture, evident in his notes
to *The Words upon the Window-Pane* and elsewhere,
has hardened into a reactionary contempt for modern
democracy and the ignoble and uncultured Irishmen
who have been elevated to political power by the successful struggle for independence. Fortunately, Yeats's
artistic tact, conscious or unconscious, has subordi-
nated the political and social implications of *Purgatory*
to its human interest. They constitute only one aspect,
though an important one, of what is undoubtedly a
brilliant piece of theater.

An eminent critic of Irish literature, Vivian Mercier, saw a production of *Purgatory* at the Abbey in
December, 1938. This was not the original production
that Yeats, in his last public appearance, had attended
on August 10 of the same year, and recorded as "a
sensational success so far as the audience went." But
Mercier was sufficiently impressed to recall the play as

. . . one of the most shattering experiences that
the modern theater has to offer. Into some 240
lines the dying poet put everything he knew about
stagecraft, so that in a bare fifteen or twenty minutes, without any feeling that the exposition has
been hurried, we learn of three generations' suf-
ferings from a family curse and see its culmination

in the third. What is more, Yeats perfected for this play an entirely new dramatic meter, a four-stress unrhymed verse that adds its speed to the dizzying pace of the exposition. . . . I believe a good contemporary director could make [*Purgatory*] as exciting to the younger generation as Beckett or Genet.[20]

IX. YEATS'S ACCOMPLISHMENT AS A DRAMATIST

There is virtual unanimity about Yeats's status as a poet—he is universally acknowledged to be one of the greatest of modern poets; indeed, he is often reckoned to be the greatest poet of our time. There is not the same consensus of opinion, however, about Yeats the dramatist. In fact, Yeats's plays have, on occasion, been summarily dismissed as bizarre, inhuman, and esoteric, or as interesting and worthy of study only insofar as they bear on his poetry. The first objection usually rests on a narrow conception of drama, one that places an unduly high value on realism, the second depends on a questionable value judgment about the relative merits of literature and drama.

It is essential to remember that Yeats was committed to a symbolic and spiritual form of drama; it seems misguided, therefore, to judge his work by the criteria of realism that he explicitly rejected from the beginning of his career as a dramatist:

> Our unimaginative arts are content to set a piece of the world as we know it in a place by itself, to put their photographs as it were in a plush or a plain frame, but the arts which interest me, while seeming to separate from the world and us a group of figures, images, symbols, enable us to pass for a few moments into a deep of the mind

that had hitherto been too subtle for our habitation.[1]

The expectations of an audience accustomed to the tradition of the mainstream of western drama are defeated not only by the virtual absence in a Yeats play of the quasi-photographic realism Yeats attacks, but more importantly, by the absence of the psychological, social, and moral aspects of human relationships. Yeats concerns himself with something quite different: "In Yeats the new subject for observation is the life of the soul and spiritual powers, and so the progression is from inward to outward, unseen to seen, a sensuous world of drama shaping itself upon an ideal world of spirit." [2]

The basic structure and function of a Yeats play is, then, often radically different from what most theater audiences expect to encounter. Yet while Yeats's dramatic theory and technique is revolutionary, it is also intellectually and aesthetically coherent and impressive. Yeats creates a new form in which, as one critic succinctly puts it, "symbolic significance of action, schematic relationships of character, sculptural quality of the playing area, rhythm of bodily movement, harmony of music and song, patterns of colour in costume and setting, and unifying texture of language . . . join together in the expression of some hidden truth or reality of the imagination." [3]

The historical significance of Yeats's theory and practice and his anticipation of contemporary European drama are only beginning to be appreciated. Yeats's anti-illusionistic technique prefigures the Theater of the Absurd; his emblems of tramp, beggar, and blind man have become "the most potent Icon of the modern stage—in Beckett and Genet, Pinter and Ionesco, the lineaments traced by Yeats maintain their form." [4] Several of Yeats's plays, indeed, may be seen

as the precursors of those plays that are the most intensely and movingly dramatic in our modern
theater:

> [Yeats's] plays . . . tap a reservoir of feeling that
> current dramatic literature seldom reaches in
> depth and intensity. Perhaps, seeing *Waiting for
> Godot* with its terrible-tender parody of human
> religious hope, we might observe a similarity of
> motive that would lead us to remember that the
> man who first among modern authors set an action
> of doomed spiritual attendance by an ancient tree
> (in *At The Hawk's Well*) was also Irish. I don't
> think it unreasonable to assume that the theatrical
> tradition of *Godot* and *Fin de Partie* derives from
> *At The Hawk's Well, The Cat And The Moon,*
> and *The Herne's Egg.* The same savagery and
> tenderness are at work, and the same basically
> religious motivation.[5]

Yet, despite the affinity with the Theater of the Absurd that we find in a number of Yeats's plays, and the
striking anticipation of experimental theater by so
many of them, Yeats's work for the stage continues
to be neglected by the modern theater. The reasons
might be summarized as follows. First of all, almost
all of Yeats's plays are in verse. This in itself, some
would argue, make them at best an acquired taste
for the modern playgoer, at worst archaic, contrived,
and artificial. Then the concerns of the plays seem
esoteric, involving as they do Irish mythology and
Yeats's own "private" mythology, neither of which
appear to have anything to do with the human condition in the twentieth century. The suspicion is that
appreciation of Yeats's plays requires membership of
a cult. Aesthetically, too, Yeats's drama, with its emphasis on music, dance, and masks, seems to have been
designed for a coterie theater. Of course, the practical

difficulties of mounting such productions often constitute an added objection. And what is one to do, finally,
about the inconvenient brevity of most of Yeats's
plays? (Certainly a single Yeats play is not long enough
for an evening at the theater.)

There appears at first sight to be an element of
truth in each of these objections; enough, certainly,
to make anyone who admires Yeats's drama attempt
to refute them. The objections are lent plausibility by
being based on widely shared, if narrow, assumptions
about the nature of drama.

Yeats's use of verse in his plays should alert us to the
fact that he is creating drama, that is, literature *and*
theater. As Eric Bentley points out: "Where literature
and theatre overlap, you have drama. The plays of
Yeats are an instructive case in point."[6] Yeats's plays,
indeed, connect the theater with resources of language and stage technique from which it had all but
severed itself in his time; he seeks to attain in them the
richness of language and technique of the ancient
Greek, or the Elizabethan, or the Japanese stage.
Yeats's success in creating verse drama is eloquently
and forcefully attested to by T. S. Eliot:

> We can begin to see now that even the imperfect
> early attempts he made are probably more per-
> manent literature than the plays of Ibsen and
> Shaw; and that his dramatic work as a whole may
> prove a stronger defense against the successful
> urban Shaftesbury Avenue vulgarity which he op-
> posed as stoutly as they. . . . the idea of the poetic
> drama was kept alive when everywhere else it had
> been driven underground. I do not know where
> our debt to him as a dramatist ends—and in time,
> it will not end until that drama itself ends.[7]

It is the naturalistic play and not the poetic drama,
Yeats would claim, which is eccentric in its relation to

the golden ages of European and world drama. To exclude verse, dance, mask, and music from the theater is to rule out realms of expression and ways of feeling that were, and still can be, among the very richest aspects of drama.

So it is with Yeats's use of Irish mythology and his own mythology, set forth in *A Vision*. The use of myth, insofar as myth tends to universalize human experience, gives drama one of its greatest and most ancient strengths. Yeats's plays are, by and large, successful in their use of myth, so that one can argue that their action, characters, and setting tend to be archetypal, not merely Irish or Yeatsian. This is not to say that Yeats expects his audience to *identify* with the patterning of human experience embodied in a particular Irish myth; on the contrary, he usually employs various distancing techniques that result in his audience being *confronted* with myth. This technique, as a critic of Yeats's plays has recently pointed out, is shared by those culture heros of the contemporary theater, Antonin Artaud and Jerzy Grotowski.[8]

Though Irish myth and history are very important in any consideration of Yeats's work, they are important not because of their intrinsic value, but because they give Yeats, so often, a subject that is perfectly suited to the kind of symbolic, ritualistic drama he wanted to create. The element of ritual, the sense that drama has a religious significance in the way that it recreates myth and history, is, again, an important aspect of Yeats's plays, and one which, while it goes back to the origins of the drama, is virtually absent from modern drama. Thomas Parkinson explains that Yeats's use of myth was designed to

> . . . restore drama to its original sources and theater to its only valid function, the evocation of a

sacred presence. Then he [Yeats] might see what he so missed in West End and Abbey theater, an audience exalted by the contemplation of glorious images of possibility and attainment. The quality to be restored could only be embodied by all the devices of ceremonious mystery, the shapes of dance and poetry fashioning with the art of the designer an image of mankind ritualized and liberated.[9]

The rare exceptions to Yeats's successful use of mythology do not indicate that Yeats is writing for a coterie, or that his drama is, in any real way, esoteric.

As for the brevity of most of Yeats's plays—it is, first of all, the nature of symbolic drama to be brief. Realistic drama requires a certain length because everything must be explained and accounted for, whereas symbolic drama operates in a different, archetypal realm, one to which details of time, place, and motivation are largely irrelevant. Moreover, when brevity is a concomitant, as it almost invariably is in Yeats, of such striking intensity and concentration, then brevity is not to be considered, necessarily, as a shortcoming. From the practical point of view, it is obvious that more than one Yeats play should be staged at a time; this would seem to be an axiom of recent, successful productions. There are various, natural groupings of these short plays that enhance the effect of each of the plays in the group and establish a formal, dramatic continuity. There can be no doubt that any intelligent grouping of a series of Yeats plays provides at least as great an emotional and intellectual effect as any one play of conventional length by a modern dramatist.

It is, fortunately, becoming less and less necessary to defend Yeats as a dramatist. The number of books and articles that convincingly demonstrate the importance of Yeats's plays and dramatic theory is on the rise. Katharine Worth, a British drama critic, reminds us how far Yeats was ahead of his time:

> In those last twenty years since *Waiting for Godot* first appeared, the entire European theatre has experienced the revolution which Yeats carried through single-handed in Dublin in the first two decades of the century. We have become accustomed to the ideas of Artaud and Grotowski, read Peter Brook on the "empty space" and followed his explorations in theatre of cruelty, in ritual and improvisation. We have seen the symbolist doctrine of the concrete establish itself, seen the diaphanous imaginings of that arch-prophet, Apollinaire, realised in exquisite patterns of colour, light and sound on the stage of the Aldwych Theatre in one of those World Theatre seasons which have also familiarised us with the techniques of Japanese Nō and much of the important avant garde-theatre of Europe. We have become used to a bare, open stage, direct address to the audience, invitations to collaborate with the actors. We have seen the ideas of Gordon Craig, long thought of (except by Yeats) as an inspired but ineffectual dreamer, realised in many types of experiment with masks and marionettes, notably Tadeusz Kantor's strange, hypnotic representation of life as a death class, where adult people carry round with them their puppet alter ego. And all the time we see the frontiers of drama and ballet, drama and opera dissolving in works like Lindsay Kemp's balletic adaption of Genet, *Flowers,* and the Bond/Henze *We Come to the River,* which the collaborators describe as 'Action with Music.'
>
> Now we can look again at Yeats and see how amazingly he anticipated all that is most original in the European theatre.[10]

Yeats's plays are staged now, too, with a greater understanding of his art than previously. As more of his plays are accorded the informed, sympathetic treatment they deserve, Yeats's reputation as a dramatist is certain to increase. Yeats himself, as he movingly asserted not long before his death, was ultimately indifferent to the lack of popular success of his plays. He considered himself sufficiently rewarded by his memory of scenes of "tragic ecstasy" in his own and his friends' plays:

> I am haunted by certain moments: Miss O'Neill in the last act of Synge's *Deirdre* "Stand a little further off with the quarrelling of fools"; Kerrigan and Miss O'Neill playing in a private house that scene in Augusta Gregory's *Full Moon* where the young mad people in their helpless joy sing "The boys of Queen Anne"; Frank Fay's entrance in the last act of *The Well of the Saints;* William Fay at the end of *On Baile's Strand;* Mrs. Patrick Campbell in my *Deirdre,* passionate and solitary; and in later years that great artist Ninette de Valois in *Fighting the Waves.* These things will, it may be, haunt me on my deathbed; what matter if the people prefer another art, I have had my fill.[11]

X. YEATS AND THE IRISH HISTORICAL AND CULTURAL BACKGROUND

Irish myth and folklore, geography, history, and politics provide the inspiration and subject matter of very many of Yeats's poems and plays, and to the end of his days, Yeats consciously defined himself not only as an Irish writer, but as one who had an important part to play in Irish public life. To appreciate fully Yeats's accomplishment as a dramatist and poet, then, we should reach some understanding of the course of Irish history, and the evolution of Irish culture and society.

Ireland was settled during prehistoric times by successive waves of Stone and Bronze Age peoples. The first to arrive in Ireland, about 6000 B.C., were the Middle Stone Age people, who have left behind only flint implements and middens as evidence of their existence. The New Stone Age settlers, who came to Ireland about 3000 B.C., erected great stone monuments to their dead. A large number of these megalithic tombs, among the oldest in western Europe, dot the landscape of Ireland to this day. County Sligo, the landscape of which played an important role in the forming of Yeats's imagination, contains one of the highest concentrations of these remains, as well as the massive and spectacular cairn, high on top of the mountain of Knocknarea, in which Queen Maeve of Connacht is reputed to be buried. The stones of the cairn, incidentally, have been estimated to weigh forty thousand tons. The other most impressive of these ancient monuments is the passage-grave at Newgrange, County Meath, where the stones that comprise the memorial are decorated with mysterious spiral and lozenge patterns. These patterns "must have had a religious significance, and some are thought to be highly stylized versions of the human face and figure. They may represent the death-goddess worshipped for so long in the Mediterranean world." [1]

About 2000 B.C. the first metal workers arrived in Ireland; they left behind golden jewelry and decorated pottery, and there is evidence that they engaged in trade with the Middle East. Indeed, by 1500 B.C., "Ireland had become one of the chief gold-producing countries in Europe. Gold was exported to the Mediterranean—most of the gold found in Mycenae is said to have come from Ireland—as well as to Britain, Germany, and Scandinavia." [2] The artifacts and treasures of this culture are displayed in the National Museum in Dublin, along with those of a later group of Bronze Age people who came to Ireland about 1200 B.C. Their adornments are sumptuous and magnificent. The large, heavy neck ornaments of beaten or twisted gold, called torques, the gold bracelets, dress fasteners and hair ornaments, the shields of bronze and leather, must have given them a splendid and formidable appearance.

It was the Late Bronze Age people whom the Celts, the iron-using warrior tribes from central and western Europe, conquered when they invaded Ireland about 300 B.C. The Celts not only assimilated the culture of these people, but, paradoxically, seem even to have venerated them. In all likelihood, it was an elite group of these defeated people, banished to the hills and caves of Ireland, who were mythologized by the imaginative Celts as the godlike Tuatha de Danaan.

If the Danaan were conquered and dispossessed, they in turn invaded the imagination of the Celts, who conceived of them as sorcerers and of their remote inhabitation as a beautiful, joyful world of eternal youth named Tir na nOg.

The quasi-supernatural Danaan eventually became the "little people" of folk belief; Christianity probably had a lot to do with their diminution. Mythology evolved into folklore, and only a residual sense of the power of the Danaan is retained in most Irish fairy tales. As a child in Sligo, Yeats was enthralled by the stories he heard from servants and local people, and included some of them in his first published prose work, *Fairy and Folk Tales of the Irish Peasantry* (1888). Yeats's early poetry in particular is also filled with references to the supernatural inhabitants of Ireland. Consciously or otherwise, he sought to restore to the fairies some of the beauty, dignity, and power of the Danaan. For instance, when Yeats describes, in the poem "The Unappeasable Host," fairy children laughing in "cradles of wrought gold," we see him implicitly equating the fairy world with the Danaan civilization distinguished by its golden artifacts.

The Celts mythologized the early experience of their own race mainly in two cycles of epic literature that deal with the adventures of their heroes Cuchulain and Finn MacCool. While the first of these cycles recounts events of the historical period approximately contemporary with Christ's lifetime, and the second of a period about two hundred years afterwards, they appear not to have been written down until much later—until the twelfth and fifteenth centuries respectively, in fact. The myths and legends of the Celtic heroic age (which ended about 450 A.D.) probably reflect historical reality in something of the same way that Homer's *Iliad* does. Just as archaeological evidence in Asia Minor substantiates the story of the Trojan War, so the ornamental war regalia found in Ulster and Connacht tends to verify the battle described in the saga of the *Tain Bo Cualgne* (*The Driving Away of the Bull of Cooley*).

The story of this epic battle between Cuchulain, the champion of the northern kingdom of Ulster, and Maeve, queen of the western kingdom of Connacht, as well as the other tales of the Cuchulain cycle, were translated from the Irish by Yeats's contemporaries, Standish O'Grady and Lady Gregory. To the end of his career, Yeats was fascinated by the figure of Cuchulain, seeing in him the heroic purposefulness, the passion, the stoicism in the face of suffering and death that he sought to emulate in his own life. Yeats's poems and plays also draw on the stories and characters of the later heroic cycle, which portrays the adventures of the Fianna, who are led by Finn Mac-Cool and his son Oisin, the poet and warrior.

The Celts dominated Ireland for more than a thousand years, until the invasion of the Vikings at the end of the eighth century, and even then their social organization survived into the seventeenth century in the west of Ireland.[3] In the Celtic heroic age, Ireland was divided into the five kingdoms of Connacht, Meath, Munster, Leinster, and Ulster; Emain Macha, the capital of Ulster, largest of these kingdoms, is mentioned by Ptolemy in the second century A.D. In the postheroic age, these kingdoms evolved into loose confederations of smaller principalities, but a surprisingly high degree of cultural unity was maintained. The people of Ireland shared an animistic, druidic religion, the same Gaelic language, and a sophisticated rule of law; there existed, too, an aristocracy of men of learning and art—poets, lawyers, harpists and genealogists.

This Celtic culture, in which art and heroic action were so highly esteemed, informed the imagination of

the cultural and political organizations that dominated Irish life at the end of the nineteenth and beginning of the twentieth centuries. The prestige of
the poet in Celtic society clearly appealed to Yeats.
In his play *The King's Threshold,* he obviously identifies with the Celtic poet's role in society as the dis-
seminator of truth and knowledge. The tactic of hunger strike that Seanchan resorts to in this play was a
legitimate recourse for the assertion of one's rights
in Celtic society; indeed, it was institutionalized in
the complex Celtic legal system, known as the Brehon
laws. (These laws also forbade capital punishment,
gave women virtually equal rights with men, and
stated that all of the land was held in common by the
people.) The tradition of the hunger strike as a recourse against political maltreatment was widespread
in Yeats's own day among Irish political prisoners
jailed by the British. The death in 1920 of Terence
MacSwiney, Mayor of Cork, after a hunger strike of
more than ten weeks, prompted Yeats to revise the
ending of *The King's Threshold* and give the play a
tragic resolution.

When Christianity was brought to Ireland by St.
Patrick in the second half of the fifth century, it did
not, of course, instantly supersede the pagan beliefs
of Celtic society. There is plenty of evidence of pagan
belief and culture in what ostensibly had become a
Christian country. One can see this in ecclesiastical
art of the early Christian period, in which Celtic,
pagan motifs are mixed with specifically Christian
ones. Christian saints tended to be made over in the
image of the Celtic heroes, praised for their unsaint-
like virtues of physical courage, cunning, and hospitality. On an ancient cross at Drumhallagh in
County Donegal, the carved figures are obviously
Christian clerics, except for one who is sucking his
thumb. This incongruously infantile activity identi-

fies the figure as the pagan hero, Finn MacCool, who sucked his thumb when he was seeking after knowledge. Yeats characteristically identified with pagan, rather than with Christian Ireland. When he portrays the legendary encounter between Oisin and St. Patrick in *The Wanderings of Oisin* (1889), he elicits the reader's sympathy for the heroic pagan poet, not for the censorious Christian saint.

The Irish Church cherished its independence from Rome in many matters, and retained its monastic structure at a time when most other churches in Europe were organized into an episcopal hierarchy. In the period between the sixth and eighth centuries, Irish monks carried learning and the gospel to western Europe, founding such famous monasteries as Luxeuil in France and Bobbio in Italy. The seventh and eighth centuries have often been described as the golden age of Ireland; Ireland was then, as Samuel Johnson put it, "the school of the West, the quiet habitation of sanctity and learning." [4]

It was during this period, when Ireland was commonly known as the "island of saints and scholars," that such magnificent ecclesiastical art as the Book of Kells and the Book of Durrow were produced. These and many similar books, which can be seen today in Trinity College, Dublin, are copies of the gospels, remarkable for their colorful and elaborate calligraphy and stylized drawings. Giraldus Cambrensis vividly recorded his reaction to one of these books in 1185: "if you take the trouble to look very closely and penetrate with your eyes to the secrets of the artistry you will notice such intricacies, so delicate and subtle, so close together and well knitted, so involved and bound together, and so fresh still in their colourings that you will not hesitate to declare that all these things must have been the result of the work, not of men, but of angels." [5] The sacred objects of the altar were also beautiful artifacts. One can see in the National Museum in Dublin such splendid examples of this art as the Ardagh chalice, a silver vessel exquisitely ornamented with gold filigree, precious stones, and enamel.

James Joyce, often conceived of as a quintessentially modern writer who owed nothing to the culture of ancient Ireland, described the Book of Kells as "the most purely Irish thing we have" and acknowledged its influence on his own elaborate creations.[6] The modern Irish poet, Austin Clarke, has seen in this period of Irish history an ideal both of art and sanctity that is distinctly Irish, an ideal that faded as the Irish church fell under the domination of Rome and gradually became more puritanical. There can be little doubt that even very early Irish culture and art is capable of exerting a singular influence on the work of modern Irish artists, and that it particularly influenced and inspired the Irish writers of the late nineteenth and early twentieth centuries.

The precious ornaments and altar vessels of the monasteries were often plundered by the warriors popularly known as the Vikings, who came from western Norway. They first raided the Irish coast in 795 A.D. There followed a series of wars during the ninth and tenth centuries between the Irish and these invaders, many of whom settled in Ireland and established the coastal townships of Dublin, Waterford, Wexford, Cork, and Limerick. Not until 1014 were the Norse decisively beaten at the battle of Clontarf by Brian Boru, who managed to unite Ireland under his high-kingship. There was a reciprocal process of assimilation at work between the Norse who remained after this time and their native Irish neighbors. The Norse establishment of towns significantly altered the nature of a hitherto purely rural Ireland, making

Dublin and the surrounding area the social and political focus of the country.

The circumstances of the next invasion of Ireland, by the Normans, were both romantic and tragic. In a dispute between two warrior kings, Dermot Mac-Murrough and Tiernan O'Rourke, Dermot kidnapped his enemy's wife, Dervorgilla, reputedly with her compliance. O'Rourke recovered her within a year and forced Dermot to flee Ireland. In his desire for revenge, Dermot appealed to Henry II, king of England, who invited his subjects to help Dermot. Henry had already received a commission from Adrian IV, the only Englishman ever to be Pope, to "reform" the church in Ireland. The Norse and the native Irish proved no match for the disciplined, armored Norman forces under Strongbow, the Earl of Pembroke, to whom Dublin fell in 1170. The Normans established fortresses to keep the territory they had won, built inland garrison towns, churches, roads, bridges, and also systematized agriculture. By the fourteenth century they controlled much of the country, although the Gaelic chieftains were not conquered and continued to attack them from their hideouts. Many of the Normans became more Irish than the Irish themselves, intermarrying with the Gaelic nobility, speaking Irish, and resenting the English king's attempts to curb their power in Ireland.

The Norman invasion was, nonetheless, the beginning of the English domination of Ireland, and Yeats fully appreciated its significance for his own time, when many Irishmen were once again struggling to eject the English from Ireland. In Yeats's play *The Dreaming of the Bones,* the action centers on the plea for pardon made by the guilty ghosts of Dermot (Yeats uses the variant "Diarmuid") and Dervorgilla to an Irish revolutionary soldier who has just taken part in the Easter Rising of 1916. The ghostly lovers realize that they have been responsible for first bringing the English into Ireland, and therefore responsible, too, for the whole bloody history of oppression and rebellion from their time until the present.

The English kings of the fifteenth century were in a quandary about Ireland. Clearly, the Anglo-Irish lords (descendants of the Normans) could rule Ireland more effectively than the English. But these lords did so by means of various, dubious agreements with the native Irish chieftains. There was danger, then, as well as expediency in having them rule Ireland, and they were capable of wielding power in Ireland for their own ends. Thus it was the determined policy of the Tudors to conquer Ireland and bring it under a strong, central, English government.

Henry VIII decided to take a commanding role in Ireland's affairs. In the same year that he broke with Rome (1533), he called the Earl of Kildare, governor of Ireland, to London. On report of the false rumor that he had been executed by Henry, Thomas Fitzgerald, the earl's son (often referred to as Silken Thomas, from the fringe of silk his men wore on their helmets) rebelled against the English king. The rebellion was brutally crushed and its leaders executed. It was clear to Henry that the Anglo-Irish lords could no longer be trusted with the government of Ireland, and a strong military presence in Ireland was the only way of persuading them, as well as the Gaelic chieftains, to obey English law. One consequence of Henry's determination to control Ireland has been the presence of an English army in Ireland from the early sixteenth century until 1922—indeed, until the present in Northern Ireland.

Henry's daughter, Elizabeth I, continued her father's policy of seeking to anglicize the Irish culture, its laws and language, and even its dress. The exter-

mination of the native Irish was widely advocated in
Elizabethan England, and the Elizabethan armies in
Ireland often did their utmost to accomplish this goal.
Though Elizabeth maintained political and mili-
tary power over much of Ireland—a rebellion by the
Desmonds of Munster gave her the excuse, in 1584, to
confiscate half a million acres of fertile land in Mun-
ster—Ulster was the notable exception to her rule.
Ulster's fate was to decide whether Gaelic civilization
would survive in Ireland or be displaced by the alien
English culture.

In 1595, the Ulster chieftain Hugh O'Neill took
arms against Elizabeth and was more than able to
hold his own in the military struggle against the English until 1601. But in that year, Spanish troops
landed at Kinsale with the aim of helping the Irish
rebels against England, and the leaders of Ulster,
O'Neill and O'Donnell, marched south to meet
them, collecting an Irish army on the way. This aban-
donment of a defensive position was a great tactical
blunder; the Irish were, as a consequence, utterly defeated at the battle of Kinsale. In the wake of the
battle, Lord Deputy Mountjoy introduced a scorched-
earth policy that left Ireland devastated. Six years later "the flight of the earls," as the poignant self-exile
of the proud Ulster chieftains is known, marked the
virtual end of Gaelic culture as a vital element in
Irish society.

England was doubtless moved, in some measure, to
subjugate Ireland in the interests of her own national security, fearing that enemies might use Ireland as a base from which to attack her, but there
were other, more important motives: Ireland was the
first of many English colonies deliberately acquired
and exploited. Ireland's wealth was its land, and English policy in the seventeenth century sought to gain
control of it by dispossessing Irish landowners. This

policy was more ruthlessly applied in the case of Ulster by James I than it had been in Munster by his predecessor. The land of Ulster, two million acres, was taken away from its Catholic owners and given to Protestants (mostly Scottish) on the understanding that they would recruit their co-religionists as tenant farmers. The plantation of Ulster, beginning in 1608, thus served a double purpose, for it "solved" the religious problem (as the English saw the Irish rejection of the Reformation), and transformed Ulster, formerly the chief source of resistance, into a loyalist garrison committed to maintaining English rule in Ireland.

The military subjugation of the Irish was continued after the English Civil War, when Oliver Cromwell came to Ireland with a Puritan army in 1649, mercilessly laying waste to town and country in retribution for Irish support of the Catholic king, Charles I. Cromwell used the excuse of Irish disloyalty to seize almost all the arable land in Ireland that was not yet held by the English: "the Cromwellian settlement . . . envisaged the annexation of almost eight million acres of Irish soil—about half the cultivable land in the island." [7] The dispossessed Irish were forced to Connacht, the most barren of Ireland's provinces, or remained as menial laborers on what had been their own land.

It is important to note that English colonial policy resulted in two quite different restructurings of Irish society. In the greater part of Ireland, the Elizabethan and Cromwellian confiscations resulted in the establishment of an elite class of English Protestant landlords. But the plantation of Ulster had a significantly different result: the numerous Protestant Scottish colonists themselves farmed the land that had belonged to the native Irish, and installed, ultimately, a wholly alien culture in most of that province.

The military importance of the plantation of Ulster

became apparent in the war fought in Ireland between the Catholic James II and his Protestant son-in-law, William of Orange, both of whom were supported by a variety of Irish and continental allies. James's sieges of Derry and Enniskillen in Ulster failed, and contributed to his defeat by William in 1690 at the battle of the Boyne. The native Irish had depended on a victory by James to redress their economic and religious grievances, but his defeat doomed their cause. The century that followed was the age of Protestant ascendancy and the infamous penal laws that were designed to degrade the Catholic Irish, "to brutalize a race of aristocratic and learned tradition and reduce it to peasant status and ignorance." [8]

From 1691 to 1778 laws were in effect in Ireland that prohibited Catholics from exercizing the most basic rights: they were forbidden to practise their religion, attend school, hold any government office, enter Parliament or the legal profession, and so on. In short, despite the fact that four-fifths of the population of Ireland was Catholic, Irish Catholics were virtually legislated out of existence. By 1778 a bare five percent of the land of Ireland, the only economic resource of the country, was held by Catholic owners. The degradation and poverty of the native population at this time inspired one famous member of the Protestant ascendancy, Jonathan Swift, Dean of St. Patrick's in Dublin, to write his famous satire, "A Modest Proposal," which scathingly indicts English policy in Ireland as cannibalistic and genocidal.

If the native Irish were almost completely degraded in the eighteenth century, the Anglo-Irish flourished. Swift was not the only famous member of this class; it also included the dramatists Farquhar, Sheridan, and Goldsmith, the philosopher Berkeley, and the political theorist Burke. In the latter part of his life, Yeats claimed a spiritual kinship with these men, seeking to unite their reason and integrity with the passion that distinguished the Ireland of his generation. It was Swift whom Yeats admired in particular, and whose tragic figure is at the center of his play *The Words upon the Window-Pane.*

For a brief period at the end of the eighteenth century, the liberal Protestant Irish parliament, led by Henry Grattan, appeared to have gained substantial independence from a British government willing to grant concessions in Ireland because it was preoccupied by the French and American revolutions. Inspired by the republican ideals of these revolutions, the United Irishmen under Theobald Wolfe Tone staged a rebellion. The insurrection of 1798 was brutally crushed by the largest military presence England had ever billetted in Ireland, an army larger than any with which she had opposed Napoleon. This army was responsible, after the rebellion had been suppressed, for cruelly terrorizing the Irish population at large. Successive generations of Irishmen admired the romantic, revolutionary ardor of the leaders of the 1798 rebellion, and Yeats was to find himself, in 1898, though not altogether without mental reservations, involved in organizing the centenary commemoration of this insurrection.

In the aftermath of the rebellion of 1798, the British prime minister, William Pitt, decided that formal incorporation of Ireland into the United Kingdom of England, Scotland, and Wales would effectively deal with the Irish problem. Thus the Act of Union was passed in 1800; Ireland was henceforth to be governed by the British Parliament. Despite Pitt's contention that the Act of Union would ensure complete emancipation for Irish Catholics, the British Parliament passed additional oppressive measures against what was now a totally demoralized country.

It was Daniel O'Connell, known as The Liberator,

who organized the Catholics. In 1829, after huge, peaceful demonstrations, Catholic Emancipation, that is, the elimination of most of the discriminatory laws, was secured. This accomplishment was brought about by the involvement, for the first time, of the Irish peasants in the political process. O'Connell failed, however, to secure repeal of the Act of Union by using the same tactics of massive public demonstrations that had won Catholic Emancipation. Like many Irishmen of his generation, Yeats rather disliked O'Connell's inglorious practical politics, favoring instead the romantic, revolutionary idealism of the 1798 rebellion, and of his own time.

By 1845, the population of Ireland had reached eight and one-half million, and most of it depended on the potato for subsistence. Potato blight and the consequent failure of the crop four years in succession (1845–48) resulted in the deaths of at least one million and the emigration of at least another million. The horrors of the Famine, "the worst event of its kind recorded in European history at a time of peace," and the forced emigration to America on overcrowded, pestilent ships in which so many died, are deeply imprinted on the Irish mind.[9] There can be little doubt that the Famine deeply scarred the Irish psyche, altering attitudes to sex and marriage, money and land.

It seems possible that sexual inhibition and guilt in the Irish was, for many generations, a direct and understandable legacy of the Famine, when so many children starved to death. And the late or loveless marriages that emerged as an institution of Irish life (they figure prominently in Synge's plays), were due in large part to an equally understandable fearful prudence. The Catholic peasant was compelled to wait for his parents to die so that he could inherit the land, or, in the interests of economic security, acquire land by marriage. One of the central conflicts in Synge's plays, indeed in much modern Irish drama and literature, would seem to stem from this national trauma: the experience of famine lies behind the struggle between a natural affirmation of life and love, and the crippling puritanism, often promulgated by the Catholic church, that would deny both. An awareness of this terrible period of Irish history helps also to illuminate the concerns of Yeats's first play, *The Countess Cathleen,* in which the heroine sells her soul to save the starving peasants of Ireland.

In the years after the Famine, that is, in the second half of the nineteenth century, three political movements dominated the Irish scene; all three were given crucial moral and financial support by the millions of Irish who had emigrated, mainly to America, in the two generations after the Famine. The first was the Land League, founded by Michael Davitt in 1879 to combat evictions, rack-renting, and other outrages perpetrated by landlords on their tenants. At this time, many tenants were evicted from their small holdings for nonpayment of rent, or to cut losses, or increase profits. These evictions were carried out on a large scale, as indicated by the fact that "between 1869 and 1882 some 130,000 people were forcibly evicted from their holdings." [10] The outcome of the increasingly violent struggle between tenant and landlord (rent strikes were succeeded by murder and arson) was the passage of legislation that was ultimately to inaugurate peasant ownership of the land.

The Anglo-Irish did not have to be landlords on a grand scale to be affected by this social upheaval. John Butler Yeats, the writer's father, was politically very liberal and certainly did not think of himself as a landlord; yet the modest income from inherited lands, heavily mortgaged though they were, helped support the family for some years. Synge's mother and brother defended the brutal evictions because the Synge family was wholly dependent on the income received from their small estate in Galway; but Synge himself, in his life and work, was to reject everything associated with such narrow self-interest. Sir William Gregory, the husband of Lady Gregory, Yeats's friend and patron, had in the years of the famine "promoted the iniquitous 'quarter-acre' clause, which pauperized large numbers by obliging them to divest themselves of holdings above a quarter of an acre before admission to relief." [11] Lady Gregory herself, of course, was not involved in such abuses (she did not marry her much older husband until 1880), and her role as landlord was rather to be on the receiving end of legislation that was passed as a result of the land agitation. She was one of very many landlords who were practically required, by a land act of 1903, to sell their estates to the tenant farmers.

The conclusion of the second movement to dominate the late nineteenth century was less happy. Charles Stewart Parnell headed the constitutional Irish parliamentary party that sought home rule for Ireland through its participation in, or most often, obstruction of, the British Parliament. Liberal opinion in England was in favor of granting a measure of independence and repaying the debt of social justice to Ireland, and Gladstone, the British prime minister, championed the cause of home rule. But the discovery of Parnell's adulterous affair with Kitty O'Shea lost the movement much of its moral force and support both in England and Ireland. The Catholic clergy played a key role in Parnell's downfall, denouncing him from the pulpit as immoral and unworthy to lead Ireland. Parnell died in 1891, worn out by the struggle to maintain the leadership of his party.

The integrity of Parnell's idealism, apparently unique among politicians, and the heroic aloofness and defiance he showed in his tragic downfall, were

admired by Joyce and Yeats. Joyce saw Parnell's defeat as the Judas-like betrayal by the Irish people of
their great and noble leader. The national quarrel between the opponents and supporters of the charis-
matic figure known as "the Chief" and "the un-
crowned king of Ireland" is brilliantly dramatized in
the Christmas dinner scene of Joyce's *A Portrait of the
Artist as a Young Man.* Yeats wrote poems early and
late in his career that bitterly compared Parnell with
contemporary public figures; he also contrasted him,
as tragic hero, with O'Connell, whom he termed "the
Great Comedian."

The third major political movement of the late
nineteenth century in Ireland was Fenianism, named
after the legendary warriors of Celtic Ireland, the
Fianna, and inspired by the republicanism of 1798.
The aim of the Fenian brotherhood, founded simultaneously at Dublin and New York in 1858, was Irish
independence, and its methods were violent. For the
first time in Ireland, an avowedly revolutionary group
enlisted its members in large part from the working
classes. While the Fenian rebellion of 1867 was little
more than a futile gesture, Fenianism survived in
the organization called the Irish Republican Brotherhood, whose members were largely responsible for the
Easter Rising of 1916. This rebellion, too, was a failure in the military sense, but it was the catalyst for
the events that led to the eventual independence of
Ireland.

As a young man Yeats was deeply involved in the
nationalist cause; a police report in Dublin Castle as
late as 1899 describes him not only as a literary per-
sonage, but as "more or less of a revolutionary."
The qualification "more or less" is accurate, for
Yeats's revolutionary predilections, if not his nationalism, were in large measure designed to win the ap-

proval of Maude Gonne. Maude Gonne and John
O'Leary were to Yeats the incarnation of the romantic, political Ireland of his youth.

The purely political movements that dominated the
late nineteenth century in Ireland were complemented
by the growth of a fervid cultural nationalism. The
Irish Literary Revival began in the 1880s and flourished in the years after Parnell's death, when constitu-
tionalism was discredited as the method for redressing
Ireland's wrongs. Though the intention of the cultural and literary societies was not political, the result
of their successful attempt to awaken in Irishmen a
keen sense of their national identity was decidedly
separatist and political in effect. In Standish O'Grady's
histories of the Celtic heroic age (the last volume published in 1880), his treatment of Cuchulain and other
Irish heroes was calculated, in O'Grady's words, "to
make this heroic period once again a portion of the
imagination of the country." [12] The measure of
O'Grady's success, and that of others such as Dr.
George Sigerson, can be seen in the person of Padraic
Pearse; commander of the rebel forces in the insurrection of 1916, Pearse invoked in his call to arms the
heroic example of Cuchulain and the other Celtic
heroes.

Douglas Hyde's translation of Irish poetry in *The
Love Songs of Connacht,* published in 1893, was of
comparable influence and importance to O'Grady's
history. Hyde's rendering of Irish into English significantly influenced the poetic idiom of Synge's plays,
and Lady Gregory's own translations. Hyde was the
chief propagandist for the de-anglicizing of Ireland
and the restoration of the Gaelic culture which had
been almost completely destroyed in Ireland by the
start of the eighteenth century. Interestingly enough,
it was to the Irish National Literary Society, which

Yeats was so instrumental in founding, that Hyde de-
livered in 1892 the famous lecture entitled "The Necessity for de-Anglicizing Ireland."

This lecture was "from first to last a plea to Hyde's
fellow-countrymen to turn away from things English
before they lost irretrievably the sense of a separate
nationality." [13] It was a plea to which Irishmen were
particularly receptive at this point in their history. The
popular enthusiasm aroused by Hyde's ideas enabled
him to found the Gaelic League, in 1893, for the purpose of promulgating Irish cultural nationalism. The
organization was enormously popular: the concerts
and lectures it sponsored were greeted with widespread enthusiasm, as was its program to revive the
Irish language and the ancient games of Ireland, such
as hurling.

The appeal of the League was particularly strong
among young people: "Many a young clerk or shop
assistant, attending evening classes after a day spent
behind desk or counter, felt in his daily life the power
of a new inspiration. . . . It was a protest against the
petty jealousies of . . . politicians, against the general
stagnation of Irish life, and against the commercialism
of the English popular press, which was beginning
just then to inundate Ireland." [14] Hyde was to become the first president of Eire, the new name for
the twenty-six county Free State, from 1939 until
1945; the appointment was an acknowledgment of
Hyde's having helped restore to Ireland a sense of
national identity and honor.

Dr. George Sigerson, president of the National Literary Society, helped promote the idea of an Irish
national literature written in English. His collections
and translations of Irish poetry and his elucidation of
its elaborate techniques made it possible for Irish
poets, even if they wrote in English, to feel that they
belonged to a tradition different from that of English

literature. The first literary production of the Revival was *Poems and Ballads of Young Ireland* (1888), which contained poems by Sigerson, Hyde, Yeats, and others. Under the auspices of the National Literary Society, the Irish Literary Theatre was founded in 1899 by Yeats, Lady Gregory, and Edward Martyn. Yeats and Lady Gregory were particularly concerned that their theater should create a body of dramatic literature that was distinctly Irish in its reliance on Irish legend and folklore.

Other notable figures of the Revival were James Stephens, George Moore, AE (the pseudonym of George Russell), Oliver St. John Gogarty, and, of course, John Millington Synge. Sean O'Casey and James Joyce rejected what seemed to them the provincial romanticism to which the Revival writers subscribed, and while they themselves were clearly part of the flowering of Irish literature and drama in the early twentieth century, it is inaccurate to consider them as members of this movement. (The term Irish Renaissance, however, could be used to include both Revival writers and others such as Joyce and O'Casey.)

Some sense of the way in which the cultural movement inevitably overlapped the radical political movement can be seen in Hyde's failure to preserve the purely cultural identity of the Gaelic League. Despite Hyde's best efforts, by 1915 the Gaelic League had become a revolutionary, political organization. That Yeats himself was a member not only of the National Literary Society, but of the revolutionary Irish Republican Brotherhood, also shows the difficulty of maintaining an effective distinction between cultural and political nationalism in the Ireland of his day.

Some of Yeats's early poems and plays were nationalistic enough to make him suffer remorse years later; he asked himself guiltily about *Cathleen Ni Houlihan,* "Did that play of mine send out / Certain

men the English shot?" ("The Man and the Echo").
The answer is that its passionate patriotism certainly
helped create the sacrificial mentality of the men who
fought and died in the Easter Rebellion of 1916.
Yeats knew the men and women who led the insurrection, and though he was aware how closely their
heroism skirted fanaticism, he celebrated the courage
that ennobled them in one of his finest poems, "Easter, 1916".

One can find another indication of the convergence
of literary, cultural, and political influences of the
period in the figure of Padraic Pearse. Pearse was poet,
translator, member of the Gaelic League, founder of
schools in which the language of instruction was Irish,
and seems to have conceived of himself as embodying
the spirit of the Celtic heroes, particularly Cuchulain,
in his leadership of the Easter Rising. It seemed apparent to Yeats also that the heroism of Cuchulain had
renewed itself in the self-sacrificial commitment of
Pearse and Connolly. In his last play, *The Death of
Cuchulain,* Yeats wonders

> What stood in the Post Office
> With Pearse and Connolly?
> What comes out of the mountain
> Where men first shed their blood?
> Who thought Cuchulain till it seemed
> He stood where they had stood?

It should be pointed out that the ghosts of Marx
and Engels, as well as that of Cuchulain, were present in the Post Office during the Rising, for James
Connolly and the Citizen Army he led were avowed
socialists. Marx and Engels had taken a keen and sympathetic interest in Ireland's plight in the late nineteenth century, and had hopes that a socialist revolu-
tion might begin in Ireland. But it was nationalism

that was to become the dominant political ideology in Ireland after the Rising.

Ireland was shaken by the consequences of the Rising for the next seven years. The rebels were initially unpopular with many Dubliners because the insurrection provoked the British army to retaliate with sufficient force to devastate the center of the city (the gunboat *Helga* bombarded Dublin from the river Liffey). But they soon assumed the status of martyrs as fifteen of their leaders were executed. The execution protracted over ten days and carried out in a cold-blooded manner—Connolly was suffering from wounds received in the battle, but was shot anyway, strapped to a chair—aroused a great deal of revulsion against the English and sympathy for the rebels. The political party of Sinn Fein (We Ourselves), led by Arthur Griffith, won an overwhelming electoral victory only two years after the Rising and set up an Irish government designed to replace English rule and institute an Irish republic.

The British attempted to destroy Sinn Fein, but they were met with armed resistance from the Irish Republican Army, led by Michael Collins. The Anglo-Irish war was a guerilla war; like most struggles of national liberation, its stock in trade involved ambushes, assassinations, the taking of hostages, executions, and reprisals. Yeats was witness to the atrocities committed by the hated Black and Tans, a British auxiliary force whose name derived from their half-police, half-army uniforms. From his home in Galway he heard the screams of young men in the nearby village being dragged behind the trucks of the Black and Tans, who murdered more than one innocent in the neighborhood, including a tenant of Lady Gregory's named Ellen Quinn. In the poem "Nineteen Hundred and Nineteen," Yeats uses the circumstances of her death to capture the atmosphere of terror in which the people of Ireland lived at this time, and to symbolize what he saw as a widespread, anarchic dissolution of order and civilization.

The 1921 treaty that ended the Anglo-Irish war gave limited independence—dominion status within the British Empire—to twenty-six counties of Ireland. The other six counties formed the quasi-independent state of Northern Ireland. Disagreement over the terms of this treaty caused the civil war of 1922–23, in many ways a more bitter and devastating conflict than the war against the English. Those who accepted the treaty and the establishment of a twenty-six county Free State of Ireland were led by Arthur Griffith and Michael Collins, who maintained that it gave the Irish "the freedom to achieve freedom." [15] Eamon de Valera, a veteran of the 1916 Rising, led the faction which was determined to fight on for a thirty-two-county republic. Almost 4,000 lives were lost, the cost to the Free State government of waging their military campaign was £17 million, and property damage amounted to more than £30 million.[16]

After the Republicans negotiated a truce in 1923, de Valera reentered the political arena. Under his leadership the twenty-six counties became a republic in effect in 1936, though not in name until 1949. It was under his leadership, too, that the 1930s and 1940s in Ireland were marked by an economic war with England and by neutrality during World War II. A new constitution had been ratified in 1937 that was regrettably anti-libertarian: among other things, it contained an article positing a special relationship between church and state. While this article of the Irish constitution has recently been repealed, very close ties between church and state still remain. In the Republic of Ireland today the control of education is in the hands of the church, divorce and contraception are outlawed, and there is still considerable censorship. When Yeats served as senator for six years in the Irish parliament (1922–28) he fought energetically against the introduction of such measures, though his own inclination in politics, particularly at that time, could not be described as liberal.

The recent violence in Northern Ireland can be seen as a result of the tragically unresolved complex of Irish history. Just as the seventeenth-century Protestant plantation of Ulster was an important factor in the defeat of James II, and with him, the defeat of the native Irish cause for over two hundred years, so Ulster's existence in the years following the Easter Rising in 1916 resulted in the partition of Ireland. The one million Protestants of Northern Ireland (they outnumber the Catholics in that state by about two to one) are committed to resisting political unity with the overwhelmingly Catholic Republic of Ireland. The dates of 1690 and 1916 are potent symbols for the opposing sides in the civil strife that began in Northern Ireland in 1969 and still shows no signs of abatement. One can see this demonstrated in the graffiti on gable walls in Belfast, which urge the Catholics to remember 1916 and the Protestants to remember 1690.

The Protestants and Catholics of Northern Ireland need little urging, for the ancient quarrels fuel the present conflict. Despite the passage of three hundred years, the problem remains essentially the same—economic, racial, and sectarian. Ever since Ulster was first planted by Scottish Presbyterians, the Catholic Irish who remained have been deeply embittered by their dispossession and their consignment to the role of second-class citizens. Catholics in 1969 had every reason to resent discrimination in the allocation of jobs and housing, and to demand radical changes in the electoral system.

But the nonsectarian civil rights movement which attempted to redress these grievances was inevitably superseded by historically determined responses and the emergence of paramilitary organizations committed to achieve political objectives by violence. A resurrected Irish Republican Army is pledged to fight once again for a united, thirty-two county republic, and the Ulster Defense Association, like earlier Protestant military organizations, is committed to maintaining Protestant political supremacy in Northern Ireland and to preventing any union with the rest of Ireland. To paraphrase Stephen Dedalus in Joyce's *Ulysses*, history is a nightmare from which Irishmen, especially in the north, cannot awaken. More than most peoples, it seems, the Irish are prisoners of the past.

NOTES

I. YEATS'S LIFE AND WORK

1. Cited in Michael MacLiammoir and Eavan Boland, *W. B. Yeats and His World,* p. 8.
2. Joseph Hone, *W. B. Yeats, 1865–1939,* p. 17.
3. Cited in Richard Ellmann, *The Man and the Masks,* p. 28.
4. W. B. Yeats, *The Letters of W. B. Yeats,* ed. Allan Wade, p. 63.
5. W. B. Yeats, *Memoirs,* ed. Denis Donoghue, p. 40.
6. Ellmann, p. 227.
7. Cited in Hone, p. 144.
8. A. Norman Jeffares, *W. B. Yeats: Man and Poet,* p. 121.
9. Jeffares, p. 125.
10. W. B. Yeats, Preface to *Poems 1899–1905,* pp. xii–xiii.
11. Cited in Hone, p. 199.
12. W. B. Yeats, "Modern Ireland," *The Massachusetts Review,* Winter 1964, p. 262.
13. Ellmann, p. 215.
14. *Letters,* p. 634.
15. W. B. Yeats, *The Variorium Edition of the Plays,* ed. Russell K. Alspach, p. 932.

16. Ellmann, p. 233.
17. *Letters,* p. 696.
18. W. B. Yeats, *The Senate Speeches of W. B. Yeats,* ed. Donald R. Pearce, p. 99.
19. Cited in Hone, p. 232.
20. Cited in Hone, p. 445.
21. Balachandra Rajan, *W. B. Yeats: A Critical Introduction,* p. 190.

II. Yeats and the Abbey Theatre

1. W. B. Yeats, "The Irish Dramatic Movement," in *The Bounty of Sweden,* p. 33.
2. W. B. Yeats, *The Bounty of Sweden,* p. 28.
3. W. B. Yeats, *Explorations,* p. 107.
4. W. B. Yeats, *Explorations,* p. 80.
5. W. B. Yeats, *Explorations,* p. 92.
6. Lady Gregory, *Our Irish Theatre,* p. 20.
7. W. B. Yeats, *Dramatis Personae,* pp. 20–21.
8. Andrew E. Malone, *The Irish Drama,* p. 66.
9. W. B. Yeats, *Explorations,* p. 73.
10. Roger McHugh, Foreword to Lady Gregory's *Our Irish Theatre,* p. 7.
11. W. B. Yeats, *Dramatis Personae,* p. 78.
12. W. B. Yeats, *Explorations,* p. 108.
13. Lady Gregory, pp. 157–58.
14. W. B. Yeats, *Explorations,* pp. 86–87.
15. W. B. Yeats, *Explorations,* pp. 176–77.
16. Lady Gregory, pp. 168–69.
17. Lady Gregory, p. 61.
18. *The Abbey Theatre 1904–1966,* ed. Gabriel Fallon, p. 6.
19. Richard Ellmann, *The Man and the Masks,* p. 1.
20. Cited in James W. Flannery, *W. B. Yeats and the Idea of a Theatre,* p. 224.
21. Lady Gregory, p. 67.
22. Lady Gregory, p. 67.
23. Lady Gregory, p. 8.
24. Cited in Lady Gregory, p. 103.

25. Cited in Michael O hAodha, *Theatre in Ireland,* p. 83.
26. Flannery, pp. 360–61.
27. W. B. Yeats, *Explorations,* p. 250.
28. Lady Gregory, p. 52.
29. Anne Saddlemyer, "'Worn Out With Dreams': Dublin's Abbey Theatre," *The World of W. B. Yeats,* ed. Skelton and Saddlemyer, p. 124.
30. Samuel Beckett, *Murphy,* p. 269.
31. W. B. Yeats, *Explorations,* pp. 254–55, p. 257.
32. W. B. Yeats, at Stratford-on-Avon, May, 1901, cited in *The Abbey Theatre 1904–1966,* p. 3.
33. *The Village Voice,* November 29, 1976.
34. Ghassan Maleh, "Synge in the Arab World," in *A Centenary Tribute to John Millington Synge,* ed. S. B. Bushrui, pp. 245–252.
35. Flannery, p. 236.

III. PRELUDE TO PLAYWRITING

1. W. B. Yeats, *Autobiographies,* p. 60.
2. F. R. Leavis, *New Bearings in English Poetry,* p. 37.
3. W. B. Yeats, *The Letters,* ed. Allan Wade, p. 87.
4. Richard Ellmann, *The Man and the Masks,* p. 35.
5. W. B. Yeats, *Letters to Katharine Tynan,* ed. Roger McHugh, p. 90.
6. W. B. Yeats, *Letters to Katharine Tynan,* p. 147, p. 90.
7. Harold Bloom, *Yeats,* p. 53.

IV. FOLK AND MORALITY PLAYS

1. Peter Ure, *Yeats and Anglo-Irish Literature: Critical Essays,* ed. C. J. Rawson, p. 194.
2. W. B. Yeats, *The Variorum Edition of the Plays,* ed. Russell K. Alspach, p. 173.
3. Cited in Peter Ure's *Yeats the Playwright,* p. 16.

4. W. B. Yeats, *Dramatis Personae*, p. 39.
5. Joseph Holloway, *Joseph Holloway's Abbey Theatre*, ed. Robert Hogan and Michael O'Neill, p. 74.
6. Klaus Völker, *Irisches Theater I: Yeats und Synge*, p. 97.
7. *Variorum*, p. 212.
8. Cited in Walter Starkie and A. N. Jeffares, *Homage to Yeats 1865–1965*, p. 20.
9. *The Irish Independent*, cited in Thomas Mac-Anna, "Nationalism from the Abbey Stage," *Theatre and Nationalism in Twentieth Century Ireland*, ed. Robert O'Driscoll, p. 93.
10. *The United Irishman*, May 5, 1902.
11. *Variorum*, p. 232.
12. J. I. M. Stewart, *Eight Modern Writers*, p. 326.
13. *The United Irishman*, May 5, 1902.
14. *Variorum*, p. 233.
15. *Variorum*, p. 254.
16. *Variorum*, p. 254.
17. W. B. Yeats, *The Letters of W. B. Yeats*, ed. Allan Wade, p. 503.
18. *Variorum*, p. 713.
19. Holloway, p. 96.
20. Klaus Völker, *Irisches Theater I: Yeats und Synge*, p. 97.
21. Much has been written on Yeats's revisions of this play. See, for example, *Druid Craft: The Writing of The Shadowy Waters*, by Sidnell, Mayhew and Clark and *Yeats's Verse Plays: The Revisions, 1900–1910* by Bushrui. John Rees Moore points out in *Masks of Love and Death* that between 1885 and 1900 *The Shadowy Waters* grew "into a kind of dramatic encyclopedia of Yeats's knowledge and theories of symbolism; it was to be the culminating masterpiece of the theatre of symbolism" (p. 79).
22. J. I. M. Stewart, p. 318.
23. *Letters*, p. 459.
24. Thomas Parkinson, *W. B. Yeats Self Critic and The Later Poetry*, p. 75.

25. *Variorum*, p. 341.
26. T. S. Eliot, "The Poetry of W. B. Yeats," in *The Permanence of Yeats*, ed. Hall and Steinmann, p. 301.
27. W. Y. Tindall, "The Symbolism of W. B. Yeats," rpt. in *The Permanence of Yeats*, ed. Hall and Steinmann, p. 239.
28. Wildred Scawen Blunt, *My Diaries;* cited in Peter Kavanagh's *The Story of The Abbey Theatre*, p. 37.
29. *Variorum*, p. 645.
30. Una Ellis-Fermor, *The Irish Dramatic Movement*, p. 108.
31. Cited in George Brandon Saul's *Prolegomena to the Study of Yeats's Plays*, p. 63.
32. Karen Dorn, "Dialogue into Movement: W. B. Yeats's Theatre Collaboration with Gordon Craig," in *Yeats and the Theatre*, ed. Robert O'Driscoll and Lorna Reynolds, p. 125.
33. Klaus Völker, *Irisches Theater I: Yeats und Synge*, p. 97.
34. *The Irish Times*, July 14, 1976.

v. Heroic and Tragic Plays

1. Thomas Parkinson, *W. B. Yeats Self Critic and The Later Poetry*, p. 54.
2. W. B. Yeats, "The Legendary and Mythological Foundation of the Plays and Poems," *The Variorum Edition of the Plays*, ed. Russell K. Alspach, p. 1282.
3. Henry Popkin, "Yeats As Dramatist," *Tulane Drama Review*, 3 (March 1959), p. 77.
4. W. B. Yeats, *Dramatis Personae*, p. 70.
5. Cited in Liam Miller, *The Noble Drama of W. B. Yeats*, p. 63.
6. Proinsias MacCana, *Celtic Mythology*, p. 111.
7. *The Freeman's Journal*, October 22, 1901.

8. Joseph Holloway, *Joseph Holloway's Abbey The-atre*, ed. Robert Hagan and Michael O'Neill, p. 26.
9. *Variorum*, p. 315.
10. Roger McHugh, "The Plays of W. B. Yeats," *Threshold*, 19 (Autumn 1965), p. 7.
11. Maire Nic Shiubhlaigh, *The Splendid Years*, pp. 59–60.
12. W. B. Yeats, *The Letters of W. B. Yeats*, ed. Allan Wade, p. 444.
13. Parkinson, p. 80.
14. James W. Flannery, *W. B. Yeats and the Idea of a Theatre*, p. 306.
15. Cited in Joseph Hone, *W. B. Yeats, 1865–1939*, p. 205.
16. Reg Skene, *The Cuchulain Plays of W. B. Yeats*, p. 158.
17. Cited in Peter Ure, *Yeats the Playwright*, p. 222.
18. Hone, p. 212.
19. *Variorum*, p. 389.
20. *Letters*, p. 482.
21. Cited in Lennox Robinson, "The Man and the Dramatist," in *William Butler Yeats: Essays in Tribute*, ed. Stephen Gwynn, p. 96.
22. W. B. Yeats, *Essays and Introductions*, p. 255.
23. David R. Clark and James McGuire, "Yeats's Version of Sophocles: Two Typescripts," in *Yeats and the Theatre*, ed. Robert O'Driscoll and Lona Reynolds, p. 222.
24. *New York Times*, December 12, 1926.
25. Alec Reid, in a review of *Sophocles' King Oedipus*, *Canadian Association of Irish Studies Newsletter*, No. 4, June 1974, p. 19.

VI. NOH PLAYS

1. W. B. Yeats, *The Variorum Edition of the Plays*, ed. Russell K. Alspach, p. 415.
2. W. B. Yeats, Introduction to *Certain Noble Plays of Japan* by Pound and Fenollosa, rpt. in *The Classic Noh Theatre of Japan*, p. 151, p. 156.

3. W. B. Yeats, Introduction to *Certain Noble Plays of Japan,* p. 155.
4. *Variorum,* p. 417.
5. Ernest Fenollosa, "Fenollosa on the Noh," *The Classic Noh Theatre of Japan,* p. 61.
6. Pronoti Baski, "The Japanese Noh: A Survey," *Threshold,* 19 (Autumn, 1965), p. 80.
7. Baski, p. 86.
8. Fenollosa, pp. 69–70.
9. *Variorum,* p. 805.
10. Cited in Ann Saddlemyer, " 'The Heroic Discipline of the Looking-Glass': W. B. Yeats's Search for Dramatic Design," *The World of W. B. Yeats,* ed. Skelton and Saddlemyer, p. 97.
11. W. B. Yeats, Introduction to *Certain Noble Plays of Japan,* pp. 159–60.
12. Shotaro Oshima, "Yeats and the Japanese Theatre," *Threshold,* 19 (Autumn, 1965), p. 100.
13. Katharine Worth, *The Irish Drama of Europe from Yeats to Beckett,* p. 216.
14. *Variorum,* p. 566.
15. Joseph Hone, *W. B. Yeats, 1865–1939,* p. 297.
16. Hone, p. 297.
17. Shotaro Oshima, pp. 89–102.
18. Richard Ellmann, *Yeats: The Man and the Masks,* p. 215, p. 212.
19. W. B. Yeats, Introduction to *Certain Noble Plays of Japan,* p. 159.
20. *The Irish Times,* October 28, 1968.
21. *Variorum,* p. 567.
22. *Variorum,* p. 567.
23. W. B. Yeats, *Wheels and Butterflies,* p. 62.
24. Peter Ure, *Yeats the Playwright,* p. 75.
25. James W. Flannery, *W. B. Yeats and the Idea of a Theatre,* p. 47.
26. *New York Times,* March 25, 1970.
27. *New York Times,* April 26, 1970.
28. W. B. Yeats, *Mythologies,* pp. 354–55.
29. Micheal O hAodha, *Theatre in Ireland,* p. 95.
30. W. B. Yeats, *The Letters,* ed. Allan Wade, p. 788.

31. David R. Clark, "Yeats, Theatre, and National-ism," in *Theatre and Nationalism in Twentieth Century Ireland,* ed. Robert O'Driscoll, p. 152.
32. W. B. Yeats, *Mythologies,* p. 354.
33. James W. Flannery, "Action and Reaction at the Dublin Theatre Festival," *Educational Theatre Journal,* vol. 19 (March, 1967), p. 77.
34. Cited in Flannery, "Action and Reaction at the Dublin Theatre Festival," p. 75.
35. *Variorum,* p. 805.
36. Baski, p. 82.
37. *Variorum,* p. 805.
38. *Variorum,* p. 1308.
39. *Variorum,* p. 805.
40. *Irish Independent,* July 14, 1976.
41. Walter Sorell in *Dance News,* April, 1975.
42. *Variorum,* p. 1009.
43. *Variorum,* p. 1010.
44. *Letters,* p. 826.
45. Denis Donoghue, *The Third Voice,* pp. 56–7.
46. *The Toronto Telegraph,* February 12, 1971.
47. James Revson in *Our Town,* April 30, 1976.
48. Clark, pp. 147–48.
49. Flannery, *W. B. Yeats and the Idea of a Theatre,* p. 40.
50. Reg Skene, *The Cuchulain Plays of W. B. Yeats,* p. 54.
51. Skene, p. 56.

VII. TRAGI-COMEDIES

1. That Yeats had in mind a special understanding of the term "farce" is indicated in his observation on affinities between farce and tragedy. Farce, he claims, is capable of attaining the simplicity, compression and intensity that is the essence of tragic drama: "A farce and a tragedy are alike in this, that they are a moment of intense life." (*Explorations,* p. 153).

2. Peter Ure, *Yeats and Anglo-Irish Literature: Critical Essays,* ed. C. J. Rawson, p. 185.

3. James W. Flannery, *W. B. Yeats and the Idea of a Theatre,* p. 311.

4. Reg Skene, *The Cuchulain Plays of W. B. Yeats,* pp. 38–71, *passim.*

5. W. B. Yeats, *Essays and Introductions,* p. 523.

6. John Jay, "What Stood in the Post Office," *Threshold,* 19 (Autumn, 1965), p. 36.

7. Micheal O hAodha, *Theatre in Ireland,* pp. 97–98.

8. Robert Langbaum, "The Exteriority of Self in Yeats's Poetry and Thought," *New Literary History,* 3 (Spring, 1976), p. 581.

9. W. B. Yeats, *Mythologies,* p. 334.

10. W. B. Yeats, *The Variorum Edition of the Plays,* ed. Russell K. Alspach, p. 761.

11. Vivian Mercier, "In Defense of Yeats as a Dramatist," *Modern Drama* 8 (September, 1965), p. 163.

12. Peter Ure, *Yeats the Playwright,* p. 146.

13. *Variorum,* p. 1311.

14. *The Irish Times,* October 30, 1950.

15. J. I. M. Stewart, *Eight Modern Writers,* p. 405.

VIII. SUPERNATURAL PLAYS

1. James W. Flannery, "Action and Reaction at the Dublin Theatre Festival," *Educational Theatre Journal,* 19 (March, 1967), 75.

2. Peter Ure, *Yeats the Playwright,* p. 112.

3. Vivian Mercier, "In Defense of Yeats as a Dramatist," *Modern Drama,* 8 (September, 1965), 164.

4. Cited in Rose Pfeffer, *Nietzsche: Disciple of Dionysus,* pp. 46–7.

5. W. B. Yeats, *The Variorum Edition of the Plays,* ed. Russell K. Alspach, p. 935.

6. Mercier, p. 166.

7. *Variorum,* p. 1308.

8. *New York Times,* November 20, 1934.

9. Flannery, p. 74.

10. Flannery, p. 74.
11. *Variorum,* p. 967.
12. *Variorum,* p. 969.
13. David R. Clark, *W. B. Yeats and the Theatre of Desolate Reality,* p. 84.
14. *Variorum,* p. 958.
15. *Variorum,* p. 958.
16. *New York Times,* November 19, 1930.
17. *New York Times,* January 4, 1931.
18. T. S. Eliot, "The Poetry of William Butler Yeats," in *The Permanence of Yeats,* ed. Hall and Steinmann, p. 304.
19. William Butler Yeats, *On the Boiler,* p. 10.
20. Mercier, p. 164.

IX. YEATS'S ACCOMPLISHMENT AS A DRAMATIST

1. W. B. Yeats, *Essays and Introductions,* pp. 224–25.
2. Ronald Peacock, *The Poet in the Theatre,* p. 127.
3. Richard Taylor, *The Drama of W. B. Yeats,* p. 1.
4. M. C. Bradbrook, *English Dramatic Form,* p. 139.
5. Thomas Parkinson, "The Later Plays of W. B. Yeats," in *Modern Drama: Essays in Criticism,* ed. Bogard and Oliver, p. 392.
6. Eric Bentley, "Yeats as a Playwright," in *The Permanence of Yeats,* ed. Hall and Steinmann, p. 223.
7. T. S. Eliot, "The Poetry of William Butler Yeats," in *The Permanence of Yeats,* ed. Hall and Steinmann, p. 306.
8. James W. Flannery, *W. B. Yeats and the Idea of a Theatre,* p. 368.
9. Parkinson, pp. 388–89.
10. Katharine Worth, *The Irish Drama of Europe from Yeats to Beckett,* pp. 2–3.
11. W. B. Yeats, *On the Boiler,* pp. 13–14.

X. YEATS AND THE IRISH HISTORICAL AND CULTURAL BACKGROUND

1. G. F. Mitchell, "Prehistoric Ireland," in *The Course of Irish History*, ed. T. W. Moody and F. X. Martin, p. 38.

2. Giovanni Costigan, *A History of Modern Ireland*, p. 4.

3. Costigan, p. 6.

4. Cited in Una Ellis-Fermor, *The Irish Dramatic Movement*, p. 14.

5. Cited in Kathleen Hughes, "The Golden Age of Early Christian Ireland," in *The Course of Irish History*, p. 88.

6. Cited in Richard Ellmann, *James Joyce*, p. 558.

7. Costigan, p. 80.

8. Edmund Curtis, *A History of Ireland*, p. 280.

9. Curtis, p. 368.

10. Costigan, p. 236.

11. Frank Tuohy, *Yeats*, p. 96.

12. Cited in Alex Zwerdling, *Yeats and the Heroic Ideal*, p. 39.

13. F. S. L. Lyons, *Ireland Since the Famine*, p. 228.

14. Costigan, pp. 260–61.

15. Treaty debates, cited by Patrick Lynch in "Ireland Since the Treaty," in *The Course of Irish History*, p. 325.

16. Lyons, p. 468.

BIBLIOGRAPHY

1. Dramatic Works by Yeats

The Countess Cathleen. In *The Countess Kathleen and Various Legends and Lyrics.* London: T. Fisher Unwin, 1892.

The Land of Heart's Desire. London: T. Fisher Unwin, 1894.

Cathleen Ni Houlihan. In *Samhain,* 1902.

The Hour-Glass. London: Heinemann, 1903.

On Baile's Strand. In *In the Seven Woods.* Dundrum: Dun Emer Press, 1903.

The Pot of Broth. In *The Hour-Glass and Other Plays.* London: Macmillan, 1904.

The King's Threshold. New York: Printed for Private Circulation, 1904.

The Shadowy Waters. London: A. H. Bullen, 1907.

Deirdre. Dublin: Maunsel, 1907.

The Unicorn from the Stars. New York: Macmillan, 1908.

The Green Helmet. In *The Green Helmet and Other Poems.* Dundrum: Cuala Press, 1910.

At the Hawk's Well. Dundrum: Cuala Press, 1917.

The Only Jealousy of Emer. In *Two Plays for Dancers.* Dundrum: Cuala Press, 1919.

The Dreaming of the Bones. In *Two Plays for Dancers.* Dundrum: Cuala Press, 1919.

Calvary. In *Four Plays for Dancers.* London: Macmillan, 1921.

The Cat and the Moon. In *The Cat and the Moon and Certain Poems.* Dublin: Cuala Press, 1924.

The Player Queen. In *The Cat and the Moon and Certain Poems.* Dublin: Cuala Press, 1924.

Sophocles' King Oedipus. London: Macmillan, 1928.

The Resurrection. In *Stories of Michael Robartes and his Friends.* Dublin: Cuala Press, 1931.

Sophocles' Oedipus at Colonus. In *The Collected Plays of W. B. Yeats.* London: Macmillan, 1934.

The Words upon the Window-Pane. Dublin: Cuala Press, 1934.

The King of the Great Clock Tower. Dublin: Cuala Press, 1934.

A Full Moon in March. London: Macmillan, 1935.

The Herne's Egg. London: Macmillan, 1938.

Purgatory. In *Last Poems and Two Plays.* Dublin: Cuala Press, 1939.

The Death of Cuchulain. In *Last Poems and Two Plays.* Dublin: Cuala Press, 1939.

The Collected Plays of W. B. Yeats. London: Macmillan, 1952.

The Variorum Edition of the Plays of W. B. Yeats, ed. Russell K. Alspach. New York: Macmillan, 1966.

The *Variorum Plays* includes four early dramatic poems omitted from the *Collected Plays—The Island of Statues* (1885), *The Seeker* (1885), *Mosada* (1886), and *Time and the Witch Vivien* (1889). This text also contains *Where There Is Nothing* (1902), which Yeats rewrote as *The Unicorn from the Stars* (1908), and *Diarmuid and Grania* (first published in 1951), on which he collaborated with George Moore, and possibly Lady Gregory and Arthur Symons.

2. Nondramatic Works by Yeats— Poetry and Prose

The Bounty of Sweden. Dublin: Cuala Press, 1925.

Dramatis Personae. Dublin: Cuala Press, 1935.

A Vision. London: Macmillan, 1937.

On the Boiler. Dublin: Cuala Press, 1939.

Letters to Katharine Tynan. New York: McMullen Books, 1953.

The Letters of W. B. Yeats. Ed. Allan Wade. London: Hart-Davis, 1954.

Autobiographies. London: Macmillan, 1955.

The Collected Poems of W. B. Yeats. New York: Macmillan, 1956.

The Senate Speeches of W. B. Yeats. Ed. Donald R. Pearce. Bloomington: Indiana University Press, 1960.

Mythologies. London: Macmillan, 1959.

Essays and Introductions. New York: Macmillan, 1961.

Explorations. London: Macmillan, 1962.

The Variorum Edition of the Poems of W. B. Yeats. Ed. Peter Allt and Russell K. Alspach. New York: Macmillan, 1966.

Memoirs. Ed. Denis Donoghue. London: Macmillan, 1972.

3. Works Relating to Yeats's Plays

Beum, Robert. *The Poetic Art of William Butler Yeats.* New York: Frederick Ungar, 1969.

Bloom, Harold. *Yeats.* New York: Oxford University Press, 1970.

Bogard, Travis and William I. Oliver, eds. *Modern Drama: Essays in Criticism.* New York: Oxford University Press, 1965.

Boyd, Ernest A. *Ireland's Literary Renaissance.* Dublin and London: Maunsel, 1916.

Bradbrook, M. C. *English Dramatic Form: A History of its Development.* New York: Barnes and Noble, 1965.

Brown, Malcolm. *The Politics of Irish Literature: From Thomas Davis to W. B. Yeats.* Seattle: University of Washington Press, 1972.

Bushrui, S. B. *Yeats's Verse Plays: Revisions, 1900–1910.* Oxford: Clarendon Press, 1965.

————, ed. *A Centenary Tribute to J. M. Synge 1871–1909*. New York: Barnes and Noble, 1972.

Clark, David R. *W. B. Yeats and the Theatre of Desolate Reality*. Dublin: Dolmen Press, 1965.

Costigan, Giovanni. *A History of Modern Ireland*. New York: Pegasus, 1970.

Curtis, Edmund. *A History of Ireland*. London: Methuen, 1936.

Donoghue, Denis, ed. *The Integrity of Yeats*. Cork: Mercier Press, 1964.

————. *The Third Voice: Modern British and American Verse Drama*. Princeton: Princeton University Press, 1959.

————. *William Butler Yeats*. New York: Viking Press, 1971.

Donoghue, Denis and J. R. Mulryne, eds. *An Honoured Guest: New Essays on W. B. Yeats*. New York: St. Martin's Press, 1965.

Ellis-Fermor, Una. *The Irish Dramatic Movement*. London: Methuen, 1939.

Ellmann, Richard. *Eminent Doman: Yeats Among Wilde, Joyce, Pound, Eliot and Auden*. New York: Oxford University Press, 1967.

————.*The Identity of Yeats*. New York: Oxford University Press, 1964.

————. *Yeats: The Man and the Masks*. New York: Macmillan, 1948.

Fallon, Gabriel, ed. *The Abbey Theatre 1904–1966*. Dublin: The National Theatre Society, n.d.

Fay, Gerard. *The Abbey Theatre*. London: Hollis and Carter, 1958.

Fay, W. G. and Catherine Carswell. *The Fays of the Abbey Theatre*. New York: Harcourt Brace, 1935.

Flannery, James W. *Miss Annie F. Horniman and the Abbey Theatre*. Dublin: Dolmen Press, 1970.

————. *W. B. Yeats and the Idea of a Theatre: The Early Abbey Theatre in Theory and Practice*. New Haven: Yale University Press, 1976.

Friedman, Barton R. *Adventures in the Deeps of the Mind*. Princeton: Princeton University Press, 1977.

Gregory, Lady Augusta. *Our Irish Theatre*. Ed. Roger McHugh. New York: Oxford University Press, 1973.

Gwynn Stephen L., ed. *William Butler Yeats: Essays in Tribute*. Port Washington: Kennikat Press, 1965 (originally published as *Scattering Branches,* 1940).

Hall, James and Martin Steinmann, eds. *The Permanence of Yeats*. New York: Macmillan, 1950.

Harper, George Mills. *The Mingling of Heaven and Hell: Yeats's Theory of Theatre*. Dublin: Dolmen Press, 1975.

Hogan, Robert G. and James Kilroy. *The Irish Literary Theatre*. Vol. 1 in *The Modern Irish Drama, A Documentary History*. Dublin: Dolmen Press, 1975.

Holloway, Joseph. *Joseph Holloway's Abbey Theatre: A Selection From His Unpublished Journal "Impressions of a Dublin Playgoer."* Ed. Robert Hogan and Michael J. O'Neill. Carbondale: Southern Illinois University Press, 1967.

Hone, Joseph. *W. B. Yeats, 1865–1939*. London: Macmillan, 1965.

Jeffares, A. Norman. *W. B. Yeats, Man and Poet*. New York: Barnes and Noble, 1966.

Jeffares, A. Norman and A. S. Knowland, eds. *A Commentary on the Collected Plays of W. B. Yeats*. London: Macmillan, 1975.

Kavanagh, Peter. *The Story of the Abbey Theatre*. New York: Devin Adair, 1950.

Leavis, F. R. *New Bearings in English Poetry*. Harmondsworth, Middlesex: Penguin Books, 1963.

Lyons, F. S. L. *Ireland Since the Famine*. Glasgow: Fontana/Collins, 1973.

MacCana, Proinsias. *Celtic Mythology*. London: Hamlyn House, 1970.

MacLiammóir, Micheál. *Theatre in Ireland*. Dublin: Three Candles, 1964.

MacLiammóir, Micheál and Eavan Boland. *W. B. Yeats and His World*. New York: Viking Press, 1972.

Malone, Andrew E. *The Irish Drama*. London: Constable, 1929.

Marcus, Philip L. *Yeats and the Beginning of the Irish Renaissance*. Ithaca: Cornell University Press, 1971.

Maxwell, D. E. S. and S. B. Bushrui, eds. *W. B. Yeats, 1865–1939: Centenary Essays on the Art of W. B. Yeats*. Ibadan, Nigeria: Ibadan University Press, 1965.

Miller, Liam, ed. *The Dolmen Press Yeats Centenary Papers*. Dublin: Dolmen Press, 1968.

————. *The Noble Drama of W. B. Yeats*. Dublin: Dolmen Press, 1977.

Miner, Earl. *The Japanese Tradition in British and American Literature*. Princeton: Princeton University Press, 1958.

Moore, George. *Hail and Farewell!* 3 volumes. London: Heinemann, 1947.

Moore, John Rees. *Masks of Love and Death: Yeats as Dramatist*. Ithaca: Cornell University Press, 1971.

Moore, Virginia. *The Unicorn: William Butler Yeats's Search for Reality*. New York: Macmillan, 1954.

Nathan, Leonard E. *The Tragic Drama of William Butler Yeats: Figures in a Dance*. New York: Columbia University Press, 1965.

Nic Shiubhlaigh, Maire. *The Splendid Years*. Dublin: James Duffy, 1955.

Oates, Joyce Carol. *The Edge of Impossibility: Tragic Forms in Literature*. New York: Vanguard, 1972.

O'Connor, Frank. *My Father's Son*. New York: Knopf, 1959.

O'Driscoll, Robert, ed. *Theatre and Nationalism in Twentieth Century Ireland*. Toronto: University of Toronto Press, 1971.

O'Driscoll, Robert and Lorna Reynolds, eds. *Yeats and the Theatre*. Toronto: Macmillan, 1975.

O hAodha, Micheal. *Theatre in Ireland*. Totowa: Rowman and Littlefield, 1974.

Parkinson, Thomas. *W. B. Yeats: Self Critic and The Later Poetry*. Berkeley and Los Angeles: University of California Press, 1971.

Peacock, Ronald. *The Poet in the Theatre*. New York: Harcourt Brace, 1946.

Pound, Ezra and Ernest Fenollosa. *The Classic Noh Theatre of Japan*. New York: New Directions, 1959.

Qamber, Akhtar. *Yeats and the Noh*. New York: Weatherhill, 1974.

Rajan, Balachandra. *W. B. Yeats: A Critical Introduction*. London: Hutchinson, 1965.

Robinson, Lennox. *Ireland's Abbey Theatre: A History 1899–1951*. London: Sidgwick and Jackson, 1951.

Ronsley, Joseph. *Yeats's Autobiography: Life as Symbolic Pattern*. Cambridge: Harvard University Press, 1968.

Saul, George Brandon. *Prolegomena to the Study of Yeats's Plays*. Philadelphia: University of Pennsylvania Press, 1958.

——. *Prolegomena to the Study of Yeats's Poems*. Philadelphia: University of Pennsylvania Press, 1957.

Sidnell, Michael J., George P. Mayhew, David R. Clark, eds. *Druid Craft: The Writing of "The Shadowy Waters."* Amherst: University of Massachusetts, 1971.

Starkie, Walter and A. Norman Jeffares, eds. *Homage to Yeats 1865–1965*. Los Angeles: University of California, 1966.

Stewart, J. I. M. *Eight Modern Writers*. Oxford: Clarendon Press, 1963.

Skelton, Robin and Ann Saddlemyer, eds. *The World of W. B. Yeats: Essays in Perspective*. Victoria: University of Victoria, 1965.

Skene, Reg. *The Cuchulain Plays of W. B. Yeats: A Study*. New York: Columbia University Press, 1974.

Taylor, Richard. *The Drama of W. B. Yeats: Irish Myth and the Japanese Nō*. New Haven and London: Yale University Press, 1976.

Tuohy, Frank. *Yeats*. London and New York: Macmillan, 1976.

Thompson, William I. *The Imagination of an Insurrection, Dublin, Easter 1916: A Study of an Ideolog-*

ical Movement. New York: Oxford University Press, 1969.

Ure, Peter. *Yeats the Playwright: A Commentary on Character and Design in the Major Plays*. New York: Barnes and Noble, 1963.

―――. *Yeats and Anglo-Irish Literature: Critical Essays by Peter Ure*. Ed. C. J. Rawson. New York: Barnes and Noble, 1974.

Vendler, Helen Hennessy. *Yeats's "Vision" and the Later Plays*. Cambridge: Harvard University Press, 1963.

Völker, Klaus. *Irisches Theater I: Yeats und Synge*. Velber bei Hannover: Friedrich Verlag, 1967.

Weygandt, Cornelius. *Irish Plays and Playwrights*. New York: Houghton Mifflin, 1913; rpt. Port Washington: Kennikat Press, 1966.

Whitaker, Thomas R. *Swan and Shadow: Yeats's Dialogue with History*. Chapel Hill: University of North Carolina Press, 1964.

Wilson, F. A. C. *W. B. Yeats and Tradition*. New York: Macmillan, 1958.

―――. *Yeats's Iconography*. London: Victor Gollancz, 1960.

Worth, Katharine. *The Irish Drama of Europe from Yeats to Beckett*. New Jersey: Humanities Press, 1978.

Zwerdling, Alex. *Yeats and the Heroic Ideal*. New York: New York University Press, 1965.

See also the special issues of *Modern Drama* (December, 1964), and *Threshold* (Autumn, 1965).

INDEX